Other Books by Charles Rubin

Thinking Small: The Buyer's Guide to Portable Computers

The Endless Apple

AppleWorks: Boosting Your Business with Integrated Software

Command Performance: AppleWorks

Microsoft Works on the Apple Macintosh

Macintosh Hard Disk Management

Running Microsoft Works

The Macintosh Bible "What Do I Do Now?" Book

The Macintosh Bible Guide to System 7

The Macintosh Bible Guide to FileMaker Pro

The Macintosh Bible Guide to System 7.1

The Macintosh Bible Guide to ClarisWorks 3.0

The Little Book of Computer Wisdom: How to Make Friends
with Your PC or Mac

GUERRILLA MARKETING ONLINE

The Entrepreneur's Guide to Earning Profits on the Internet

Jay Conrad Levinson
and Charles Rubin

HOUGHTON MIFFLIN COMPANY
Boston New York 1995

For information about permission to reproduce selections from
this book, write to Permissions, Houghton Mifflin Company,
215 Park Avenue South, New York, New York 10003.

Library of Congress Cataloging-in-Publication Data
Levinson, Jay Conrad.
     Guerrilla marketing online : the entrepreneur's guide to earning
profits on the Internet / Jay Conrad Levinson and Charles Rubin
          p.   cm.
     Includes index.
     ISBN 0-395-72859-2
     1. Marketing – Data processing. 2. Internet advertising.
I. Rubin, Charles 1953– .   II. Title.
HF5415.125.L48   1995
 658.8'00285'467 – dc20   95-6335   CIP

For information about this and other Houghton Mifflin
trade and reference books and multimedia products, visit
The Bookstore at Houghton Mifflin on the World Wide Web
at (http://www.hmco.com/trade/).

Printed in the United States of America
MP 10 9 8 7 6 5 4 3 2 1

Contents

Acknowledgments ix

I THE ONLINE MARKETPLACE

1 Attacking the Online Marketplace 3
2 Understanding the Online Marketplace 15
3 The Electronic Battlegrounds 33

II STRATEGIES FOR ONLINE BATTLES

4 E-mail and Mailing Lists 57
5 Electronic Storefronts 85
6 Classified Ads and Billboards 113
7 Forums and Newsgroups 129
8 Bulletin Boards 148
9 Boosting Your Online Reputation 163
10 Seventy-five Online Guerrilla Marketing Weapons 179
11 Twelve Strategies for Online Success 192

III MANAGING YOUR ATTACK

12 Planning the Attack 209
13 Secrets of a Successful Attack 230
14 Sustaining the Attack 241
15 Using Online Information 249
16 Leveraging Your Online Advantage 260

Glossary 275
Appendix: The Information Arsenal 282
Index 294

Acknowledgments

I would first like to thank Jay Levinson for making this project such a pleasure. I'm also grateful to Michael Larsen for introducing me to Jay, whose work I've admired for a long time. My thanks as always to Claudette Moore, my agent, for her continuous friendship and advice.

It would have been impossible to do this book without a lot of help from members of the online community. These Champions of Cyberspace offered insights and direct support simply because of a desire to be helpful, and they exemplify the spirit of the online community. My thanks to Joe Andreiu, Dave Asprey, Mike Bauer, Barbara Byro, Mark Campbell, David Cordeiro, Mary Cronin, Daniel Dern, Adam Engst, Glenn Fleishman, Karyn German, Larry Grant, Harley Hahn, Steven Heath, Walt Howe, Arnold Kling, Cliff Kurtzman, Steve Lambert, Albert Lunde, Tom McSherry, Mary Morris, Andrew Payne, Casey Peffers, John Quarterman, Rob Raisch, Rosalind Resnick, Lew Rose, Margaret Ryan, Murph Sewall, Bruce Speyer, Jim Sterne, Rick Stout, Michael Strangelove, Dave Taylor, Chris Tillman, and Mike Walsh.

Finally, a special thanks to Orvel Ray Wilson for his encouragement, and for showing me the difference between publishing and promotion.

CHARLES RUBIN

I offer acknowledgment and gratitude, not to mention a tip of my mouse, to Charles Rubin, internaut supreme, who has enlightened me about the capabilities of online marketing just as this book will enlighten you. I also offer my thanks to Mike Larsen and Elizabeth Pomada, my agents, who pointed out Charlie and said, "That guy knows the Net, knows computers, knows how to write, and is a terrific guy. You ought to do a book with him." And I want to thank my wife, Pat, not only for learning about online life but for becoming an onliner herself.

JAY LEVINSON

PART I

The Online Marketplace

1

Attacking the Online Marketplace

Success in business means selling, and that usually means putting your message, your company identity, and your product or service before as many prospective customers as possible. Since the 1970s, technologies like cable television, fax-on-demand, and 800- or 900-number service have given guerrilla marketers more ways than ever to get their messages out to a wide audience quickly and at lower costs. But nothing we've seen so far comes close to the potential of the online marketplace. Imagine:

- putting your message before a million prospects, or being able to target promotions at very specific groups of prospects in seconds, and for pennies
- opening virtual storefronts in dozens of locations around the world, having instantaneous control over the look and content of your store displays, and being able to take orders day and night
- competing on equal terms with companies ten times the size of yours
- being able to win head-on battles through superior customer service and attitude

The online marketplace makes all this possible. In the online world, you leverage your savvy, guts, and marketing budget far more effectively than you ever have before.

But success in the online marketplace isn't a sure thing, any more than opening a storefront with a good idea is a guarantee of early retirement. The online world has great potential, but in many ways it's a more perilous place than traditional marketing battlegrounds. Already, dozens of would-be millionaires have tested the online waters and have been severely burned.

In this book, we'll show you how to fight and win in the online marketplace. You'll learn how the marketplace is organized, how different areas of it demand different strategies, how to pick your battlegrounds for maximum success, and how to press your attack for continuing victories and profits.

ABOUT THE ONLINE MARKETPLACE

Anyone who hasn't lived on Mars during the past year or so has heard a lot about the "information highway." Technologies as diverse as computer networks, interactive television, and two-way video telephones have been lumped together under the information-highway banner. Vice President Al Gore has promoted the National Information Infrastructure as a means to streamline the flow of information among businesses and consumers and to make American companies more competitive.

In the broadest sense, the information highway includes any form of interactive communications technology. That includes everything from the 800 number you dial today to order from a catalog to the interactive TV setup of tomorrow where you point to pizza toppings on the screen to order a hot one from Domino's.

Eventually, interactive computer and television communications may change the way people shop. Already, there are interactive TV trials where you can browse on-screen menus of restaurants or entertainment events and make reservations or order tickets with your TV remote control. Futurists envision a time when you will instruct software "agents" to do your shopping for you. For example, you could have an agent search all online sources for a specific size of refrigerator with certain features and give you a list of options. The agent might suggest the model with the most bang for the buck, or you might even tell it to go ahead and order the appliance for you.

Yes, the future of shopping looks incredible, but if you're planning to leverage online technologies for your business, you'll have to separate what's possible today from what you might be able to do tomorrow. For our purposes, today's information highway, or infobahn, is the online marketplace: people using computers and computer networks to connect with one another. This marketplace includes:

- online computer services such as Prodigy, CompuServe, and America Online, whose combined subscriber base is more than six million people
- bulletin board systems that host some 20 million regular callers in the United States alone

- the Internet (or simply the Net), the international matrix of computer networks that links millions of people at university, government, and corporate networks, in addition to subscribers to the major online services and many bulletin board systems

The online marketplace is, obviously, changing rapidly. Nevertheless, we've focused on marketing avenues and strategies that should stand the test of time, and we'll show you how to stay in touch with new developments on the information highway.

A MARKET TOO BIG TO IGNORE

Willie Sutton said he robbed banks because that was where the money was. Guerrilla marketers go online because that's where the customers are. Using marketing techniques detailed in other Guerrilla Marketing books, you can reach hundreds, thousands, or even tens of thousands of potential customers by spending a few hundred dollars a month. But with a personal computer and a modem, you can go online and reach a community of millions for pennies. Your message will probably appeal to only a tiny fraction of the online population, but with millions of people out there, a tiny fraction is plenty. And, as we'll see, the online marketplace is neatly segmented into special-interest groups, so it's easy to find the groups that will most likely buy your products.

The number of people online is staggering. As of September 1994, there were an estimated 30 million people connected to the Internet in 148 countries, and the Internet's growth is accelerating.

- Every thirty minutes, a new network joins the Internet. Among the commercial networks that make up more than half of the Internet's population, the growth rate is 10 percent per month.
- According to *Internet World* magazine, two new user accounts are added to the Internet every four minutes, and one of those accounts is a commercial user.
- According to *Boardwatch* magazine, most of the 60,000 bulletin board systems in the United States will be connected to the Internet by the end of 1995.
- America Online, just one of the major online services, doubled its membership between 1993 and 1994 alone, and now has over 2 million subscribers. CompuServe and Prodigy each boast more than 2 million, and the other players (GEnie, Delphi, eWorld, Ziffnet, and

so on) have another million or so among them. Online service sub-scribers are ready and able to buy, with median annual household incomes of more than $50,000.

- The *Internet Business Report* newsletter predicts that commercial activity on the Net could top $100 million by the end of 1995.

The numbers game

Any subscriber numbers reported about the online market are suspect for a variety of reasons. But the numbers are big even when you allow for a reality check.

First, the estimates of Internet users are based on assumptions about the number of users on each host computer that joins the Internet. The assumption is that there are about ten users per host computer, but many connected hosts don't have any connected users — they're just collections of files. On the other hand, other hosts like Prodigy and CompuServe host millions of users.

Second, the numbers include any user or computer that has ever joined an online service, bulletin board, or the Internet, whether or not that user is active or has multiple accounts. In a 1994 study, the Software Publishers Association found that 20 percent of online service users had more than one account. And when Prodigy reports 2 million subscrib-ers, that number includes every subscriber Prodigy has ever had since it was founded, including those who logged on once and never used the service again.

But even if we allow for those who have dropped out of the online life, those who have multiple accounts, and errors in estimating the Internet's population, there are easily millions of people in the online marketplace, and that makes it a place worth exploring.

OPPORTUNITIES FOR A GUERRILLA MARKETER

The size of the online market is impressive, but size alone is only the beginning of what makes it attractive for guerrilla marketers. After all, opening a storefront in Los Angeles doesn't guarantee you'll reach even a fraction of your potential customers in southern California. The In-ternet beckons because it gives you incredible leverage over your time and money, lets you zero in on prospects easily, and levels the playing field between you and your competitors, no matter how large or well-financed they are.

How do you know if your product or service can make it online? Here's just a sampling of the types of goods and services available on the Internet today:

accounting, banking, brokerage, and legal services
arts and crafts
automobiles and automotive products
board games
books
CD-ROM publishing services
cemetery monuments
clothing
compact disks, laser disks, and videotapes
computer consulting and programming services
computer hardware and software
concert tickets
cosmetics
custom-stained glass
desktop publishing and graphic design services
discount telephone service
employment agencies
eyeglasses
flowers
food
ghostwriting and copywriting
insurance services
international trade consultants
jewelry
legal services
magazines and newsletters
museum reproductions
musical instruments
original artwork, posters, and prints
personal-care products
promotional products and advertising specialties
real estate
removable tattoos
research services
stamps and coins
training and educational services
travel services
vitamins
X-rated videos, photos, and adult toys

More goods and services appear every day, often with impressive results. For example:

- 800-THE-ROSE, one of America's largest flower delivery services, doubled its sales after it went online.
- Ceram Corporation of San Diego, California, sells $3 million worth of technical workstations and other components a year through its Internet marketing campaign.
- Alain Pinel Realtors was a struggling real estate company in San Jose, California, three years ago, but thanks to its Internet business pres-

ence, it now has two hundred agents selling $600 million in properties per year to customers across America, Europe, and Australia.

The Internet abounds with success stories like these, and you can write one of your own.

An advertiser's dream

As with television, radio, or newspaper advertising, on the Internet you can broadcast your message to thousands or millions of people at once. But instead of paying big money to produce an ad, you can create your own online information package and post it yourself. You can change your message whenever you like. You can post different messages in different locations to reach different audiences. You can instantly tell which messages are working best, which are losers, and how many people respond to each one.

Even with a $20-per-month Internet account, you can post as many marketing messages and send as much electronic mail as you like for nothing. The prices of print ad pages and TV time place severe limits on just how much you can say about your product or service in these media, but you can deliver details, competitive comparisons, testimonials, and even provide catalogs and order forms for customers online for almost nothing. Online florists show color samples of their arrangements, and auto companies like Ford and GM offer interactive demos of cars that you can retrieve and run on your home PC. You can also accept credit cards online.

Finally, the targets of your online advertising are paying attention. People watching TV or skimming through a magazine might devote only a fraction of their attention to any particular ad, but online prospects have chosen to read your ad.

Location, location, location

You can be in several places at once in the online marketplace. No matter how adept you are at selling in person, you're limited by your ability to talk with customers one at a time. On the Internet, your message can reach thousands of people at any time of the day or night anywhere around the world.

And with a minimum of expense, your product presentation can be as polished as one from a company ten times the size of yours. The online marketplace puts the smallest company on equal terms with the largest ones.

Niche marketing

While magazine advertising and direct mail can help you focus on particular markets, the Internet lets you attack markets with laserlike precision, and for free. You might pay hundreds or thousands of dollars for a focused mailing list, spend more on producing a direct-mail package, and then spend more on postage. But online buyers have already sorted themselves into topic-specific interest groups. You can place your message on only the groups that promise high interest in your products. As members of these groups respond to your messages, you automatically build a mailing list of prequalified prospects for future announcements.

Competitive intelligence

By joining the right online discussion groups, you can find out what people are saying about your competitors' products, or respond to questions or complaints about your own. Major companies like Microsoft and Apple Computer host their own discussion groups to help customers with questions or to conduct focus groups on new products, and you can do the same. Not sure if a particular marketing message is appropriate? Post it to a discussion group and ask for feedback first. Or, as companies like Dell Computer do, you can pay one or more employees to surf the Internet constantly, looking for scuttlebutt about your company or your competition and responding when appropriate.

You can also dig through thousands of computer databases containing millions of reports on business and market activity, corporate financial performance, labor statistics, and other facts that can help you understand and respond to changing markets.

THE PITFALLS OF ONLINE MARKETING

As with the great California gold rush of 1849, there's a lot of profit to be had in online markets, but it doesn't come without risk. True guerrilla marketers survey the terrain and understand the risks going in, so they can anticipate and avoid the many traps that lie ahead.

Net savvy

To win in the online market, you must understand the online world: how to connect, how to explore and exploit various market battlegrounds, and which battlegrounds to choose for maximum return on your investment. If you're not computer-literate already, you'll have to invest in some computer and communications equipment and choose a method of going online, or else pay someone else to do it for you. Once you are computer-literate, you must become *Net-literate*, understanding the online marketplace, how to navigate it, and how to express yourself effectively in it.

When in Rome . . .

Marketing techniques that might seem perfectly natural in the outside world can ruin your reputation online. In a well-publicized case, the Phoenix law firm of Canter & Siegel *spammed* the Internet, indiscriminately posting advertisements for their immigration law services on thousands of Internet discussion groups. Most of these groups had rules prohibiting such advertising, and most of these groups were about topics that had nothing to do with immigrating to the United States. The spam attack generated a tidal wave of *flames*, or hate mail, back to Canter & Siegel's electronic mailbox. Their Internet access was revoked by their service provider, and although the firm claims to have generated $50,000 worth of business through the effort (and, ironically, the two partners have written a book about how to make money online), their online reputation has been severely damaged.

Bad news travels quickly

Just as the online market allows you to deliver your marketing messages quickly and easily, it also allows your detractors to spread false or damaging information about you just as quickly and easily. One dissatisfied customer, or one prospect who's offended because you posted a marketing message on a particular discussion group, can pass a summary judgment of you and spread that judgment among thousands of people in seconds with the click of a mouse button. Canter & Siegel and other firms have found this out the hard way. As you pursue your marketing attack, it might be difficult to avoid being flamed entirely, but you can choose your battlegrounds and tailor your strategies to minimize the risk.

The world's largest anarchy

The Internet has been described this way because unlike on a television network or a newspaper, on the Internet nobody is in charge. When you place an ad in a newspaper, for example, the paper's staff will help you choose a location for maximum impact. On the Internet, you're on your own. Mistakes can be costly to your reputation and future efforts, so it's important to do your homework.

The online market isn't a mass market; it's not one giant fishbowl where you can cast your net for customers. Rather it's hundreds of smaller sub-markets. Many of the market's citizens may never frequent the areas where you post your information. You have to learn how to identify the markets with the greatest interest in your product or service, and how to reach them most effectively.

A thousand words are worth more than one picture

Your marketing efforts must be adapted to the physical realities of the electronic world. You might use photos or pictures liberally in print ads or on television, but these can be costly and time-consuming for prospects to read online. While there are ways to view graphics or even video online, most of the online customers these days don't have those capabilities or don't use them because they're still too clumsy. Your message must be delivered in such a way that the most likely target groups can see it easily.

Being invisible

In the physical world, you can bombard customers and prospects with passive marketing messages even when they're not particularly looking for them. People see and unconsciously remember print ads, TV ads, billboards, and bus ads as part of their daily lives. But in the online world, messages you post are invisible unless the prospect takes the time to look for and read them. Again, the answer is to be careful about placing those messages in the right locations and to use messages so enticing that people will choose to view them.

Once people are reading your messages, remember that you can't smile and shake hands with customers online. You'll have to learn to engage people with well-written copy, a helpful attitude, and reliable service.

The electronic till

If you actually take orders online, you'll have to decide which payment method to use. Some online marketers only provide product information online and then direct customers to place actual orders over the phone. Others accept credit card numbers online, and still others use secure payment methods that protect financial information from potential interception by computer hackers. Online transaction systems have improved dramatically in the past year, and will continue to do so.

Paying attention

The online market is open twenty-four hours a day. As you manage your employees or deal with customers in person, it can be easy to forget that customers may also be waiting on the other side of your computer screen. You'll have to discipline yourself or your staff to monitor your online presence regularly. How often you check your electronic mail or other online communication channels depends on the specific marketing strategies and battlegrounds you choose, but all your online customers and prospects expect speedy results, and you must be prepared to oblige them. Follow-up and consistency are even more important than they are when you're selling in person.

High volume can mean high demand

In most cases, your online marketing attack will be only part of your overall business marketing plan. But the Internet market is vast, and your online attacks may generate a staggering volume of electronic mail or other electronic traffic. Your marketing plan must be designed to anticipate and deal with the load.

So while going online can boost your visibility and profits, it's also a brave new world that can reward the informed traveler and can severely punish the ignoramus. It's no place for second-best, but it promises great rewards for A students.

ABOUT THIS BOOK

The online marketplace is exploding, and as in the Wild West, there are plentiful opportunities and few rules. This book is a guerrilla's guide to that marketplace and how to successfully attack it.

There are many fine books available about personal computer communications, networking, using the Internet or using specific online services, conducting research online, setting up a bulletin board system, and even on conducting all manner of business activities on the Internet. This book is not one of them. Our focus is on applying proven guerrilla marketing strategies to the online marketplace.

If you haven't been online or have only explored a small part of the online world, you'll need to get your bearings as to the scope and layout of the overall marketplace. We'll give you enough information to get oriented, but you also need a more detailed and technical guide to using the online world.

HOW TO BEGIN

In this book, we'll cover the realities of online marketing. We'll explore detailed weapons and strategies for fighting and winning in the online markets, producing maximum profits with minimum expense. Here are your basic marching orders:

Understand the online marketplace. The online market is a vast, diverse, and potentially confusing place. There are millions of people exploring tens of thousands of electronic locations on the Internet, online services, and bulletin boards. Chapter 2 will introduce you to this market: how it's organized, what you can do there, who can participate, and how to begin participating as quickly as possible.

Learn to navigate, communicate, and respond. Once you have a general idea of how the online terrain is laid out, your next mission is to understand the different online battlegrounds — the various online tools and services you can use to market online. Chapter 3 is your guide.

Learn strategies for attacking specific battlegrounds. Chapters 4 through 9 offer detailed strategies for winning online battles. In these chapters, you'll find out how to maneuver in specific battlegrounds and how to use them to your best advantage.

Choose your weapons. Chapter 10 lists 75 proven marketing weapons you can use to press your attack, and Chapter 11 offers 12 strategies you can use to make the most of them

Develop a strategy. Chapter 12 offers step-by-step instructions for planning a successful online guerrilla marketing attack. You'll learn how to choose the right battlegrounds, how to build your own custom arsenal of online marketing weapons, and how to create an attack calendar.

Implement that strategy consistently. Chapters 13 and 14 show you how to launch and maintain your marketing attack.

Leverage your online presence. Chapters 15 and 16 show you how to use your online presence to boost other marketing efforts, and how to use online resources to gain vital intelligence about your business, your customers, and your competition.

Armed with the resources in this book, you can create an online market presence that will become a significant part of your overall business strategy. You can expand your markets by reaching customers you could never reach before, increase sales by handling many more transactions than you could before, and boost your bottom line by slashing sales and marketing costs to the bone.

All it takes is a commitment to winning, a modest investment in basic computer equipment and services, and the willingness to take action.

2

Understanding the
Online Marketplace

The online market exists because millions of people use their computers to communicate. If your computer is connected to a network (either directly or via a dial-up connection with a modem), you can exchange messages with other computer users or gather information from other computers. And where there is communication, there's commerce.

THE BIRTH OF ONLINE SHOPPING

In personal computing's misty past — around 1975 — most communications were private. Companies had their own networks designed for employees only. Universities and government agencies had their own networks that were linked by a government-sponsored data pathway, or *backbone*, so they could exchange research information. There were online information services, but these were basically collections of statistical data, legal citations, or business-related articles.

As personal computers began to catch on in households and small businesses, some of the companies that had built online business information services opened them up to individual users. CompuServe and others began offering services and information for consumers, such as games, weather, news, encyclopedias, and discussion groups on various subjects, all via a phone call from a personal computer. To make connecting as easy and inexpensive as possible, the online services established local telephone numbers in every major city, so subscribers could dial in without having to make a long-distance call.

And when John and Jane Public subscribed to these services and went online, there were marketers ready there to greet them. Right there with the games, news, reference libraries, and discussion groups, there were electronic shopping malls through which shoppers could get product information and order goods. Most online services have electronic shopping malls where you can browse and order everything from compact disks or tapes to flowers, from financial consulting or legal services to computer dating. All you need is a subscriber account to the service, a personal computer and modem, and a telephone line.

Today's online services have millions of subscribers and offer a wide range of services in an effort to appeal to the masses. Subscription fees run around $10 to $15 a month, in general, but you may pay extra for accessing special information or discussion areas on these services, or for connecting for more than a few hours per month.

BULLETIN BOARDS

As the big online services were getting off the ground, early electronic entrepreneurs saw a separate market for more specialized online information. Using personal computers and bulletin board software, these guerrillas set up their own online services. Instead of trying to cover every subject and appeal to everyone with a personal computer, a bulletin board system (BBS) offers a more focused collection of information to a smaller group of subscribers.

Besides limiting themselves to specific topics, most BBS systems serve a particular city or portion of a state. And instead of having local dial-in numbers all over the country, most BBSs are reached by only one phone number, so the call is a toll call for anyone outside the immediate area.

Today there are about 60,000 BBSs in the United States alone, serving around 20 million regular callers. Some bulletin boards don't charge users for access at all — the operators make money selling advertising space or they simply offer the information as a hobby — but most charge from $20 to $100 a year for membership. A typical bulletin board has 1000 or so subscribers, and BBS topics run the gamut from aviation and astrology through Zen and zoology. But nearly half of the BBSs in the United States specialize in relationships and sex.

ADVENT OF THE INTERNET

In the 1970s and 1980s the online marketplace was a series of islands, large and small, isolated from one another. The online continents were CompuServe, Prodigy, GEnie, America Online, Delphi, AppleLink, Dow Jones News/Retrieval, and other major information services. The islets were bulletin boards. But along with these islands was a worldwide computer information pathway now called the Internet.

The Internet is a data backbone. Originally called ARPAnet, it was designed as a holocaust-proof communications system for researchers at universities, research labs, defense contractors, military installations, and government agencies. The idea was that computing resources were distributed across the country, so that an attack in any one city wouldn't cripple defense research and computer communications.

In the 1980s the National Science Foundation (NSF) expanded the ARPAnet backbone by setting up regional networks. These networks were tied together into an entity called NSFnet, which made it easier for universities to connect with each other. However, commercial activity was still prohibited on this government-funded, research-oriented system.

In the 1990s this network of networks (now called the Internet) has been opened up to commercial services and individuals. Along with the NSFnet that still links most universities and government agencies, today's Net includes a group of regional network service providers. These service providers maintain portions of the commercial Internet backbone or major networks linked to it and also offer connections to corporations, organizations, and individuals.

Once commercial traffic became possible over the global Internet, online services and bulletin boards began hooking up to it so their subscribers could communicate with people on other services and bulletin boards. In addition, companies large and small began tying their networks to the Internet so their employees could exchange information with customers on other company networks or peruse the vast stores of information available on university and government computer systems.

Today the Net has become the bridge that links all the islands and continents of the online marketplace into one colossal whole. As of mid-1994, there were over 31,000 networks connected via the Internet.

WHO'S WHO ON THE INTERNET

So who are all these people and who runs all these networks? Let's look at some of the types of networks that provide access for individual Internet citizens, whom we also call *internauts* or *netizens*.

Educational networks have been on the Internet for years. Nearly every major university in the world is connected to the Internet, and in the United States, most state colleges and even some high school networks are also connected. As a result, thousands of research papers and statistics compiled by educational researchers are available on university *servers,* which are computers set up to make files available to others. Using the Internet, for example, a biotechnology researcher in northern California can sniff out papers on the latest genetic engineering techniques located on servers in universities in the United States, Europe, Latin America, and Asia.

Also, many of the most popular Internet utilities and navigational tools were developed at universities, and copies of these programs are available for free from university networks as well. For example, the Gopher data indexing system, which lets you locate information across the Net, was developed at the University of Minnesota, and the Veronica program you use to search it for information is available from a server there.

Government agency networks were also some of the earliest members of the Net. The United States Census Bureau, Department of Labor Statistics, Library of Congress, Federal Register, Securities and Exchange Commission, Commerce Department, National Weather Service, Smithsonian Institution, and the White House are just a few of the government entities that make information available over the Internet. You can see daily transcripts of White House press briefings, view electronic images from the Library of Congress collection of documents and artwork, look at color satellite weather maps that are updated constantly, or send an electronic mail message to President Clinton or to your congressional representative.

Company networks have been joining the Internet in droves since commercial access became available in the early 1990s. Today thousands of companies large and small have their networks connected to the Internet. Some companies go on the Net so their employees can directly communicate with customers and suppliers or conduct online research. Others establish a Net presence to present their products or services to the Internet community. You can send e-mail to Bill Gates at Microsoft, request a quotation on a new minicomputer from Digital Equipment Corporation, or see the week's menu specials from the Country Fare restaurant in Palo Alto, California.

Regional backbone providers such as Performance Systems International, UUNet Technologies, BARRnet, and CERFnet maintain regional portions of the commercial Internet backbone and also offer provider services to companies and individuals. Employees of these companies sometimes sponsor Internet discussion groups on various topics.

Internet service providers (ISPs) like Portal, Netcom, and Panix don't maintain parts of the Internet backbone, but they have high-speed connections to the Internet and they provide access to the Net via dial-up or leased-line connections with individual computer users or corporate networks. Employees of these companies also sponsor Net-based discussions to help others learn about the Net.

Online computer services such as Prodigy, CompuServe, GEnie, America Online, and Delphi started life as islands in the cyberstream, but most now offer some sort of link with the Internet. Different online services offer different levels of Internet services, but the level of service is increasing all the time. For example, every online service has an Internet mail gateway so you can exchange electronic mail with other Internet citizens, but MCI Mail only allows you to exchange electronic mail, while America Online lets you search among Internet servers or participate in Internet discussion groups as well. Of all the new Net members in the past year or so, online services have had the most profound impact, bringing millions of consumers onto the Net at large.

Bulletin boards are smaller and usually localized and subject-specific versions of online services. Most will provide at least Internet mail access to their subscribers by the end of 1995.

Individual users are people who are connected to the Net, either via a corporate or educational network or an ISP. Some of these netizens are old hands who use the Net primarily for research, while others are subscribers to online services who now want fuller access to the Net.

Individual servers don't provide Net access for subscribers or groups of users, but instead offer collections of data or programs for others on the Net to use. For example, the National Center for Supercomputing Applications (NCSA) at the University of Illinois maintains an Internet server so users can get copies of its Mosaic software, which provides a graphical interface to the Net. Silicon Graphics, Digital Equipment Corporation, Adobe Systems, Apple Computer, and other companies maintain servers that offer product information and technical support for customers or prospects. There are thousands of such servers on the Internet.

WHAT YOU CAN DO ONLINE

There are several areas and services you can use to promote your company in the online marketplace. Here's a quick look.

Electronic mail (*e-mail*)

Any Internet user can send electronic mail messages to any other Internet user. You can quickly communicate in writing with people all over the world for little or no cost. All the major online computer services are on the Internet now, so CompuServe users can send mail to America Online or Prodigy users, and Internet users on corporate or university networks can freely exchange mail with everyone else.

E-mail is the common denominator among all Internet citizens, allowing you to send your product information or sales pitch to anyone. And even if many of your messages aren't promotional, you can use a signature line that is on all of them. You can also receive mail: customer feedback or orders, for example. As we'll see in Chapter 4, you can join an e-mail-based discussion group called a *mailing list*, and you can even set up a *mailbot* program that intercepts messages from prospects and automatically sends product information to them.

Mailing lists

A mailing list is a group of people who all send e-mail to one address, and who all get copies of the mail sent to that address. Mailing lists always focus on a particular topic. There are thousands of mailing lists on the Net on hundreds of specific topics, so they're excellent places to reach specific target markets.

There are three main advantages in using mailing lists. First, you can connect with dozens or hundreds of people who share a common interest, and you can do it all through e-mail. Since e-mail is a common denominator regardless of what type of Internet connection you have, mailing lists often have members from online services or bulletin boards that you wouldn't be able to reach through a newsgroup, server, or other means.

Second, all mailing list postings are automatically sent to your e-mail address, so they're there waiting for you to read each time you check your mail. This is simpler than having to navigate to a newsgroup each time you want to check on reactions to your last posting. *(See Forums and Newsgroups.)*

Third, lists are topic-specific, so they offer a prequalified group of prospects when the list's topic is in some way related to the product or service you're selling. *(See Chapter 4 for details about marketing with mailing lists.)*

Electronic storefronts

Electronic storefronts give you a location in cyberspace where you can present your company or product information for shoppers to browse. A storefront can sit by itself on an individual server on the Net; it can be part of an online shopping mall on the Net; or it can be in an online service or BBS. Online services and BBS systems usually charge a fee to participate in their malls, but on the Net you can set up your own server to display your wares or simply list a description of your offering for free and direct prospects to your e-mail address. If you plan to set up your own server, you can do the whole thing yourself or pay an ISP or consultant to set one up for you. Costs vary from a few hundred to several thousand dollars.

On the Net there are three types of servers you might set up for your electronic storefront: an *FTP server*, a *Gopher server*, or a *Worldwide Web site*.

If you use an FTP (File Transfer Protocol) server, you can store text and graphics files so users can retrieve them. Customers can use search utilities called Archie or Anarchie to locate your FTP server, or you can direct customers to the server's location.

On a Gopher server, you typically store text-only information that customers can actually view from across the Net, which is faster than having to retrieve files to their own computers. As with FTP servers, prospects can use search programs (such as Veronica) to locate your server, or you can direct them there in your promotional announcements.

On a Worldwide Web (WWW) server, customers use special graphical software that lets them locate your server and view text, graphics, or even video about your products. WWW servers use a system called the Hypertext Transfer Protocol (http) that automatically links a document on one server with a document on another. For example, you might look at a menu on a server that lists auto information, but when you select the option for Chevrolet, you're transferred to the main menu of Chevrolet's own information server. The connection happens automatically, so it makes navigating to servers around the world easy. In order to access

WWW servers, you need special http-compatible software. Some of the popular http packages are Mosaic, Netscape Cello, Lynx, and MacWeb. *(See Chapter 5 for more details on electronic storefronts.)*

Forums and newsgroups

Forums and newsgroups are subject-specific electronic discussions on the Internet. A forum (on an online service or BBS) or newsgroup (on the Net) works like a community bulletin board: you post a message with a specific topic, and others can respond to that topic. Each time you connect to a newsgroup, you can see only the messages that have been posted since you last checked, or you can browse through all postings to view messages posted weeks or months ago. At this writing, there are more than 12,000 Internet newsgroups.

For example, alt.architecture discusses building design and construction. Alt.bbs.lists contains regional BBS names and phone numbers. Alt.dads-rights is for fathers trying to win custody of their children. Alt.business.misc is a place where you'll find business opportunities of all sorts. There are newsgroups that discuss scientific topics (alt.sci.physics.new-theories) and others that focus on leisure activities (alt.beer and alt.music.progressive). Many groups are devoted to computer hardware and software. In the online services there are hundreds of forums that cover similar topics.

Chat sessions are online conferences in which several people can be connected and exchange text messages at once. The major online services have dozens of chat rooms, and the Net itself has over 400 individual conferences, or *channels*, in use around the world via a service called Internet Relay Chat (IRC). Each chat room or channel is a discussion of some topic that can include several people. Unlike newsgroups, IRC channels are live: they're like typewritten CB radios in which several people go online at once to read and respond to one another's messages as they're typed. Some chat sessions support hundreds of simultaneous participants. Your screen looks like a script from a play as user names and comments follow one another. We won't spend much time on chat sessions as a marketing tool, however, because they're mostly free-for-all discussions on relatively inane subjects. You might make a sale or two by participating in a chat session, but the time you spent to do it wouldn't be worth it.

However, chat technology is also used in *online conferences,* special events where an authority on a particular topic meets in a chat session with those interested. These are indeed good marketing vehicles, and we'll learn more about them in Chapters 3 and 9.

To participate in newsgroups, your Internet connection must allow access to them. To participate in a forum, you must be a subscriber to the BBS or online service that hosts it.

Most forums and newsgroups prohibit blatantly commercial announcements, but by participating in ones related to your business and becoming a source of information, you can develop a positive reputation that will result in sales. *(See Chapter 7 for details.)*

Online services and BBSs

Along with shopping malls and electronic mail, the online services and BBS systems offer ways to promote your business. For example, most online services and some BBSs have forums, e-mail, classified advertising sections, and online conferences. The major online services also have What's New boards that list special promotions or contests. *(See Chapter 6 for details.)* Prodigy allows you to put up an electronic billboard or ad that borders the screen as subscribers use other services. *(See Chapter 6.)* And finally, you can always start your own bulletin board system on a topic near and dear to your business identity to build online credibility and sales. *(See Chapter 8.)*

Telnet

Telnet isn't a key marketing tool (unless you're selling software that you want people to be able to test-drive on the Net), but it is a major Internet service, so we'll cover it here. Telnet is a program that allows you to connect with a remote computer and run a program on it. For example, the Worldwide Web system was developed in part by researchers at CERN, the European Community's laboratory for high-energy physics in Geneva, Switzerland. If you have Telnet service, you can navigate to the CERN server and run a program that lets you search the Worldwide Web.

This gives you an idea of how information is displayed and transferred online, but your ability to use these options will be determined by the type of connection you have.

CONNECTING TO THE INTERNET

To become an internaut, you don't call the Internet's phone number and ask for an account, because there is no such number. Instead, you gain access to the Internet through a network that's connected to it. There are three ways to do this:

1. Use a computer that's directly wired to a corporate, government, or university network that is connected by a leased telephone line to the Internet.
2. Use a modem on your PC to dial into a corporate or university network, an online service, or a bulletin board that is connected by a leased telephone line to the Internet.
3. Use a modem on your computer to dial into an ISP's network.

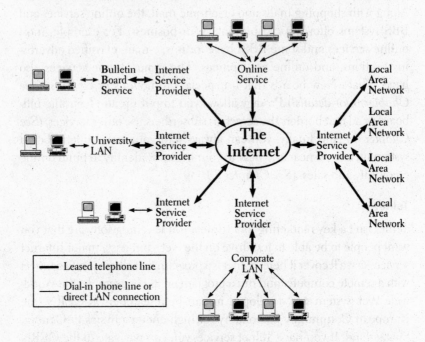

Every network or individual PC that connects to the Internet does so through an ISP. But there are different connections to ISPs, and different ISPs offer different services. The connection you choose depends on which Internet services you want to have and the speed of access you want.

As the diagram shows, for example, an ISP may provide a *direct connection* to a local area network (LAN) via a leased telephone line. If a company or university LAN is connected to the Internet, then any computer on it can have access to the Internet, although it's up to the LAN administrator to actually set up access to the Net for individual network users. LAN connections at large companies and universities are *continuous* connections. If your computer is set up for Internet access from the LAN and you have the right navigational programs on your computer, you can cruise the Internet anytime.

ISPs also provide *dial-up* connections. In this case, an individual PC user or a network server dials into the ISP's host computer whenever its user wants to get on the Internet. If you're connecting from a personal computer with a modem, there are three types of dial-up connections.

The first is a *shell account*, the most popular type of connection between an ISP and an individual PC user. You dial into the ISP's host computer and you see a menu of services available. You then choose menu options to send mail, search for information, or perform other activities on the Internet. With a shell account, however, your Internet abilities are limited to the services provided by that ISP's host computer.

Most ISPs offer relatively full access to the Net. For example, firms like Netcom or PSILink give you electronic mail, newsgroup access, Telnet, FTP, and IRC from within a shell account. Online services, on the other hand, give you more limited Internet access. For example, at this writing America Online lets you send and receive electronic mail over the Internet, browse through a selection of newsgroups, and search for information on certain types of information servers, but you can't use Telnet. Prodigy offers e-mail connections, newsgroups, and access to the Worldwide Web. A shell account at an ISP is easy to set up and usually costs $20 per month or less.

The bad news about a shell account at an ISP is that you'll probably have to deal with a text interface and learn some Unix commands in order to use it. This is often not fun and not for the technically faint at heart. A few ISPs like Netcom, Intercon, and Pipeline now have graphical user interfaces on their host computers so you can use menus and icons to perform Internet tasks. Most online services have graphical interfaces as well.

A *SLIP* (Serial Line Internet Protocol) or *PPP* (Point-to-Point Protocol) connection is a more direct connection with the Internet. Instead of asking the ISP's host computer to perform Internet chores for you (which is what happens with a shell account), you run a program on your own PC to perform a particular Internet activity. When you want to send mail, transfer a file, or surf the Worldwide Web, for example, you run programs on your own computer to do these things. You can access any service or information available on the entire Net as long as you're running the necessary program on your own computer. With a SLIP or PPP connection, you can choose the specific programs you want for Internet functions. Most of the programs you'll need are available in Internet starter packages or books. *(See Appendix.)*

SLIP and PPP accounts can be more expensive. Usually, ISPs charge from $10 to $50 to set up such an account, and they charge a monthly service fee plus an hourly rate for more than a certain amount of access per day. For example, a typical SLIP account at this writing costs $20 a month and includes three to five hours' access per day, with additional hours costing $2 or so.

The third kind of dial-up connection, a *UUCP* (Unix-to-Unix Copy Protocol) connection, is usually for bulletin boards or other networks that want to transfer large batches of mail or newsgroup updates. It requires special UUCP software, and it provides you with electronic mail and newsgroup services only. When your computer connects with the ISP, the UUCP automatically sends all your outgoing mail and receives any incoming mail as well as new postings to newsgroups since the last time you connected. Your computer then disconnects from the ISP.

CHOOSING AN INTERNET SERVICE PROVIDER

Unless you're reaching the Net through a corporate or university network or a SLIP or PPP account, your ability to send, receive, search for, and display information on the Internet depends on the variety of services your ISP makes available to you. Here's what to look for in an Internet connection.

Services

Decide which Internet services you want and make sure the connection method offers them. Every ISP and online service offers e-mail, for example, but smaller ISPs may offer only mail and a selection of newsgroups, while larger ISPs offer all newsgroups, Gopher and WAIS databases, Worldwide Web, Telnet, FTP, and IRC. Along with these basic Net services, find out if the provider can help you with your Internet presence and marketing. Some of the marketing services to look for are:

- *domain name* service, where you get a network address for your company *(See About Internet addresses below.)*
- mailbot services
- FTP, Gopher, or Web servers

When shopping for an ISP, don't just look for a laundry list of services. Get some customer references or ask for a trial account and find out what it's like to use the services. One ISP's e-mail system may be much more cumbersome to use than another's, for example. Check out some of the ISP's other customers and find out if they're happy with its services. Consider any new online account a trial — you can always change your mind and go with another ISP or online service if you don't like the first one.

Acceptable use policies

Another consideration in choosing an ISP is whether or not the ISP will permit you to conduct the kind of marketing program you want. Every ISP has *acceptable use policies*, or AUPs, that spell out such things as how many addresses you can send an e-mail message to at once (which might limit bulk e-mailings), how many different newsgroups you can post the same message to, how much disk storage you can use, and so on. Get a copy of your ISP's policies and read them to make sure your marketing plans won't be limited.

Reliability and performance

Conducting an online marketing program requires you to have frequent online sessions. Just as you wouldn't use a long-distance provider whose lines went down regularly, you shouldn't go with a cut-rate ISP if that means dealing with a system whose access number is frequently busy, whose Internet connection fails now and then, or whose equipment is so overloaded that your customers can't reach you easily. Ask the ISP for customer references, and check them out to see what sort of experience they've had.

User support

Larger ISPs have full-time technical support staffs who can help you with access or Internet navigation problems. Some offer training sessions, and some even distribute regular newsletters offering tips about surfing the Net. Some ISPs bill themselves as Internet Presence Providers (IPPs), which specialize not simply in giving you access to the Net, but in helping you design and create an electronic storefront. Your own level of technical savvy should determine the amount of service you demand from an ISP or IPP. If you think you'll need a lot of help, make sure the ISP or IPP offers it.

Cost

Unless you're connecting through a university or a corporation where you're not directly paying the bills, an Internet account will cost you something. You'll pay a monthly service charge, and there's an hourly rate on top of that for certain types of accounts. Find out what types of account the ISP offers, how each account's services differ, and what they cost.

If you're thinking about a dial-in account, find out whether or not the ISP has a local phone number in your area. Having to dial a long-distance number to access your ISP's computer will add significantly to your monthly Internet connection costs. Some ISPs have 800 numbers you can call to connect for a flat fee ranging from $5 to $12 per hour, but most use commercial data networks like Tymnet or SprintNet, which have local numbers in most major cities.

If you're planning to use a continuous leased-line connection, find out from the ISP and your local telephone company about the cost to set up and maintain such a connection. Depending on the speed of the line, these can cost from $200 to over $1000 a month. (*For more information about choosing an ISP, see Choosing an electronic storefront in Chapter 5, or pick up one of the Internet user guides listed in the Appendix.*)

ABOUT INTERNET ADDRESSES

With millions of users, thousands of servers, and thousands of networks, nobody would be able to find anything on the Net without addresses. (As it is, finding things is hard enough, which is why the Internet has been called "an endless line of information Dumpsters you can pick through.") Every network, server, or individual PC connected to the Net has a specific address. The address can tell you a lot about how or whether someone is connected, where they're physically located, and which Internet service you use to reach them.

If your online connection is through an online service, you have a user name, or screen name, that identifies you on that service, and to which others on that service send electronic mail. For example, Guerrilla Marketing International is a subscriber on America Online, and its screen name there is GM INTL.

However, because America Online (let's call it AOL for short) is connected to the Internet, every AOL subscriber also has an Internet mailing address. An Internet address includes:

- the user's name
- the name of the network (or *domain*) through which the user is connected
- the type of network it is

For example, the Internet address for Guerrilla Marketing's mailbox on AOL is gmintl@aol.com. Notice that the address is in all lowercase letters. Most Internet-connected systems aren't case-sensitive, but it has become a widely followed convention to use lowercase letters for addresses.

In Guerrilla Marketing's Internet address, the space between *gm* and *intl* has been eliminated. While AOL allows spaces in screen names, the Internet doesn't, nor do most of the systems connected to it. So in this case, the two parts of the screen name are combined.

The "at" sign (@) separates Guerrilla Marketing's user name from the network (or domain) name, aol.com. A netizen would pronounce Guerrilla Marketing's Net address as "GM INTL at AOL dot com."

Online services and Internet services providers like Netcom have simple one-word domain names. But some networks have zones or subsections that make an address longer. For example, *NBC Nightly News*'s address is nightly@nbc.ge.com. In this case, *nightly* is the mailbox address, and *nbc* is a subsection of the *ge* network.

Domains

All Internet networks are grouped into different domain types. The addresses we've seen so far end with *.com*, but the suffix identifies the type of domain, as follows:

.com	commercial
.edu	educational institutions
.gov	government agencies
.mil	military agencies
.net	network support centers
.org	other organizations (nonprofits, etc.)

By recognizing these domain types, you'll know if someone sending you e-mail is from a commercial, government, or educational network, for example. There are also geographic domains, which usually show up in addresses from countries outside the United States. For example, a user in Canada might have the address abc1234567@freenet.carleton.ca, where the *.ca* at the end indicates that the network is in Canada.

You can make your one-person company look as large as General Motors by applying for your own domain name. Most ISPs offer *domain name services*, which provide your own unique network name even though you're actually connecting via somebody else's network. For example, if you sell clothing, you might apply for the domain name gladrags.com, and then have a series of mailboxes in that domain, such as info@gladrags.com or sales@gladrags.com, even though you're actually connecting through an ISP like Netcom or PSI. With a custom domain name, your Net address contributes to your marketing effort.

Server addresses and URLs

Network or server addresses follow the same syntax as mailbox addresses, but without the @ and user name. For example, a server called Sudsly at the Old Reliable Brewing Company might be called sudsly.olrel.com.

Along with the address of a server, you need to know which of the Internet utilities or searching programs you use to access it. For example, if a server is available via the Gopher search utility, the address might say, "gopher to sudsly.olrel.com" or "gopher: sudsly.olrel.com." If the server is accessed with the Telnet program, the address would say, "telnet to sudsly.olrel.com" or "telnet: sudsly.olrel.com."

An increasingly popular alternative for specifying server addresses, especially for Web servers, is a Universal Resource Locator (URL). The URL has a standard format that indicates the type of program you need to reach it, followed by the server's address, and (if necessary) the specific location of a file on that server. For example, the address http://www.marketplace.com tells you that you need an http-compatible utility like Mosaic to reach the Worldwide Web (www) server on the network *marketplace.com*. URL addresses always follow this format. Here are two other examples:

gopher: //nstn.ns.ca

ftp://wonders.com/excerpts/android

In the second example, the URL tells us to use the FTP service to reach the *wonders.com* server and then look inside the directory *excerpts* for the file *android.*

FROM NEWBIE TO INTERNAUT IN SIX STEPS

It's easy to ruffle people's feathers by barging onto mailing lists or into newsgroups and asking all sorts of questions that immediately identify you as a novice, or *newbie,* in cyberslang. If you're careful about your approach to the Internet, on the other hand, you can learn what you need to launch an effective marketing attack without even tipping off the competition that you're coming.

Here's a six-step approach to experiencing the Net and preparing for your marketing attack:

1. Do your homework. Before you go online, finish this book, get your hands on a good Internet user's guide, and start reading at least one magazine devoted to Net happenings. *(See Appendix for suggestions.)* No single book can tell you everything about the Net, and the pace of new developments is such that you'll need a magazine at first, and ultimately the Net itself, to keep track of what's going on. Magazines will give you an overall perspective about Net trends, and they'll also show you how to reach Net-based resources you can use to stay on top of new developments.

2. Get an Internet account. Once you have a beginning idea of what's on the Net and which areas of it you'd like to explore, sign up for an account with a large ISP. *(See Appendix for more information.)* You'll get access to all the major Internet services at a low price, and you'll also get good support if you run into problems. If you don't want to jump in with both feet at first, join an online service that offers more limited Internet access, such as e-mail, newsgroups, and Gopher services.

3. Send some e-mail. Try out the e-mail system and get used to sending, receiving, reading, forwarding, and deleting mail. Start exchanging e-mail with friends, or at least send a few messages to yourself so you get the hang of it. Don't send marketing messages yet, however, or add your e-mail address to your stationery or print advertising. Your explorations may lead you to settle on a different ISP eventually, and you should be sure you want to use a particular ISP before you begin marketing or publicizing your Net address. Mail will be a fundamental feature of your marketing arsenal, so you should learn to use it as naturally as you use the phone.

4. Explore mailing lists and newsgroups. Use the ISP's search facilities to locate mailing lists and newsgroups on subjects related to your business or marketing plans. For the time being, be a *lurker* and just read the newsgroup or mailing list postings. Get a sense of what sorts of things people post, how they express themselves, and what they talk about. Learn from other people's mistakes by observing. Don't make your own contributions yet — save those for the days and weeks down the road when you're more experienced and you know exactly what your marketing plan will be.

5. Explore FTP and Gopher sites. Use your ISP's search facilities to look for FTP and Gopher sites that contain information in your area of interest. Check out some files on those sites so you'll be familiar with the process. Also, you'll get a sense of what these sites look like and what it's like to view information on them. *(See Chapters 5 and 6 for more examples.)* Think about how your own information could be presented more attractively or made easier to find.

6. Prowl the Web. If your ISP permits Web access, check out some sites mentioned in the magazines you've begun reading, or that are mentioned on newsgroups or mailing lists you're reading.

If you don't like the experience you have with one online service or ISP, try another. Most Net access providers these days have free trial periods, and even if they don't, you can always cancel one account and open another. Once you've become familiar with the various Net services and you're happy with the service you're using, you'll be ready to move ahead with your marketing plans.

3

The Electronic Battlegrounds

Marketing is war. It is war against a host of competitors in the same business as yours who are competing with you for the same customers and the same sales dollars. As in the off-line world, the online market isn't just one big battlefield; it's dozens of smaller battlefields, each of which has a unique terrain. And as in any war, the success of your online marketing attack will depend largely on your ability to choose battles you can win using tactics you can apply skillfully.

The first key to success in the online marketplace is understanding the characteristics of every battlefield so you can choose the ones where your unique product, service, and marketing skills can compete most effectively. In this chapter, we'll look at the online battlefields and see how they're being used to market products and services.

As mentioned in Chapter 2, the online world sorts itself into three main areas: online services, the Internet, and bulletin boards. Although the Internet is now providing a link between these three areas, it's useful to look at them separately in terms of their marketing possibilities.

ONLINE SERVICES

In many ways, online services represent the richest marketing opportunities for the electronic guerrilla. Although even the largest online service is fairly small compared with the total online marketplace, you'll find a high concentration of high-quality customers on these services. Here are some of the factors that make online services promising places to market your company:

1. The services are consumer-oriented. Online services cater to consumers with shopping, games, special-interest forums, and other services. People who join online services want these types of service, so your promotion or ad won't come as a shock, as it might in some Internet locations or bulletin boards where users frown on blatant

commercial activity. Shopping has always been a major attraction for online subscribers.

2. Online services have built-in mechanisms for marketing your wares, including classified ads, billboards, and shopping malls. The marketing staff at each service will help you set up an electronic storefront or promotion.

3. Subscribers to most online services have high educational levels and high average incomes. For example, a spring 1994 study showed that Prodigy subscribers had median household incomes of over $57,000, and nearly half were college graduates. Demographics for CompuServe's subscribers were similar.

4. Each online service has dozens of special-interest forums that help you focus your marketing attack on audiences who are already interested in your product.

5. Online services get lots of traffic. A busy server on the Internet might get 10,000 accesses (or *hits*) a day; each of the major online services gets far more traffic than that. According to the Software Publishers Association, 6 percent of United States households subscribe to an online service. The mean log-on rate for online service subscribers is eleven times per month and about twenty-five minutes per session. Online services have menus and icons that make it easy to notice and locate shopping or other services, so the chances of your attracting subscribers to your store are better than they are on the Internet.

Online services vs. the Net

Some analysts say there are now too many online services in the world. After all, there are now graphical interfaces available for accessing the Internet, and Internet access is getting cheaper all the time. As a marketer seeking maximum exposure, you might prefer to put your promotions on the Net itself, where the potential for visibility is much higher.

At this point, however, potential isn't the same as reality. The online services promise a higher hit rate than the Net because they're easier to use. The technical roots of the Internet and its vastness will present challenges for many years. Even though there are simplified user interfaces for the Net like Mosaic, it's still far more difficult at this point for a would-be shopper to find your store on the Net than it is to find it on an online service. You can't simply connect to the Net and click the "shopping" button to see all the businesses there, as you can in an online service.

In fact, rather than retreating, the online services business is expanding. Each of the three biggest online services reached new highs in subscribers during 1994, and two major computer companies are moving in for a share of the market. In 1994, Apple Computer launched its own online service, eWorld, and in 1995 Microsoft will reportedly include access to its new Microsoft Network service in the new version of Windows it will be shipping.

Our guess is that online services will be with us for many years yet because they give most people what they want in the easiest possible way. Just as people buy magazines because they want a certain selection of news or information on a particular topic in a particular package, they will continue subscribing to online services because they like a service's look, feel, and its collection of services and information.

Marketing on the online services

Jump onto any online service and you'll find marketing in the picture from the very first screen you see when you sign on to the very last screen you see when you sign off.

This "What's New" window automatically appears whenever you connect to CompuServe. The list changes from day to day, but you can see that it promotes eighteen activities, services, or events. In fact, selecting the Special Events/Contents item near the bottom takes you to announcements of other promotions.

Promotional messages like these appear on all the major online services. They change daily, and you can arrange for your new storefront or forum or any special promotions or contests you run to be listed here. *(See Chapter 6 for details.)*

Classified ads

Classified ads are a tried-and-true method of marketing at low cost, and ads are free on some online services. On America Online, for example, the classified ad section looks like this:

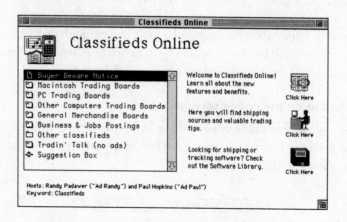

As in a newspaper or magazine, ads are broken up into categories. Here's a list of ads in the Special Holiday Gifts section of the General Merchandise Boards category shown above:

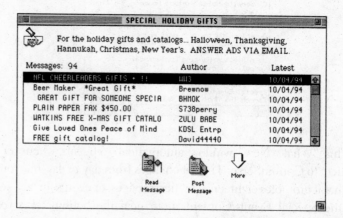

Each ad has a title or subject line. Unlike with newspaper ads, readers can't see all the text of an online classified as they browse the section;

your ad title must prompt them to open up your ad and read on. In addition to a general classified ads area, online services may have topic-specified classifieds in some of their forums *(see Forums below)*. *(For more on using classified ads, see Chapter 6.)*

Forums

Forums, also called *special interest groups* (SIGs) or *roundtables*, are the clubhouses of online services. Most services have at least fifty forums in a wide variety of topics. Here's an example from America Online:

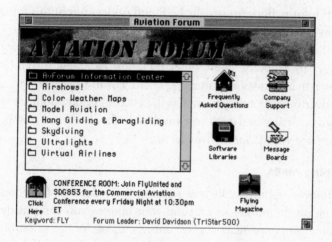

The Aviation forum's main screen shows eight subsections. Each subsection has message boards, software libraries, frequently asked question (FAQ) areas, and general information. There's also a classified ad section specifically for aviation-related items, and a conference room where forum members can gather online in a group chat session to exchange views on a particular topic. In this example, there's a Commercial Aviation conference held every Friday night at 10:30 P.M.

This forum is actually a collection of even more specific forums. There are seventeen message boards on such topics as military aviation, commercial aviation, and air shows. Many online forums are just as detailed and specific, so you can target customers with great precision. For example, if you have a great product for ultralight aircraft, you would zero in on that area and its message board to hobnob with other ultralight enthusiasts and build your company or product's image.

On most forums, direct advertising is prohibited. Here's a typical advertising policy example from the PR/Marketing forum on CompuServe:

```
SOLICITATION IS PROHIBITED ON OUR FORUM'S MESSAGE BOARD
This means that our forum members should not actively promote
their respective businesses on the message board. A member
may upload a brief piece publicizing his/her biz in LIB 5,
provided it's related to the field of professional
communications. And, of course, members are always free to
discuss their work, responding to queries. If anyone has a
question about the policy, ask a sysop for clarification.
```

This information can usually be found under "About this forum" or "Forum Information."

In this case, forum participants are asked to put their promotional messages in a library where other members can view it, rather than posting it to a discussion or message board. Forums may ban indiscriminate advertising, but they're an excellent way to build public awareness of your company and give you invaluable feedback and competitive intelligence. *(See Chapter 7 for details.)*

Shopping malls

Electronic shopping malls host storefronts for dozens of vendors. Depending on the online service and your budget, you can put up your own storefront or participate in an online catalog. With a storefront, you can offer product information, online ordering, and even photos of your products. Here's the shopping area from America Online:

Each listing here is an individual store or business. Let's go inside the America Online Store:

Each product has a separate listing, and clicking on a listing reveals specific information and lets you order. For example, if we were interested in the sweatshirts, clicking on the America Online Sweatshirts item would reveal a selection of shirt sizes. After selecting the Large size listing, we would see this:

Here, you can specify the quantity of large shirts and see how much your total order of shirts in this size will be. The Display Your Shopping Cart icon at the right shows how many items you've added to your order from the America Online Store. The Checkout item collects your credit card or payment information and your mailing address.

The America Online Store is one of several dozen on America Online, and each store has its own screens and ordering setup. America Online's is pretty fancy, but you can be successful with a far less elegant look to your store. Each online service lets you set up stores like this. *(For more information on strategies and techniques, see Chapter 5.)*

Billboards

Of all the online services, Prodigy is currently the only one that will actually rent you billboard space. With a billboard, your message appears at the bottom of the screen a certain number of times per day, week, or month. Here's an example:

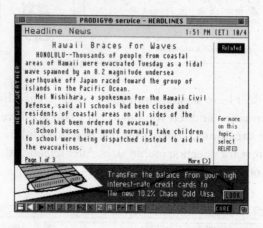

When you read the top headline news item shown on Prodigy's main screen, there's a teaser for a low-interest credit card at the bottom. If you click the Look button, you see a billboard like this:

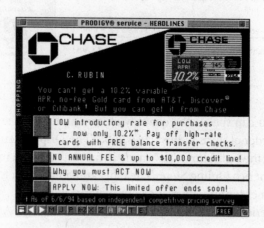

The lower half of this bulletin board has four sections, each of which has a button you can click to see more detailed information or fill out an application. Many of Prodigy's areas have advertising running across the bottom like the news item above, and they usually offer you a quick way to view more information and even order products.

No other online service lets you grab the user's undivided attention like this, but it comes at a pretty high price. Prodigy charges from $2000 to more than $50,000 per month for such billboards, depending on their display frequency, the number of places they appear, and whether the billboards appear in regional or national "editions" of Prodigy. *(See Chapter 6 for more information.)*

Online conferences

If you have some expertise that may be of interest to lots of online subscribers, you may be able to schedule a special online conference. Such conferences are usually promoted in the opening or closing screen of a service, such as this one from America Online:

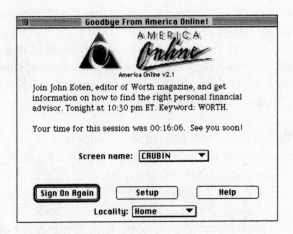

In a conference, an expert on a particular topic enters a chat room at a certain time, and you're invited to join him or her there to ask questions. Everyone in the conference sees all the comments or questions as they scroll down the screen, each preceded by the person's name or conference "handle." Here's a sample from Jay's session on AOL. (His "handle" here is AGuerrilla.)

```
Question        What are your best suggestions on how a small
independent retail store (craft supplies) can best compete
with discount mail order suppliers?

AGuerrilla      Offer better service, more convenience, more
flexibility, and go one-on-one with customers. Offer more
speed, using your customer's names. Learn personal data about
them. Small companies can cream big ones by using those
guerrilla weapons. The big guys can't match that.

WaltFT    What you're describing seems to be wrapped up in
one word, Jay. Attitude!

AGuerrilla      Attitude is part of being a guerrilla Walt.
```

If your expertise is subject-specific, you may be able to schedule a conference on a particular forum or special interest group and promote it just within that group. *(See Chapter 9 for more information.)*

THE INTERNET

The Internet is a relative newcomer to marketing, having been around only since 1991. As a marketing venue, it offers the advantage of reaching millions of people around the world. The key disadvantage is that many of them aren't likely to be interested in or aware of your product. Unlike online services, the Net is an open community, and your marketing messages won't automatically jump in front of a user when he or she signs on. It takes more effort to draw customers to your messages on the Net.

Nevertheless, the Net's potential for commerce is growing by leaps and bounds. Commercial domains joining the Net are growing at about 10 percent (about 1,500 new domains) per month. The Worldwide Web now boasts more than 6 million users, and total Web traffic grew by 1800 percent during 1994. Another sign of growing commercial activity is Dave Taylor's Internet Mall, a free service that lists Net-accessible businesses. During one three-month period in the fall of 1994, the Mall's listings grew 30 percent every two weeks.

Such growth spells opportunity, but it also spells confusion. While online services have offered a handful of workable marketing tools for many years, these tools are still evolving on the Net. Internet shopping malls come and go, for example, and last month's hot marketing vehicle is replaced by something better next month. Some companies flourish by using electronic mail alone, and others do most of their promotion through newsgroups.

But despite the Net's state of flux, there are some basic services whose marketing potential is unlikely to diminish over time.

Mailing lists

There are about 10,000 mailing lists on the Net currently, and that number is sure to rise. Some lists are very specific and are sent only to a group of hand-picked recipients, while others are more general and have hundreds of readers. As explained in Chapter 2, mailing lists are groups of people who all read one another's mail. Any mail addressed to the list's address is sent to every subscriber of the list.

The main advantages to mailing lists are that anyone with e-mail access to the Net can participate in them, and they're easy to work with. Of all the Net services, mailing lists have the widest possible audience, since everyone on the Net has e-mail access at a minimum. Also, it's simple to set up a mailing list program on any Net server. You can do the whole thing yourself using shareware or freeware list management programs if you have a Windows or Unix-based server connected to the Net, and if you don't, many ISPs can set up a mail server for you for less than $100.

Most mailing lists frown on blatantly commercial announcements, but participants often use signatures (or .*sigs*) that are like online business cards which explain their business. And it's not uncommon to see mailing list participants offering advice on a subject close to their own business, thereby encouraging requests for business by direct e-mail response.

To find out which mailing lists are out there, you can:

- search for lists by name using a mailing list search utility from your ISP
- participate in newsgroups that match your interests and watch for mentions of particular mailing lists on the same topics, or post a message asking if anyone knows of some
- check a "list of lists" maintained by someone on the Net *(See Appendix.)*

Once you subscribe to a mailing list, you receive copies of all the mail posted to that list. Depending on how active the list is, that could be one or two messages a day or dozens a day. Some particularly active lists have a Digest option, in which all the day's messages are compiled into one document and sent to you that way. In any event, joining a mailing list means paying attention to your electronic mailbox on a daily basis to check for new messages you've received. *(See Chapter 4 for more on using mailing lists for maximum marketing impact.)*

Newsgroups

Newsgroups are the special interest groups of the Net. There are currently more than 12,000 such groups on just about any topic you could name. As in an online service, a newsgroup is like a message board where participants post and read messages. You can read one message and post a reply to it, or you can add a new message (or *post*, as it's often called). Every message has a subject name.

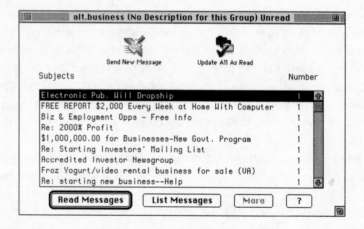

This is a view of the alt.business newsgroup as viewed from America Online's Internet Center. This newsgroup is devoted to business opportunities and information, and unlike most newsgroups, it mostly contains ads for products or services. There are several newsgroups like this on the Net, but most newsgroups are for discussions of a topic and prohibit ads like this.

The icons and buttons around the list of subjects will vary depending on the type of newsreader software you're using to view a newsgroup, but the list of subjects looks the same. Newsgroups can list thousands of messages stretching back for months or years, and the newsreader software will allow you to limit the selection by viewing only messages posted since a certain date, or only messages that you haven't already read.

Once you select a subject name and open it, you see the text of the message itself. Here's the text of the subject selected above:

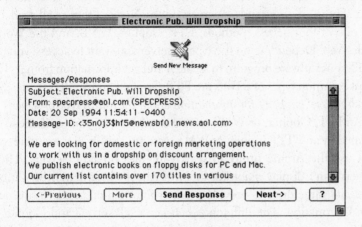

Again, the newsreader you use may look different, but the features are the same. You can jump to the previous message, move to the next message, send a response to this message, or post a new message on a different subject.

A response differs from a new message in that it's attached to the existing message. A group of responses to an original message is called a *thread*. In the alt.business newsgroup example, the Number column in the listing indicates how many messages are attached to each subject (in this case, none of them has generated a response).

Participating in newsgroups is an easy way to focus on a group of people with a particular interest. You can find out what they're saying about the subject in general, what problems or needs they have, what they're saying about your competition, and even what they're saying about you. You can conduct market research about new products or promotions, and you can offer information online that will help build your reputation as a stand-up netizen and will ultimately bring customers to your door. *(For more on newsgroup strategies, see Chapter 7.)*

FTP, Gopher, and WAIS servers

When you have a catalog, article, or other information that you want to make available to netizens at large, you can publish it by storing it on a server. This way, people don't have to ask you to send them a file via e-mail or locate a message you've posted to a newsgroup. You can simply tell people the server's address so they can view or retrieve your information. There are thousands of servers on the Net, but they're all available via one of four access methods: FTP, Gopher, WAIS, and the World-wide Web. Depending on the type of server you want to access, you use a different software program to locate it and get information from it. The most common types of servers are FTP, Gopher, and WAIS servers. *(See "Web servers" on p. 47 for information about the fourth type of server.)*

An FTP, Gopher, or WAIS server (or *site*) is a computer that can be located by an FTP, Gopher, or WAIS searching utility. For example, you can use the Archie utility to search for files on FTP servers. These servers can't display graphics, but you can list information in various files and directories to provide product information, order forms, and free information. The difference between FTP servers and Gopher or WAIS servers is how information is delivered. When you access an FTP server, you see a list of files or directories like the following:

Name	Size	Date	Zone	Host	Path
🗀 helpers	-	9/26/94	1	ftp.acns.nwu.edu	pub/newswatcher/h
🗀 inn-xpat-patch.txt	1k	10/10/94	1	ftp.acns.nwu.edu	pub/newswatcher/i
🗀 ms-word-format-docs	-	10/1/94	1	ftp.acns.nwu.edu	pub/newswatcher/m
🗀 newswatcher-20b14.sea.hqx	426k	10/1/94	1	ftp.acns.nwu.edu	pub/newswatcher/n
🗀 old-release-notes	-	10/10/94	1	ftp.acns.nwu.edu	pub/newswatcher/o
🗀 readme.txt	2k	10/10/94	1	ftp.acns.nwu.edu	pub/newswatcher/r
🗀 release-notes-20b14.txt	12k	10/10/94	1	ftp.acns.nwu.edu	pub/newswatcher/r
🗀 source-20b14.sea.hqx	534k	10/1/94	1	ftp.acns.nwu.edu	pub/newswatcher/s
🗀 user-doc-20b14.sea.hqx	103k	10/1/94	1	ftp.acns.nwu.edu	pub/newswatcher/u
🗀 user-doc-20d17.sea.hqx	77k	7/3/94	1	ftp.acns.nwu.edu	pub/newswatcher/u

ftp.acns.nwu.edu:pub/newswatcher

Here, the server name is ftp.acns.nwu.edu, and we've used the Anarchie utility to view the contents of the newswatcher directory on this server. This server offers a Net newsgroup reading program called Newswatcher, along with related files. We can view the list of files in any directory by double-clicking on the folder icon. To see what's in any individual file or to get a copy of the Newswatcher program itself, we would have to transfer, or *download,* it to our own computer and then open it up there.

On a Gopher or WAIS server, on the other hand, you can open directories and read documents immediately, but all the information is text. You can't display programs like the Newswatcher example on the

FTP server we just looked at. Here's an example of the *Internet Business Journal's* Gopher site as viewed from America Online's Internet Center:

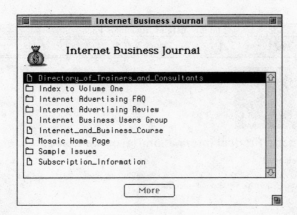

The *Internet Business Journal* is a newsletter, and the company also sells training and consulting services. In order to attract people to its site, you can see the company has posted some sample issues, a directory of Internet trainers and consultants (in which *IBJ* itself is no doubt prominently mentioned), and product information on its training sessions, business users group, and another newsletter devoted to Internet advertising. To view the document Subscription_Information, we would simply double-click on it to display the text in a window.

The *Internet Business Journal* has its own Gopher site, but you can rent space on somebody else's Gopher server to set up a "virtual server" of your own. Some companies charge as little as $100 to set up a gopher site and $30 a month to maintain it.

Gopher and WAIS sites are best for distributing text-based information. If you want to distribute graphics or programs, FTP sites are the least expensive way to go. The Net has many examples of companies that offer information about products on their FTP or Gopher sites and that use that offer of information to boost sales. (WAIS isn't used for marketing information.) *(For more information on FTP and Gopher marketing strategies, see Chapter 5.)*

Web servers

A Worldwide Web server is a computer that can be located and whose contents can be viewed by special graphical software. Web servers can display graphics and deliver sounds as well as text. Many companies are now using Web sites to display product information like the following:

This is the front door, or *home page*, for Adobe Systems's Web site. The page's URL address is in the upper right corner of the window. Each of the underlined phrases and small icons on the screen is a *hypertext link* that calls up another page of information when you click on it. In this case, each link takes you to more details about a particular software product.

Web sites make it easy for others to view lots of information about your products, ask questions, view photos, and even order products, and they're much more inviting visually. But even though a Web site contains pictures like a billboard, it's far less accessible. Unlike a Prodigy billboard that jumps out at prospects like a TV commercial, a Web site is invisible unless you tell people how to reach it. And even though the Web's graphics and sound capabilities make it the most promising marketing medium on the Net, remember that most Net surfers these days don't have access to the Web yet. *(For more information about Web sites and making them visible, see Chapters 5 and 6.)*

Internet shopping services

In the past year a number of Internet shopping malls and services have appeared on the Net. Some are collections of products or services you can look at and order right away. Others are listings of shops and services that can be reached via e-mail, FTP, Gopher, or the Web.

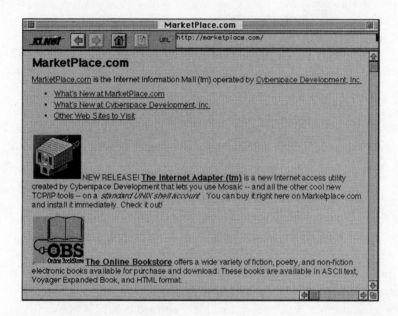

This is the home page for MarketPlace, a graphical shopping mall that displays and promotes Web sites for several businesses in one location. Each business has a hypertext link that automatically takes you to the actual server where the information is located. MarketPlace will even rent you *virtual server* space on its own computers if you don't maintain your own.

For example, clicking on The Online Bookstore on the page above automatically takes you to the OBS server, where you can browse their catalog or order. The OBS server is located on MarketPlace's own computer system.

Shopping malls make finding products on the Web easy, just as they make it easy to find lots of different stores in the physical world. You don't have to know the address of every site you want to visit — you just go to the mall's home page and then click on items you want to know more about. The disadvantage is that your business's Web link may be grouped on the same mall page with links for other companies that compete with yours.

CommerceNet, Cybermall, Branch, MarketPlace, and other malls have plans that will display your icon and link it to a Web site for as little as $50 per month. If you don't have your own Web server, you can rent a virtual server along with a Web link in a mall for as little as $100 per month, depending on the amount of information you display.

If you're not ready to jump on the Net or rent a virtual server, you can simply post a listing for your business in an online business directory. For example, the Internet Mall is a listing that describes businesses operating online. Shoppers can read about your business in an Internet Mall listing, and then contact you if they're interested in hearing more. With an Internet Mall listing, you could conduct all your business via e-mail and save the cost of servers and Web links.

You can have your business listed in the Internet Mall for free by sending a description to Dave Taylor at Netcom (taylor@netcom.com). Dave edits your business description into a one-paragraph listing and adds it to the mall list, which is distributed to a mailing list of subscribers every two weeks or made available for free to anyone who asks via e-mail. You can also see the mall on the Worldwide Web at http://www.mecklerweb.com/imall. Along with the complete Mall listing (which numbers hundreds of businesses now), Dave also sends out a biweekly listing of new Mall members. Here's a sample page from the biweekly update:

```
FIRST FLOOR: MEDIA

Books

Seaside Book & Stamp focuses on two niches: stamps and stamp
collecting supplies and science fiction and fantasy books.
The firm stocks over 10,000 titles and is accessible by
gopher (gopher.nstn.ca 70) through the Web at URL
http://www.nstn.ns.ca/cybermall/first.html or email:
gtucker@fox.nstn.ca

If your interests focus on playing Bridge, Self-Improvement,
Starting a Business, Tennis, Cooking with Herbs, Writing an
Advertisement that Works, or Maintaining Good Health --
Specialty Bookseller offers many below $9..Request by
topic/list. Email wanlitai@cybernetics.net
```

```
Meyer Boswell Books, Inc. is the only bookshop in the English
speaking world specializing exclusively in rare and scholarly
books on the law; send an e-mail message to rare-
lawbooks@netcom.com with the word "help" as the message to
learn about their on-line catalogue.
```

As you can see, businesses listed in the Internet Mall have all manner of Net presences, from a simple e-mailbox (as with Specialty Bookseller and Meyer Boswell Books above) to Web and gopher servers (as with Seaside Book & Stamp above). Going into a mall, you may have to compete with other similar businesses, but as with the Internet Mall listing on the previous page, you should be able to find a way to differentiate what you offer from what others are selling.

The Internet Mall is free, but you have little space in which to explain your product or service, and you have to rely on Dave's editing to get your message across. However, if you disagree totally with Dave's edit, you can suggest changes and come to a compromise. *(See Appendix for information about getting the Internet Mall list.)*

BULLETIN BOARDS

Compared with the Net and online services, bulletin board systems are very small slices of the online marketplace. Most BBSs have 1000 regular subscribers or fewer, although a few have more. Software Creations, the top-rated BBS in a 1994 *Boardwatch* magazine reader survey, boasts 150,000 users and 525 new callers every day.

But what you lose in numbers on most BBSs you gain in devotion. Many BBS subscribers are more active participants than their cousins on the Net or online services, so your chances of reaching any of them during a given day are better. Bulletin boards are also topic- or geography-specific, allowing you to focus on users in a particular subject area or city. Although the majority of BBSs are devoted to distributing shareware, games, pornography, or supporting adult chat lines, there are some in every part of the country that handle other topics such as religion, fishing, medicine, finance, bird-watching, scuba diving, space exploration, law, careers, reptiles, and ecology.

And if you don't find one or more BBSs whose subscribers match your target market, you can always start one of your own. The lists of BBSs in the United States are littered with boards that have been set up by companies to support and market their own products. In fact, Guerrilla Marketing International will soon join this trend with Guerrilla Marketing Online, a BBS where you can view excerpts of Guerrilla Marketing books and newsletter issues, download software, learn about upcoming seminars, collect the latest marketing tips and information, and consult with Guerrilla Marketing's staff.

The advantage of setting up your own BBS is, of course, that you have full control over the content. You can list as much of your product information as you like and take orders online. Of course, people won't want to visit your BBS much if all you're doing is selling, so you'll also have to provide some free information that makes the call worthwhile.

You can set up a BBS with an inexpensive PC, a 9600 bps modem, a phone line, and some BBS software. The whole setup shouldn't cost you more than $2000 to get started. However, you'll also have to devote a lot of time to the effort, including:

- setting the system up (or paying someone else to do it)
- deciding which information you want to offer and how to organize it
- promoting the BBS and attracting subscribers
- monitoring the BBS to make sure it's working smoothly and to see how your promotional efforts are succeeding
- continually revising the content so callers always see something new
- expanding the system as caller demand grows

To get an idea of what sorts of things you can do on a BBS, let's look at this example:

```
Caller number    :  8,797,281         |  Your total calls :  1
You are on node# :  105               |  Security level   :  5
Subscription left:  (never subscribed)|  Your last call   :  Tuesday 10/04/94
Your uploads     :  0 files           |  Your downloads   :  0 files
Download limit   :  1,000,000/day     |  Used today       :  0 bytes
------------------------- >>Demo Mode - Some Limits<< -------------------------
Exec-PC     T O P    M E N U
<F>iles ......... File Collection MENU
<M>essages ...... Message System - Conference MENU
<I>nternet ...... Access to Full Internet Superhighway
<K> QWK Mail .... Access QWK Mail - The off-line mail reader
<S>ubscribe ..... Exec-PC Membership and Renewal sign-up for full access
<R>ead mail ..... Display messages addressed to me
<D>oors ......... Doors MENU - Run PC Catalog, games, chat, more...
<W>ho ........... Show me who is on the system right now
<L>ist-user ..... Find names of subscribers to Exec-PC
<U>ser Settings . Setup MENU - Change my password, address, prompts, etc.
<A>nsi/color .... Turn on/off color and graphics from BBS
<B>ulletins ..... Information about this BBS
<H>elp .......... HELP on the most often asked questions for this BBS
<?>help ......... HELP with this menu
<G>oodbye ....... Log off of Exec-PC     <X>pert ....... Toggles short menus
(52 minutes left)  TOP Menu (?=HELP) -> _
```

This is the top menu from Exec-PC in New Berlin, Wisconsin, the number two BBS in *Boardwatch* magazine's 1994 reader survey. As you can see, it has a variety of services, including a library of files, a mail and conferencing system, Internet access, games, and a help system. This is a fairly representative sample of the kinds of services available on a BBS. *(See Chapter 8 for more about how to market on BBS systems.)*

PART II

Strategies for Online Battles

4

E-mail and Mailing Lists

Electronic mail (e-mail) is as essential to online commerce as the telephone and postal mail are to off-line commerce, so our in-depth discussion of guerrilla marketing strategies for the online market begins here.

As we've already seen, there are many different ways to market your business in the online world, but even if your online connection is limited to e-mail, you can do a remarkable amount of electronic business. You can:

- send promotional messages to individuals
- build your identity on mailing lists
- send product information
- accept orders
- offer customer support

This chapter gives an overview of e-mail and provides tips and techniques for using e-mail for maximum marketing impact.

ABOUT E-MAIL

Basically, e-mail is the electronic equivalent of postal mail. You compose a message, address it, and send it off to the recipient's address. The message is delivered to the recipient's mailbox. The recipient can check his or her mailbox at any time, read the message, and then save it, reply to it, forward it to somebody else, or toss it out.

The main difference with e-mail is that messages are delivered in seconds or hours instead of days or weeks, and the computer gives you lots of automated features that make managing e-mail much easier than paper mail.

Using e-mail

In order to use e-mail, you need an online account through an ISP, online service, or BBS. The service you choose should have an *Internet mail gateway* that allows you to send mail to anyone else on the Internet, instead of only to people on the particular service you're using. Every ISP, all of the major online services, and many BBSs provide this type of mail service, but, as mentioned in Chapter 2, you may want to ask about or test several services for yourself until you find one that has a mail system you feel comfortable using.

Composing mail

With a mail account set up, you now have access to the 30 million or so other people on the Net who have e-mail addresses. Your job will be to reach the ones who are interested in buying your product or service, who have already bought your product or service, or who can recommend your product or service to someone else.

The process begins when you compose a message. To do this, you enter the mail function of your online service, ISP shell account, or BBS, or start the mail program you're using on your computer. Here's an example from America Online's mail program:

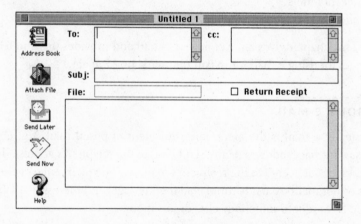

The upper portion of the message (which contains the To:, cc:, Subj:, File:, and Return Receipt boxes) is called the message's *header*. The header contains the information your mail system (or *mailer*) needs to properly handle your message.

The To: box, where you type the address or addresses of the person(s) to whom you want to send mail, can contain as many addresses as you like, but it must contain at least one.

- If you're sending only to someone on the same online service as you, you need only enter their user name on that service. For example, if you're on America Online and you want to send mail to Guerrilla Marketing's mailbox, the To: box address would read, GM INTL.
- If you're sending to someone across the Internet, you need to enter their full Internet address. For example, if Guerrilla Marketing wanted to send a message to someone named Bob Jones on Netcom, the To: box address might read, bjones@netcom.com.

As you work with e-mail, you'll build a list of addresses for people you contact all the time. You can add these to your *address book* and then quickly look up an address and copy it to your message header. In the example above, you display the address book by clicking on the Address Book icon at the left.

Some mailer programs (MCI Mail's and CompuServe's, for example) allow you to compile a list or group of addressees under one name (or *alias*) and then send to everyone on that list by simply putting the list's name in the To: box.

The cc: box is where you enter the addresses of people you want to receive copies of the notice. (*Cc:* stands for carbon copy, just as it does on a paper letter.) Some mail programs also have a bcc: (blind carbon copy) box. Bcc addresses don't show up in the address header of any delivered message.

The Subj: box is where you type a title for the message. Your message can't be delivered without a subject. The proper address ensures that your message reaches its proper destination(s), but a good subject line can be crucial if you want your message to be read. Some of your recipients will be wading through dozens or even hundreds of mail messages a day, and your subject line must work like the title of a book or magazine article, to draw them in and make them want to read the message itself.

The File: box shows the name of any file or document you have attached to the message. If you're attaching a file to your message (perhaps sending a proposal or a price list), you click the Attach File icon at the right and then select the name of the file from a list that shows the contents of your disk. That file's name then shows up in the File: box. If you're sending mail to someone on the same online service, you can attach formatted program files, graphics, or any other binary file. But if you're sending a file across the Internet, you must convert the file to a text format that the Internet's mail communication protocol will accept. Some mail programs have options for doing this automatically.

The Return Receipt box lets you request a receipt that tells you when the message is actually read by its recipient. When the message is read, you'll receive a mail message telling when this occurred. However, the Return Receipt function only works when you send mail within an online service or BBS, not when you send mail across the Net.

The body of the message, the message's content, goes in the large box below the header. You just type text into the box or paste it in from another document. Normally, you'll perform this task off-line, when you're not actually connected.

It's tempting to use the same formatting conventions you would use with paper mail, but as you'll see in *"Reading mail"* on p. 62, the sender's name and address, the date and time of the mailing, and the recipient's name and address are automatically attached to every e-mail message, so you can leave these out of the body of the message. It seems weird to just start typing the message itself without so much as a "Dear John," but you'll get used to it.

On the other hand, your signature at the end can be an important marketing tool that includes not only your name and company name, but also a promotional message. *(See "Your signature" on p. 76.)*

Saving mail

At any time after you begin creating a new message, you can save the message to your disk. You must type a name for the new file when you save the message — not the same name as the message's subject. We recommend saving early and often. There's nothing worse than getting halfway through a fabulous marketing message when you're called away by a customer in the store and you forget you were working on the message and the janitor comes by and shuts off the computer. Save any messages in progress, and save finished messages when you're done.

Sending mail

Once you've completed the header and body, you click the Send Now or Send Later icon to send the message. On America Online, the Send Now icon only works if you're currently connected. If you're not currently connected (and you probably won't be), you click the Send Later button and the message is saved for transmission the next time you do connect.

Most mail programs let you specify the exact time you want a message sent, so you can have it sent automatically the next time you connect, or you can have the program connect for you at a particular time and send the message then. It's useful to preset a time for sending messages when you use a service that is particularly busy during certain times of the day, or when you have a message that shouldn't be delivered before a certain day or time.

E-mail is remarkably reliable, but sometimes it doesn't go through. Delivery problems are most likely to happen when you send mail across one or more Net gateways, rather than when you just send a message to someone else on the same service as yours. If the delivery system is working properly and the mail was undeliverable because you used a nonexistent address, you'll receive a message that says your mail couldn't be delivered.

If the delivery problem is due to a glitch with a Net gateway or the computer that should be receiving the mail, you may not be notified. If you suspect that your mail didn't go through, however, you could try sending a message to "postmaster@network name," stating the time you sent your message and its subject and asking if the message was delivered. (Fill in the network name shown here with the actual one.) This message will go to the person responsible for the mail system at the network where you sent the message, and if this overworked person has time to check on the delivery for you, you may get a reply asking you to resend your original message, or at least one that confirms your suspicion that your original message didn't go through.

Checking your electronic mailbox

Each time you connect with your service provider, you can check for new mail you've received and then read, reply, forward, save, or delete it. Most services automatically notify you when you have unread mail waiting. Let's look at how mail works on the receiving end.

When you check your electronic mailbox, you see a window like this one from America Online:

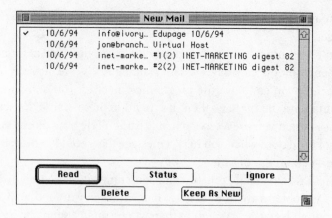

The list shows messages in your in box in the order in which they were received. You can see the receive date, sender address, and subject line for each of the four messages waiting here.

To read a message, select it and click the Read button. *(See "Reading mail" below.)* Once you've read a message, you usually see a check mark or other symbol next to its name in the in-box list, so you'll know in the future that you've already read this message. (The first message in the list above has been read.)

The Status button displays a box of information about each message, such as the exact receive time, the addressee name, and whether or not it has been read.

If you read a message and you don't want the "already read" symbol to appear by its name in your in box, you can select the message name and click the Keep As New button.

The Ignore button tells your in box to check the item as if you've read it without your having to open it.

To delete a message, select its name in your in box and click the Delete button.

Reading mail

When you select a message and give the command to read it, the message then opens in a window like this:

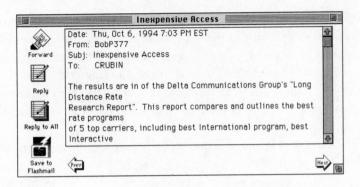

Notice the header information at the top: the receive date, the sender's address, the subject line, and the addressee. In this particular example, the lines wrap inside the borders of the message space in the window. You can make them "unwrap" by making the window itself wider. You can also scroll the window to read the rest of the message. Oddly wrapped lines may also be caused by extra line breaks in the document when it was sent by its author. *(See "The well-mannered message" on p. 75.)*

The icons at the left show you the options for dealing with this message while it's open.

The forward icon lets you forward the message to someone else. When you click this icon, you get a new message form with the previous message copied into the body and space above the forwarded message for you to type a note about why you're forwarding it. You also need to fill in the new message's header with the e-mail addresses where you want the message forwarded. The subject line of this new message is usually filled in automatically with "FWD:" followed by the old message's subject.

The reply icon displays a new mail message window with the header already filled out, like this:

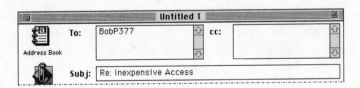

The mail program automatically puts the original sender's address in the To: box of this new message for your reply, and it fills out the subject line as well.

The **Reply to All icon** creates a new message, but instead of automatically addressing it only to the original sender, it adds the addresses of everyone who received the mail (any addresses in the original message's cc: window). When replying to mail, make sure you send it only to the person you want to send it to. It's a common mistake to reply to everyone who got the message when you really just want to respond to the original author.

The **Save to Flashmail icon** saves the message to your own computer's disk. It's important to save incoming mail to your disk, because every service provider will only store messages in your in box for a specific period of time — a week, two weeks, or a month, perhaps — and will then automatically delete them. To make sure important messages are really saved, save them to your own disk.

Other important mail features

The functions above are the bare essentials of any e-mail system. Your mail program should probably have some additional features if you want to use mail most effectively in your marketing effort. Here are a few.

Printing Every mail program gives you a way to print your messages. Some require you to save the message to your own disk first (which you should do anyway, so you don't have to wait for the document to print while you're online).

Automated sending and receiving Your computer can issue the commands to send and retrieve messages much more quickly than you can, and it can do these things when you're not around. If you have a dial-up connection, you should be able to set your computer to automatically dial your service provider, send any messages you composed earlier, retrieve any messages waiting in your in box, and then disconnect. This automated mail handling lets you make sure your mail is checked often. You can set a program to check your mailbox several times a day, every day, if you like. It also allows you to send and receive mail during late-night hours when your office is otherwise closed, and it takes care of the nuts and bolts of mail delivery while you're working on other things. The only thing you have to do is make sure your computer and modem are on during the times you've set up for mail transmissions.

Group message management This gives you options for selecting or arranging the contents of your in box. Some mail programs are quite sophisticated at this; others are rather poor. At the least, you should be able to select a group of messages in your in box and save or delete them all at once. In addition, some programs give you easier options for saving your mail in different folders or directories, sorting your in box listing in different ways — by date, sender address, or subject, for example.

Quoting Use this when you reply to a message. You quote all or part of the message to which you're replying so the reader has a frame of reference. For example:

```
On November 1, you wrote:

>I'm sure there must be a way to reform campaign spending.I'm preparing a
>new bill for the next legislative session.

I agree about the need for reform, but asking Congress to do it is like
asking the fox to voluntarily leave the henhouse.
```

The two lines preceded by > symbols are a quote from a previous message, and the response to it appears on the two lines below. Quoting is a standard practice when replying to e-mail, and the better mail programs let you do this with ease. They either quote the entire message you're replying to automatically (you then go into your reply message and delete parts of the quotation that aren't relevant to your response) or they allow you to select parts of the previous message and then add quote symbols like those above when you paste the selection into your reply message. If your mail program doesn't offer an automated quoting feature, you'll spend extra time identifying quotes yourself.

Bozo filtering This is a way to reject certain e-mail messages automatically. The best mail programs let you set up filters or screens that refuse to accept incoming mail based on the sender's address or a key word or phrase in the subject line. For example, you could set up a bozo filter to automatically reject any messages that had MAKE BIG MONEY NOW in the subject line, or that come from an address which you know only sends out crass get-rich-quick advertising. With a bozo filter in place, you won't even have to deal with messages like this in your in box, because they'll never be placed there.

Of course, you have to be careful when filtering out mail this way. Any filters you set up must be very specific so you don't end up rejecting mail that could have meant business.

ABOUT MAILBOTS

If your net connection is through an ISP, one simple way to distribute product or company information to those who request it via e-mail is to use a *mailbot*. A mailbot, or mail reflector, is a program that receives e-mail messages and then automatically sends a form letter in response to each message. Most ISPs can set up a mailbot program for you for less than $50, and you can do it yourself through an ISP shell account.

For example, suppose you have a file that describes your consulting services, and you don't want to be bothered with having to manually send it to everyone who requests it. In this case, you could set up a mailbot. The mailbot would have its own e-mail address, and it would automatically send your file in response to any mail it receives.

Sometimes mailbots respond to certain commands that must be included in the subject line or body of an e-mail message, but others simply send out a file in response to every message they receive. If you have only one information file to distribute, then a single-function mailbot with a one-track mind is all you need. In this case, your promotional mailings might contain the phrase "For more information, e-mail info@galacksy.com," where info@galacksy.com is the mailbot's address.

On the other hand, if you have several different pieces of information to distribute, your mailbot can be a multifunction one that sends different files in response to different commands. For example, your promotions might ask people to send various commands in their message subject lines or bodies to get different files, as in:

MESSAGE BODY CONTAINS	MAILBOT SENDS
send background	general info about your company
send prices	a price list
send prodinfo	product information

Once you've set up a mailbot program, you can always change the files it sends so they include the most current information. For more about mailbots, ask your ISP.

ABOUT MAILING LISTS

Mailing lists are groups of people who discuss a common topic by sending e-mail to one particular mail address. Usually, the messages (or postings) are compiled by a special *mailing list manager* program at the common address, which automatically distributes every incoming message to all members of the list.

So, for example, if you're interested in Internet marketing, you could subscribe to the Inet-Marketing mailing list, and then all mail sent to that address by the list's members would be forwarded to you. Whenever you had something to add to the discussion, you would send a message to the Inet-Marketing list address, and the message would be automatically sent to all of the list's subscribers.

Some mailing lists are unmoderated, which means all mail sent to them is automatically redistributed to all list members. Other lists are moderated, which means somebody actually reads all the messages sent to the list address and reserves the right to edit or refuse to post them.

Lists can also be open or closed. An open list can be subscribed to by anyone; a closed list has specific requirements for membership. For example, a list might focus on African archeology, and your request for a subscription may be approved or denied depending on your qualifications to discuss that topic.

Finding out about lists

Usually, you'll hear about a particular list you may want to join by participating in newsgroups on the same topic. For example, if you sell stereo equipment and you participate in the newsgroup rec.audio.highend, you may come across the name and address of a mailing list on the same topic.

However, you can also search indexes of mailing lists on the Net. For the Listserv and Listproc mailing list manager programs (the two most popular at this time), there are several indexes available on the Net that show the names and addresses of every list that uses each manager program. You can often search these indexes by keyword to see all available lists on a particular topic. For example, to find all the audio-related mailing lists that use the Listserv program, you can send the e-mail message "list global /audio" to the address listserv@listserv.net. By return mail, you'll get a list of mailing lists that have "audio" in their names.

You can also get a description of a mailing list by sending an e-mail message to the list manager. The reply will tell you what topics the list covers, whether or not it's moderated, and how to subscribe. For example, here's part of the information file on the Inet-Marketing mailing list:

```
INET-MARKETING: Internet Marketing Discussion List

List Title: INET-MARKETING: Internet Marketing Discussion List
List Owner or Contact: Glen Fleishman, fleglei@connected.com

To subscribe to this list, send e-mail to LISTPROC@einet.net; in the body of
the message, type SUBSCRIBE INET-MARKETING followed by your real name and
your organization. For example: SUBSCRIBE INET-MARKETING Jane Q. User of
Jane's Company Name.

To unsubscribe from this list, send the command UNSUBSCRIBE INET-MARKETING
in e-mail to LISTPROC@einet.net.

Send all other list-related commands to LISTPROC@einet.net. For assistance,
send the command HELP.

Send all articles to INET-MARKETING@einet.net.

It is possible to receive the contents of this list as a "digest", a
periodic collection of articles from the list traffic. You should receive
instructions on how to receive the list digest when you subscribe. If not,
you should send a politely-worded inquiry to the list contact.

This mailing list is "edited"; this means that one or more humans must
approve all articles for publication. When you submit an article, it is
reviewed by a human (or humans) who determine whether or not the article
will be distributed to the list.

This mailing list is "moderated"; that means that one or more human beings
monitors the flow of the list traffic and makes an effort to keep
conversations topical. While virtually all lists have a set number of topics
to which conversations should apply, moderated lists are more strict in
their interpretations of the guidelines. To be a good member of a moderated
list, do not go outside the topics of the list without first okaying it with
the moderator(s).

Keywords: marketing, Internet, computer, service

Description:
The INET-MARKETING list is devoted to the discussion of marketing goods and
services in an appropriate way on the Internet.
```

Subscribing to a list

Anyone with an e-mail address reachable over the Net can subscribe to a mailing list. To do this, you need to know the mailing list name, the address of the mailing list's manager program, and the command you use to subscribe to the mailing list.

Every mailing list has two addresses: the *list address,* to which you send messages you want to post on the list, and the *list manager address,* to which you send commands for getting information, subscribing, unsubscribing, and performing other administrative functions. The information file about the list will tell you how to subscribe.

When you subscribe to any list, be sure to save the list's information file or confirmation message, as these will contain all-important information about how to drop your subscription in the future, or how to use other options available for that list. For example, some lists make available an index of all messages ever posted to them, so you could search a message archive for messages on a particular topic. Some moderated lists have a Digest function that lets you receive all the list's traffic for a day or so in one e-mail package, rather than finding lots of individual messages from that list in your box every day.

Participating in a list

To participate in a list, subscribe to it and "lurk" there for a couple of weeks — just read the other messages posted to the list until you get a feel for the topics being discussed and the level of tolerance the list's members have for promotional information. Once you're satisfied that you understand the local etiquette, you can begin active participation. There are three ways to do this:

- respond to a previous post when you feel you have something to add to the discussion
- post some new information that would be valuable for other list members
- suggest a new topic of conversation or ask a question related to the general subject of the list

Make sure to send your message to the list address, and not to the list manager program's address. *(For more tips on how to say what you want to say in the most effective way, see "Marketing with e-mail" on p. 70.)*

Starting your own list

The reason there are 10,000 or so mailing lists on the Net is that you can always further subdivide topics of conversation. Someone may have started out with a list on automobiles, for example, once upon a time, only to see it generate dozens of lists about autos from different countries, auto repairs, auto racing, and so on. If after scanning the Net for lists on a particular subject, you find them all too general, you may want to start one of your own. The more tightly you can focus a group of people around a specific topic, the better your chances of ending up with a group of hot prospects for your business.

You don't need anyone's permission to start a list, but you do need three things:

1. an e-mail address to which you want the mail sent
2. access to a list manager program or the willingness to process the list's mail yourself

3. the willingness and Net contacts to promote the list so others will join it

You also need to decide whether you want to moderate the list.

To meet the first two requirements, the first place to check is your Net access provider. Most ISPs can help you access and run a list manager program to establish your list, or they can direct you to someone who can. There are several widely used mailing list manager programs, including Listserv, Listserver, Listproc, Mailbase, Majordomo, and Procmail. Your ISP should give you access to one of these. If you're running your own Net-connected BBS, you can even set up a list manager program on a PC to manage a list on your own.

Unfortunately, the online services don't support list manager programs, but some of their mail services support group mailing functions that would let you run a list manually. For example, you could set up a CompuServe account for the list address and create a mail group called List for the list's members. Then you could read all the incoming messages yourself and remail them to the List group. Of course, if your subscriber base gets big or the list has a lot of traffic, it will require a lot of effort to maintain the list (and on some online services it will cost you 25 or 50 cents to receive each message from across the Net). But if you can apply the ultimate test of guerrilla marketing (profits) and the activity generates more money than it costs, then why not?

If you do set up your own list, make sure to prepare a list description that explains the list topic, whether it's moderated or not, how to subscribe and unsubscribe, and any other list manager options. Another important item to include is a statement saying that as the list owner, you reserve the right to remove any subscriber from the list. That way, you'll be covered if you get a subscriber who spews a lot of off-topic garbage and you want to feel okay about booting him or her off the list.

MARKETING WITH E-MAIL

E-mail is so fast and convenient that you'll soon feel like firing off messages like popcorn on a hot skillet, but your marketing success demands a more cautious approach. Every aspect of e-mail has its marketing possibilities and pitfalls, including:

- subject lines
- message bodies

- signatures
- your address
- e-mail targeting
- your ability to respond quickly to the interest your mail generates

Let's look at some strategies for making the most of this messaging medium.

E-mail isn't paper mail

Aside from the method of delivery, the main difference between e-mail and paper mail is this:

With paper mail, the sender pays for delivery, but with e-mail, the recipient usually pays something for delivery. At this writing, online services like CompuServe and AppleLink charge from 15 to 50 cents *per message* to receive e-mail across their Internet gateways. So if you send mail to someone on one of these services, they have to pay a significant fee to read it.

And even if your recipient doesn't pay an extra charge to receive mail from across a Net gateway, online time costs money. Unless your recipient is using a corporate or university network where they're not billed directly for online time, each second they're connected costs something. Most people online are acutely aware that the connect-charge meter is running as they go about their online travels. The time your mail recipients take to read e-mail is time they pay for, and it's time they can't spend doing other things online.

E-mail also has the feel of a direct appeal. It's much more like getting a phone call or a knock on the door than like opening a mailbox and sorting through letters. E-mail is more immediate than forums or newsgroups or even mailing lists (where at least you know that the mail is being broadcast to many people at once). Somehow, receiving unwanted e-mail is like hitting your own personal pothole on the information highway.

Ideally, the e-mail you send for marketing online will be so useful, informative, or entertaining that the recipients will be glad to have gotten it. If you can't be sure that this is so (and you can't), the next best thing is to make sure your messages are as efficient as possible — don't bore people, and don't take up any more of their time than necessary.

From the first word in the subject line to the last letter of your signature, everything you put in every message you send either contributes to or detracts from your marketing message. The look of each message is just as important as the look of your store, the way your employees dress, or the type of phone greeting your employees give out. It's your job to make sure that every aspect of your e-mail contributes to your success.

A few words about online expression

The most important tools you'll have for getting your message across are the letters and symbols on your computer keyboard. Most of the people who frequent the online marketplace can see and transmit only these keyboard or *text* characters, so you're limited to words and standard typewriter symbols when it comes to expressing yourself.

Of course, anyone who's spent more than a few minutes online realizes that everyone else labors under the same limitations, and each of us in business seeks an attention-getting advantage. But when writing anything online, whether it's an e-mail message or subject line, a newsgroup or forum posting, or the name of your online store or departments inside it, you should follow some conventions of expression to avoid putting people off. Just as there are signage and architectural conventions you should follow when decorating a storefront (such as not painting your storefront bright red with yellow spots if you're in a neighborhood of stately brick and slate façades), there are stylistic conventions you should follow when expressing yourself online.

Follow normal rules of capitalization. Using all capital letters or asterisks is the online equivalent of shouting. Most people resent it — it's like standing in front of your store and shouting at people passing by. And if you think using all lowercase letters will make your subject line stand out, it won't. Finally, don't overdo it with emphatic symbols like exclamation points or dollar signs. Dressing up your messages with strange capitalization or extra punctuation is a poor substitute for effective writing.

Use emoticons. Since we're not all professional writers, it can be hard to convey emotions like anger, sadness, or laughter, but netizens have come up with a whole range of *emoticons* or *smileys*, combinations of text characters that look like facial expressions when viewed sideways. For example:

:=) Smiling

:=(Frowning

;=) Winking

There are several books that define hundreds of smileys, although you only need to know a few basic ones like those above to cover most situations. If you forget the smiley for a particular emotion, you can always express it as a word inside brackets, such as <grin>. As you cruise the online world, you'll see lots of examples of these and you should become familiar with them.

Use acronyms. There are several acronyms in use online that shrink common expressions to a few letters to save typing, screen space, and most important, the reader's time. Learn these and use them. Here are a few examples:

IMHO — In my humble opinion

FWIW — For what it's worth

BTW — By the way

ROTFL — Rolling on the floor laughing

FAQ — Frequently asked question (There are thousands of FAQ files that answer obvious questions about various Net services, newsgroups, or other features for newcomers.)

RTFM — Read the f—ing manual (A common response to dumb questions that are answered in an FAQ or online instruction file.)

Spell and punctuate everything correctly. Why make grade-school mistakes that will turn off 20 percent of your potential readers? Misspelled words label you as a nonprofessional, as someone who can't take the trouble or lacks the intelligence to do things right. And if your messages reflect this, prospects may think your products or services will, too. If you're not sure about the spelling and punctuation of your messages, get someone to proofread them.

The subject line is your message's front door

The subject line and your name as the sender are the envelope of your e-mail message. They're all your recipients will see when they receive your mail, and they alone must carry the burden of getting someone to actually open your message and read it. Remember, your recipient may be skimming through dozens of messages along with yours, so your subject line should stand out. A good subject line should clearly explain what the message is about; it should provide a reason to open the message; and if you're mailing to an online service, it should accomplish these things in 32 characters or less.

The 32-character limit is imposed by the e-mail medium. Those receiving your messages on online services could well be using mailer software that shows no more than 32 characters of a message's subject line (ISP mailers allow up to 80 characters). As a result, you should consider any subject descriptions that begin after the 32nd character to be potentially invisible. If you must use a longer subject line, make sure that the line works well if only the first 32 characters are showing.

The subject should give a compelling reason for the reader to open the message. The best reason is that the information inside is something the reader requested. For example, if you're responding to a request for information about your product or business, the subject might read, "Book Catalog You Requested" or "RE: Your Info Request."

If your message is a first-time contact, then it should mention a subject you know the reader is interested in, or it should refer to a message the recipient previously sent or to a subject you know the recipient is interested in. For example, "RE: Your Comment On Toys" or "Free Dollhouse Plans."

If your message is a "cold contact" and doesn't relate to a previous message you or the recipient sent, you can boost the power of your subject lines with these words from the guerrilla's vocabulary:

you	now	why	proven
money	secrets	yes	guarantee
save	results	benefits	announcing
new	health	love	how
free	easy	discovery	fast
sale	safety		

Of course, since the main reason many people cruise the information highway is to get free information, we would also add the following:

info	information	news
intelligence	report	bulletin

For example, "Free Tax Bulletin," "Home Pricing Report," or "Commodities Market Intelligence."

Subject lines shouldn't be taken lightly. Try out some potential subject lines on your associates or staff. Show subject lines around without the message they'll go with, and ask people which one makes them most likely to want to read what's behind it. Eventually you'll become a pro at crafting subject lines, but get some help and objective advice in the beginning.

The well-mannered message

Having a great subject line on a long, boring, confusing, or sloppily written message is like putting a gold-plated front door on a garbage pit. In fact, since you've managed to entice readers into opening your message (and spending a few more of those online pennies of their time), they'll resent you if your message is disappointing.

Here are two key guidelines for messages that sell:

Keep it short. If you can't say what you need to say in one page (well, okay, two at the most), then you're not sure what you want to say. This rule applies to promotional messages, not to substantive ones that thoroughly describe your products or services. The initial contact with an online prospect should be brief and inviting. If it leaves the prospect with a few questions, that only means they'll ask them, and thereby give you the opportunity to explain in detail and at greater length just what it is you're offering.

Check the format. There's nothing more annoying than trying to read a message with odd line breaks, short lines, or that is full of extraneous characters. Sometimes your mailer and online service may add line breaks or extra characters as it transmits your message, but you can try to anticipate these problems and avoid them. For example:

- Format your messages so each line is between 60 and 80 characters long, the length of a line in a typical word processing document.
- Make sure paragraphs are separated with a blank line between them so they don't run together (any indents or tabs you use may be eliminated in transmission).
- Don't use centered or justified alignment, as these formatting options probably won't survive a trip across the Net.
- Don't use special formatting characters, which are often unique to the computer system you're using and won't survive Net travel either.
- Use underline characters to indicate underlining or italics. Your computer system may let you apply boldface, underlined, or italic styles to type, but again, these don't travel in e-mail messages. To italicize

something like a book or magazine article title, put a single underline character before and after the title, like this: "See Jay Levinson's _Guerrilla Marketing_ for more information."

- Proofread the text thoroughly before you send it, to make sure there aren't any last-minute typos or problems that will interfere with the quality of your message. After all, this one message may be your only chance to reach a particular prospect.

Your signature

You can end your message with a "Sincerely yours, Jane Doe," just as you would with paper mail. But if this is all you do, you're missing a big marketing opportunity. It has become an accepted norm for people to add a *sig*, or signature, a business-card-like block of information below their signoff, and you can use sigs to provide your business name, contact information, and even a brief identity slogan in one convenient place. You can use sigs not only in e-mail messages, but also in newsgroup or forum postings where more blatant forms of marketing are frowned upon.

Here's a vertically oriented sig that spells out the person's name, company, postal (or *snail mail*) address, phone, fax, and e-mail address:

```
------------------------------
Adam Bunting
ARB Mattress Company
460 Menkin Place
Drowse, Virginia 20150

Phone  (703) 555-9247
Fax    (703) 555-4560
E-mail bedrest@arb.com


------------------------------
```

Notice the dashed lines on either end of the sig, which act like the visual edges of this electronic business card. The only problem with this sig is that it wastes screen space. Remember, the more lines you use, the longer it takes to read and transmit your sig, so the sig should be as space-efficient as possible. You won't be getting off on the right foot if your sig shows you to be an ignorant waster of precious online bandwidth.

Further, many newsgroups and mailing lists frown on sigs that are blatant wasters of screen space. Four lines is considered a safe maximum, but above that you could risk being labeled as a bandwidth hog. This sig could just as easily have been squeezed into four lines if the information was arranged horizontally. For example:

```
--------------------------------------------------------
Chris Terman, Financial Aid Advisor: chris@clarity.com
Clarity College Funding Service: For info, info@clarity.com
Quality Scholarship Search Services for USA Students
PO Box 1002, Globe, AZ    85711   (602) 555-7155
--------------------------------------------------------
```

This sig crams a lot of information into four lines. It even adds information about the nature of the service and the e-mail address of a mailbot program that automatically sends information. Still, this seems a little crowded and hard to read. How about:

```
Robin Shadegg: The Shadegg Corp.   | shadegg@mphisto.com
     Strategic Planning for        |
     Marketing Development          | Voice: 206-555-6477
8203 - 39th Street                  | Fax: 206-555-6553
Spokane, Washington 98115           | Home: 206-555-6551
```

This sig combines a lot of information in a visually appealing layout. The only problems we see here are the vertical dashes and the indenting of the company's identity statement. As you can see, the vertical lines don't quite line up (they would on some computers, but not on others), and the indenting could be thrown off in the same way. It would depend on the type of computer being used to read the message. You should make your sig format "translation-proof."

In lieu of a business mission statement like the one above, some cybernauts like to include a quotation that expresses their company's mission or their outlook on life or business, like this:

```
-------------------------------------------
Adult Literacy Consultants
415-555-8271 info@readme.com

"Knowledge will forever govern ignorance...."
-James Madison
-------------------------------------------
```

Again, notice the mail responder address in this sig. Also, the person's name isn't included in the sig itself, because it was used in a sign-off line located between the sig and the end of the message body.

Finally, some internauts like to use Ascii graphics, little pictures made up of symbols or letters from the keyboard, like this:

```
*************************************************************
_____|\ o|\   | Premier Printers & Publishing
| / |\ || \ |\ |__ |  1000 World Trade Center    ofc: 804-555-8160
| \_ |_/ .||_/ .| \|\_|  Roswell, NM 80510           fax: 804-555-7113
    | |                  http://www.ppp.com/     email: sales@ppp.com
*************************************************************
```

Ascii graphics seem like a good way to make your sig stand out visually, but they're usually more trouble than they're worth. The problems of spacing and alignment that you can have when your message is viewed on different types of computer systems make it difficult, if not impossible, to come up with a graphic that looks the way you want it to look on every computer where it might be viewed. Personally, we can't really tell what the above graphic is supposed to represent. Can you?

Nevertheless, you should definitely come up with a sig of your own. It doesn't have to be fancy; it just has to provide your name, company name, and at least your e-mail address in a compact format so your correspondents can refer to it again easily. In fact, you may want to come up with a variety of sigs for different marketing purposes. If you're in the furniture business, for example, you might have one sig that highlights your expertise in bedding, another that promotes your decorating services, and a third that stresses your financing or free deliveries.

Your address

Whether your mailbox is on an online service or you have access through an ISP, use an address that helps promote your business. If you're on an online service, use your company name or an evocative word as the mailbox name, such as gladrags@aol.com for a clothing store or literati@prodigy.com for a bookstore. If you have access through an ISP, you can go further and request your own domain name, so that it appears to all outsiders as if you have your own corporate network. For example, your bookstore might have the domain literati.com, and it could have one or a dozen different mailboxes such as sales@literati.com or info@literati.com.

Domain name service is available from most ISPs and, depending on the type of account you have, is included at no charge or costs a few dollars a month.

Provide useful content

People on the Net are usually looking for useful information — they're not just hanging around in cyberspace looking for people to talk to, or if they are, they're in chat rooms doing that. Whether you're sending mail to one individual or to a list or posting to a newsgroup, make sure your messages have a high *signal-to-noise ratio*. A high signal-to-noise ratio, the ratio of useful content to meaningless blather, is the ultimate test of any good message.

Stay on the topic. You probably wouldn't appreciate having to get up from *Monday Night Football* to take a call from a solicitor peddling municipal bonds, and most people don't like being intruded upon with messages on topics they have no interest in (or no interest in at that time or in that context). The main reason *spam attacks* — mass e-mailings or newsgroup postings of messages — don't work is that they're off the topic for 99.5 percent of the people they reach. The reason well-written messages to targeted markets *do* work is that they're on the topic — you're adding information to a discussion others are already involved with.

Obviously, you're anxious to tell the online world about your business, but you have to accept the reality that most of them just won't care. Of course, this general apathy won't matter because you can make plenty of money by reaching those who do care. The best way to make sure you stay on the topic is to use e-mail only to respond to queries from others, or to post relevant and useful information on mailing lists.

Provide information, not hype. Quote objective sources or cite objective findings rather than expecting people to take your word for it. Use statistics. If your service saves people 40 percent over another service, explain how and why. Try your best to put out messages that others will consider to be information, rather than an intrusion. For example, in the message about inexpensive phone access on p. 63, the author tells people to send him e-mail asking for his free report. He's asking people to extend themselves without much reason to do so. If, on the other hand, he included key excerpts from that free report in the initial mailing, he would have a much better chance of engaging people's interest and getting them to ask for more.

Use word-of-mouth marketing

Word-of-mouth advertising is the best kind, because it involves one friend telling another about something they found useful. The built-in forwarding function in every mail program makes word-of-mouth advertising spread even more quickly. Since it's so fast and simple to forward a message to someone else, it would be great if people to whom you sent promotional messages or product information would forward them to others they knew were interested.

Some forwarding will happen automatically. Friends on the Net are constantly forwarding information to one another, or posting something they thought was particularly interesting or useful to a mailing list or newsgroup where they felt it would be appreciated.

However, just as you might ask your in-store customers to recommend friends who might be interested in your products or services, you can come right out and ask your e-mail customers to forward your information to others who might be interested. And the beautiful thing about e-mail is that the information will be forwarded from friend to friend, associate to associate, rather than from seller to prospect.

You don't have to hit anyone over the head with the idea of forwarding your messages, but a brief "If you found this information helpful, feel free to pass it on" at the end of your mail could expand your marketing efforts with no extra effort from you.

Save messages to save hours of effort

After you've spent hours, days, or weeks coming up with a dynamite subject line, a killer message, and a sig that will live forever in your prospects' memories, it would be a real waste if you only used them once. E-mail is a fast and efficient medium, but it's even faster and more efficient when you can pull prewritten messages and sigs from your arsenal of marketing weapons and fire them off at will.

As you create messages and sigs, save them with descriptive names in directories or folders on your computer. As your marketing attack advances, you'll find yourself expanding the library with new messages, but a message you wrote weeks or months ago may be just the thing for a new prospect, or it can quickly be modified to suit a new marketing task.

If you develop a series of sigs for different purposes, create a directory for them and save them with descriptive names so you don't have to open them all up and read them each time to decide which one you want to use.

And along with your library of e-mail classics, save any customized messages you sent to specific individuals or mailing lists so you can refer to them if you need to. For example, if you sent a promotional message to a particular mailing list, save it with the name of the list you sent it to and the date so you can find it again easily. That way, when someone responds with "Regarding your message of November 20," you'll have a better chance of knowing what they're talking about. Many mail programs have an option you can set to automatically save each message you send.

Test messages before broadcasting them

You wouldn't put out a radio, TV, or newspaper ad without running it by a few friends or employees first, so don't make this mistake with e-mail you're sending to a group. Before you send the message, have others you know and trust read it and make sure the message hits the bull's-eye. Your first message is your best chance to get your online identity off on the right foot (and it may be your only chance with many prospects), so don't blow it.

Customize messages to test markets

As you craft e-mail messages for different markets, you can test which message or which market is responding the best by asking respondents to include different code numbers or key words in the subject line of their information requests. For example, if you mail to both a high-end audio mailing list and a professional audio mailing list, your messages could tell people to ask for high-end amplifier information or professional amplifier information. This way, you'll know by the number of messages using each phrase which of the two messages worked better for you.

If you're using a mailbot to dish out your product information, you can still track which markets are best by programming the mailbot to send the same document in response to two or more different messages, say "send high-end amp info" or "send pro amp info." The mailbot will keep track of how many messages it responds to, and you'll have a quick gauge of which market is working the best.

Build a mailing list and use it

The best source of future sales is people who have already bought or shown interest in your product. When you receive requests for information or orders, save the customer names and e-mail addresses, and make a note about what the customer bought or asked about. You can use the same computer you need to go online to set up a simple database of customer information. This way, you can create mailing lists that let you make the most of the information you gain from your marketing efforts.

For example, you could set up a simple database file with one field for the e-mail address, another for the person's name, a third for the date of the last contact, and a fourth for a note about what the person bought or asked for information about. If you used uniform code words to describe various customer interests in the notes field, you could later select records based on different interests. For example, if you sell books, your notes field could contain genre information such as romance, general fiction, mystery, and cooking. Then if you have a spring sale on cookbooks, you could target just that part of your list with an e-mailing.

E-mail makes it easy to gather customer information, because the person's mail address is included in the header of any message you receive. You can simply copy the address information right into your database file, and then fill out the rest of each database record by hand.

Once you've set up a simple database in which to store the information, the real strategy comes in choosing which types of addresses to use. In selecting your addresses for mailing, there are three categories of prospects:

1. People who have bought from you in the past.
2. People who have requested more information from you in the past.
3. Everybody else who might be interested (newsgroup or mailing list members, for example).

Our advice is to focus on categories 1 and 2. Doing a mass mailing to category-3 people will likely label you as a junk mailer, and will probably hurt your chances of being taken seriously in future mailings.

For the first two categories, however, it's appropriate to send special notices every few months, just to keep in touch, especially if you're really offering something special for a limited time, or which isn't part of your regular marketing effort. This could be in the nature of a "thank you" or "preferred customer" offering, or simply a brief update on what's new with your business. The point is that you maintain your relationship with previous customers and prospects. Remember, you're fighting for share of mind with dozens of other companies and thousands of other information sources on the Net, so you need to take the initiative once in a while.

One thing each targeted message should contain is an offer to drop people from the list. Some people just won't want to receive your mailings, especially if they're paying a special Internet receive fee to get the message delivered to an online service. A sentence at the end of the message offering to drop people from your mailing list lets them know that you're sensitive to their concerns about unsolicited mailings. This is much better than saying nothing and waiting for people to flame you for intruding into their mailboxes.

THE TOP TWELVE E-MAIL STRATEGIES

In summary, here are the top twelve e-mail strategies for the online guerrilla:

1. Compose and read mail off-line. Don't try to write new messages or responses to ones you've received while you're connected. Your attention will be distracted by the knowledge that you're connected and that, in some cases, the connection charge meter will be running. You're much more likely to write an effective message, correctly spelled and formatted, if you have the leisure to compose and review it without worrying about connect charges.

2. Use an effective subject line. You may not get the chance to explain further in your message if the prospect won't open it.

3. Pay attention to the message's style and clarity. You wouldn't dress like a slob at the office; don't dress your messages like slobs on the Net.

4. Use an effective signature. Everyone appreciates having a business card, and your signature is your electronic business card.

5. Use an evocative address. Choose a screen name, user name, or domain name that helps promote your business.

6. Keep messages short. Again, don't waste people's time. If they want more information, they'll ask for it and you can then take more time to explain things.

7. Provide useful information. There's a big difference between hype and information, and your readers know it.

8. Create an e-mail library. As you develop successful messages and signatures, save them and reuse them. Also, save all your outgoing messages so you'll know what you said where and when.

9. Stay on the topic. Nothing ruins your reputation more than sending messages that waste people's time because they're not interested.

10. Test messages. Try out your messages with individuals before sending them to the masses.

11. Test markets. Use slightly different response mechanisms to test the pull from different markets.

12. Build and use a mailing list. Stay in regular contact with former customers or prospects to keep your identity fresh in their minds.

5

Electronic Storefronts

An electronic storefront is a place in cyberspace where you present your wares through a catalog, product descriptions, price lists, and other information. Customers can browse in your store and perhaps order online. If you sell lots of different items, a storefront is the most efficient way to tell prospects about them. Companies now online offer books, music, flowers, food, clothing, luggage, jewelry, and many other collections of merchandise, and you can, too.

Guerrillas use electronic storefronts to expand their virtual selling space, offering their products and services to thousands of self-targeted people they wouldn't otherwise reach. A neighborhood bookstore in Berkeley, California, can gain an international marketing presence via the Net or an online service. An art gallery in New York can sell posters in Australia at three in the morning.

There is a range of options for setting up an electronic store. You can spend $50,000 for your own server equipment, graphics capabilities, a high-speed phone connection, and the capacity to handle thousands of transactions per day, or you can spend a few hundred dollars to set up shop in an electronic mall and rent space there for less than $100 a month. In this chapter, we'll look at the ins and outs of setting up, operating, and promoting an electronic storefront that matches your budget and your overall marketing plan. You'll learn how to choose the right storefront option, how to design it, and how to bring customers into it.

There are hundreds of electronic storefronts on online services and on the Net. They run the gamut from a simple collection of files at an FTP site to a color catalog on a Web server. But there are two fundamental characteristics that make or break a store's success: location and presentation.

STOREFRONT LOCATIONS

Location has a lot to do with whether your online store turns a profit. The fanciest storefront in the world won't contribute to your bottom line if people can't find it. The simplest store in the world will keep your cash register humming if it sells what people want in a place where they can find it easily. The location you choose determines how people can find and use your store, who can access it, and how you can present information in it.

In the darkness of cyberspace, some people say that all locations are equal, since every store is just one address among millions. Stores can offer thousands of items or just a handful, but their addresses are all the same size.

Still, some stores are easier to get to than others. When you dial up an online service, the Shopping button is right there on the welcome screen, so it's easy to find the mall. When you're on the Net, there is no Shopping button, although your store can be one of many at one Gopher or Web location.

The basic decision you must make is whether to move into a mall on an online service, or to put up your own storefront on the Net, either in a mall or by itself. Some online guerrillas swear by a niche in an online service's shopping mall, claiming that online services have the highest concentration of buyers. Others are striking gold on the Net because it gives them access to customers around the world.

LOCATING IN AN ONLINE SERVICE

When you locate in an online service, you put up a storefront in the service's shopping area or mall. Your "store" is actually a name on a menu or an icon in the shopping area. When customers select that listing or icon, they're taken into your store to see selections of merchandise or services.

TWO WAYS TO OPEN A STORE

Technically speaking, there are two ways to obtain space in an online service:

- rent storage space on the online service's own computer
- establish a link or *gateway* between the online service's shopping mall and a server or host computer someplace else

The advantage to setting up inside the service's own computer is that it's less hassle: the service sets up the store and takes care of maintaining the computer system. But setting up on a service's computer limits your audience to the subscribers of that particular service — your store on Prodigy's computer is only available to Prodigy subscribers.

If you set up a gateway, you take responsibility for setting up and maintaining the computer system that stores and presents your information. You also have to make sure your communications link to the online service is reliable. Larger operations like J.C. Penney have their own computers to serve such a gateway, but smaller firms pay an ISP or consultant to maintain the computer system and gateway for them. While a gateway arrangement can mean more maintenance effort for you, it has several advantages:

- You can build gateways from one computer system to more than one online service. For example, J.C. Penney has gateways to Compu-Serve and Prodigy, allowing any of those services' 3.5 million subscribers access to its wares, yet it only has to maintain one physical store on one computer system.
- You have more control over the information you provide. If you use the online service's computer, you might be allowed to "redecorate" your store — change its menu structure, for example — only a couple of times a year, whereas you could change it whenever you liked if you had your own computer linked by a gateway.

Whichever technology you use, you pay the same price for a mall store. If you want to have a gateway to more than one online service, you must pay each online service's mall charge.

To explore shopping malls on online services further, get a trial account on each of the major services and browse their shopping areas. Each service's mall has its own look and feel; one may appeal to you more than the others. Each service also has a different group of subscribers, and one service may have more hot prospects for your business than another. To find out more about the demographics, the cost, and the procedure for setting up a store in any online service, contact a mall marketing representative at the service. *(See Appendix for phone numbers and addresses.)*

PROS AND CONS

Locating in an online service has both good and bad points. Some stores come and go within months in an online mall, while others make money year after year. Here are the basic advantages to choosing an online service as your store's location.

Production services Online services like CompuServe, AOL, and Prodigy will "build" your electronic storefront for you if you rent space on their computer. These services have a standard storefront look — all you do is supply the text and graphics you want to display. The process takes a month or two, and the cost is included in the store's rental fee. (If you have a gateway, the store's setup is your responsibility.)

A captive subscriber base Online services funnel large, well-heeled groups of subscribers to your store. If you set up on the Net instead, you'll have to do more to attract them yourself.

Visibility The shopping mall is a main feature of every online service, so subscribers can find it (and your store) easily. If you're on Prodigy, you can get even more visibility by renting billboard space. Billboards pop up as subscribers move around on the Prodigy service, and they can include buttons that take interested readers directly to your store.

Promotion As part of your store agreement, you get a grand opening notice on the service's welcome screen. Every subscriber will see a message about your new store for a week or more. On CompuServe, you also get a series of marquees, which are display ads that pop up whenever a subscriber enters the shopping area.

The major drawback to having a store in an online mall is the cost. The least expensive option for having a store in CompuServe's mall is $20,000 per year plus 2 percent of sales made through the store. Other options go as high as $100,000 per year, and other major online services have similar rate structures. You have to move a lot of product to make such a store pay. Recent statistics on CompuServe's shopping area reported that only 4 percent of people browsing in the mall actually bought something.

But 4 percent is a better rate of return than most direct-mail campaigns, and when the mall has thousands of shoppers per day, 4 percent can be plenty. Penny Wise Office Products in Edmonton, Maryland, has had stores on CompuServe, America Online, and GEnie since 1991. Although the company has a multimillion-dollar direct-mail business, its online stores and bulletin board service now account for about 20 percent of its orders.

Online services also give you less control over the information your store presents and how it looks. The online service's own computer technology limits your presentation: CompuServe marquee notices can only contain text, not graphics. If you want to include pictures of your merchandise, your options for showing pictures are limited to the method by which the online service can deliver them. In some online malls, it can take a minute or more to transfer one graphical image to a shopper who wants to see it.

If you rent space on the online service's own computer, your store agreement may place a limit on the number of products you can list, the number of graphics you can use, and the number of changes you can make to the store in any month or year.

LOCATING ON THE NET

If you put up a storefront on the Net, you have more control over what it contains, where it is located, and how the information is presented. You can also set up a store for a lot less money.

The Net is a mix of different types of computers and access technologies, so you have a lot of choices about how you present your store. To set up on the Net, you need:

- a computer (or space on one) that's connected to the Net via an ISP
- a storefront on that computer, which is a system of menus or icons that categorize your store's offerings and allow customers to browse and check out the merchandise

How to get a location

If you can design a store yourself, you may need only an ISP to provide space on one of its computer systems and access to the Net. If you have your own computer system, you may need only the ISP to provide a Net connection. But guerrillas know how to make the most of their time and money, and you'll probably want to pay a consultant or Internet Presence Provider to design and set up the store for you.

To do it yourself, you'll have to learn the intricacies of Unix server technology, interface design, and Net connections. Software is available now that makes it easier to design a store, but you still need a lot of technical knowledge. You also need a network server you can use to support the store.

You could spend $5,000–$30,000 on a moderately fast Unix workstation, plus another $5,000–$10,000 to set up a high-speed telephone connection between the computer and an ISP, plus a few thousand in salaries and fees to design the store and run the system. In all, you could spend $50,000–$100,000 in the first year. Even if you already own the server and have a programmer on your staff, you're still taking on a lot of work for your company.

As a guerrilla, you'll want to gain the most market presence for the least time and money. When it comes to online markets, that means renting equipment and hiring a consultant. Depending on the size of your storefront, you can set up for a few hundred dollars. On the equipment end, you have two rental options:

- a *dedicated server* of your own
- a *virtual server*, which is space on a shared computer that looks like a separate server to your customers

Some ISPs also offer production services to help you design your store and get it up and running, especially if it's a simple Gopher site. Most ISPs can also make files available via FTP from their host computers, so you can store your catalog or product description files on your ISP's computer to create an FTP storefront. If your ISP doesn't offer production services, look up an Internet Presence Provider, a company that specializes in setting up online stores. *(See Appendix to locate an Internet Presence Provider.)*

Different servers, different stores

When you put a store on the Net, you can choose among several types of servers to present it. The server type affects how customers can find and access your store, how you present the store's merchandise, and how you promote the store's existence.

An FTP site FTP sites are reached with the FTP command from an ISP shell account (if the customer knows your site's address) or by using the Archie or Anarchie search utilities or Fetch, a file retrieval program. For example, a customer shopping for hand tools might ask Archie to search for *hand tools*, and Archie would return with a list of FTP sites that contained files or directories with that phrase in their names. The customer could then go to your site and retrieve your catalog or product descriptions from files there. But rather than waiting for people to search for your site, you would probably tell prospects about it directly through e-mail or by participating in newsgroups or mailing lists.

With an FTP site, you can create files or directories containing product descriptions, price lists, catalogs, or other information. Your files can contain text, graphics, sounds, or computer programs, too. The problem is that your customers have to download the files from the FTP site to their own computers and open them there to see what they contain. This is not an ideal situation. It's like making your customers take home a sealed box before letting them examine the merchandise. Your prospects will have to be pretty sure from looking at the names of files at your site that those files contain the information they want.

On the other hand, FTP sites are easy to set up and very inexpensive. Your Internet access account with an ISP probably allows you to store up to 5 megabytes of files on the ISP's computer at no extra charge, so all you have to do is place your files there. In a matter of minutes, you can store your files where anyone on the Net can get them via FTP. If you want to store more than 5 megabytes of data, the additional cost is from $10 a month and up, depending on the volume.

FTP sites are best when you're selling products or services to the technical community or to veteran netizens who are familiar with FTP as an Internet service. Lots of netizens don't have FTP services, or if they do, they're not comfortable using them. (Most of the major online services only began offering FTP to their subscribers in early 1995.) And even if a shopper can navigate to your site, the extra steps he or she would have to take to download files about your wares may prove too much of a bump in the road to the sale.

A Gopher server With a Gopher server, you organize your information by menu options. Each option displays different pages of text, and shoppers can see that information by simply selecting a menu option, much as they would in an online service's shopping mall. Like an FTP site, shoppers can find a Gopher server with a search utility like Veronica or you could direct prospects to your server address through e-mail, newsgroups, or mailing lists. If you rent a Gopher server or virtual Gopher server from an Internet Presence Provider, you may be able to locate in the provider's mall and gain exposure from the provider's own efforts to promote the mall as a Net destination.

Unlike a store in an online service's mall, however, Gopher servers can only display text information. You couldn't display pictures of your products.

Gopher servers are a little more expensive than FTP sites, perhaps $50–$200 per month. You'll pay a hundred dollars or so to have somebody set up such a site for you, and the process may take from a week to a month. On the other hand, Gopher servers are available to most netizens and they're easier for customers to use. Your Gopher storefront will be accessible by far more people than an FTP site.

A Web server Web servers are rapidly becoming the storefronts of choice on the Net. With a Web server, you can display graphics, sounds, or even video as well as text. If you want to give shoppers the most realistic experience of your products, the Web is for you. Along with setting up a storefront, you can build hypertext links from your store to other Web sites as long as you get those sites' permission.

Links give your storefront many different doors. Your Web site might sell sports equipment from its own server, yet have links in MarketPlace, CyberMall, Branch, or other Web malls. Each link puts your store name in another location on the Net and gives browsers an easy way to get to your store. Like banks that set up automated teller machines at shopping malls and other locations, Web links let you take your store to the customers rather than making them come to you.

Once your Web site is up and running, you can direct customers to its address, establish hypertext links to other Web sites so customers can find you from them as well, and promote your address through e-mail, newsgroups, and mailing lists.

You can rent a full Web server for $250 a month and up, depending on its capacity and speed. A virtual Web site costs as little as $50 per month, although it depends on how many pages of information your store contains.

Web usage is growing quickly. In early 1995 most of the major online services began offering their subscribers a way to prowl the Web, and some BBS systems are jumping on the bandwagon as well. However, developing a Web storefront will be more expensive than having a Gopher server, because you'll have to put more effort into the design of the store's graphical interface. Each graphical page of information on a Web site can cost $500 or more to design.

THE STORE'S PRESENTATION

Once you've determined your store's location, you can turn to the store's design, its look and feel. The look of your store on a given type of server is dictated by the type of merchandise you're selling and the people to whom you hope to sell it. There are several aspects to consider.

The front door If you're in an electronic mall, the look of your front door is limited by the capabilities of the mall itself. Online services, Gopher servers, and FTP sites offer menus of text information, so browsers will see only your store name or department names. Web malls can display graphics, so you might include your logo or an evocative picture. Here's the sign for Grant's Flowers on the Branch Mall:

Store owner Larry Grant shows his guerrilla instincts by using a logo to make his store stand out from the others.

The navigational system A trip through your store usually means selecting menu options, clicking on icons, or downloading files. The journey starts with a *home page* (if it's a Web site) or *top menu*, where browsers get an overview of your store's contents. If you're in a mall or are sharing server space with other companies, customers will have to select your store's name from a list in order to see your actual storefront.

Your store's facade is its top menu or home page. This is the place to promote what you sell. Here's one for a jewelry store:

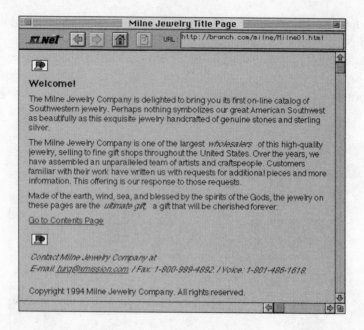

The idea here is to entice customers further into the store. Owner Sherry Milne describes her store's expertise in gathering together a collection of southwestern jewelry. If you're curious enough to want to see more, click *Go to Contents Page* to see the menu of options for browsing the store:

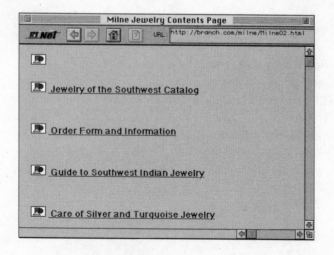

You can display each logo by double-clicking the generic icons shown, but you have to wait a few seconds for each logo to appear. There's a different logo for each of these options. Sherry has wisely used text to describe the options as well. This way, buyers don't have to spend time downloading pictures just to browse around the store. If your store uses an FTP site, browsers will have to download files before they can see your catalog or other information.

Your navigational system should be as intuitive as possible, so browsers can focus on what you're selling, rather than how to get to the information. If your store is on the Web, the Web browsing software gives people a quick way to return to the previous page or move to the next one in a chain of pages they've viewed. In the examples here, the arrow buttons at the top of the window display the next or previous page.

Also, the system should always give shoppers an easy way to order. In the example above, the order form is one of the main options.

Information presentation Depending on the type of storefront and its location, you may be limited to text descriptions, or you may be able to use graphics. But graphics cost money to design and they take time to view, so limit them if your merchandise sells well without them. Online bookstores do just fine with pithy, evocative summaries of the books they have on special, along with a catalog customers can browse for titles and prices. Florists and art galleries are selling a look, so graphics are an important part of the sale.

A lot of Web pioneers got carried away with graphics and ended up turning customers off. Graphics usually take time to transmit over a telephone line and make the customer stop and wait. When the customer is interested and ready to buy, the last thing you want to do is put up a roadblock. It's one thing to have a small, enticing logo on your home page or top menu, or to offer browsers the chance to see a picture of the merchandise, but it's another to make customers wait while a series of pictures they didn't ask for is downloaded to their screens.

If you set up a Web store, design it so customers can get the information they need with or without having to wait for graphics to download. Net malls like MarketPlace give shoppers a choice of viewing its information as text or with graphics. Instead of getting the pictures right away, customers see text and some small generic icons that show where pictures will appear if users choose to display them:

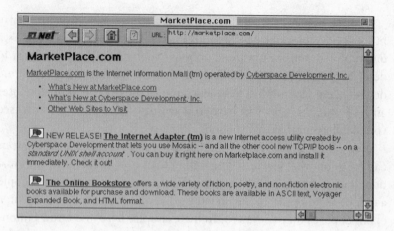

You can double-click on the graphic icons to see pictures or logos for the items mentioned, or you can use your Web browsing software to automatically download all the pictures on each page.

The ordering mechanism Decide whether you want to allow shoppers to order online, and if so, how. Will you accept CODs, credit cards, or purchase order numbers? Will you ask people to fax or phone verification of their purchase? If you're worried about hackers stealing credit card information from your storefront, ask your ISP, online service, or Internet Presence Provider about its options for encrypted transfers of sensitive financial information. Many of them offer a lot of security these days.

Also, find out exactly how you receive the orders. Orders may be sent to your e-mailbox as they come in, which means that you'll have to check your e-mailbox regularly. However, some Net malls offer to monitor your site for orders and then fax them to your store. Larry Grant of Grant's Flowers in Ann Arbor, Michigan, doesn't even have a computer in his store: he simply fills orders that are faxed to him from the Net mall where his store is located.

CHOOSING AN ELECTRONIC STOREFRONT

The best way to evaluate your store options is to surf the Net or the online services and see for yourself. If you don't have a Net account that allows you to view all the different types of servers, get one and poke around. You'll see lots of examples of different FTP, Gopher, and Web sites.

Once you have a good idea of what's out there and how your store might look on each type of server, ask yourself some questions about how you want to implement it.

How much time do you have?

Each of the options for setting up shop online requires a certain amount of time. You're already spending time to learn just what the various options are, but you'll have to spend more time to implement them. Let's look at the time requirements for each storefront option.

An FTP site Setting up an FTP site is a snap. It can probably be done within a few minutes, once the files are ready. Your effort will involve preparing each of the files you want to store at the site, uploading them to your ISP's computer, promoting the site, and adding or changing files as necessary. Customers simply grab the files they want to see, and then they can e-mail you if they want to order or ask questions.

A Gopher or WWW server This will involve researching the market for servers and virtual servers to get an idea about pricing and find the best deal, designing the server (how information is organized on menus and what the information looks like), preparing the information and uploading it to the server, and promoting and maintaining the site.

A store in an online service's mall Choosing this option means researching the costs of various plans on the major online services, designing the store (probably with help from the service itself), preparing the information and putting it up on the service's computer, and then promoting and maintaining the site.

If you're pressed for time, the simplest way out of all this is to hire a consultant or Internet Presence Provider to handle the whole thing for you. The consultant or presence provider's representative will sit down with you, analyze your marketing needs, and help you determine the best type of storefront to have, and will then research the best option and help you set it up. All you'll have to do is sit in on some meetings and provide the information you want to make available in the store when the construction gets under way.

While using a consultant is far less hassle for you, it also makes you dependent on someone else whenever you want to make changes to your store. This can mean delays in making changes you need to make if you can't reach the consultant or presence provider right away. It will also mean some additional costs when you do make changes.

If you want more control over the process, you can do it yourself. This requires learning what you need to know about setting up a server yourself or renting one from an ISP, designing the storefront's look yourself, and maintaining it yourself. You'll have more immediate control over your store and you can change it when you want without relying on a third party, but it will require much more of your time.

A half-step between these two alternatives is to use a consultant as needed. You might use the consultant to locate the cheapest or best ISP for your storefront, or for help in designing it or setting it up. You would handle the actual work of setting up the store or working with the ISP to maintain it.

To get an idea of how much time you'll need for each of these options, find some storefronts you like on the Net and contact their owners. Most owners are glad to talk about their experiences if you're in an unrelated business.

What are you selling to whom?

The best location for a service business might not be the same as the best location for a consumer goods business.

If you're in a service business, you may not want a storefront at all. Your online marketing efforts might best be handled through e-mail and participation in forums, mailing lists, and newsgroups. On the other hand, having an online storefront would give you a place to offer free information, and that would help build awareness of your services. If you're an accountant or financial consultant, your online store might offer free information about budgeting, retirement planning, etc. as a way to attract new customers.

If you're selling technical consulting services, you might reach your target market best with an FTP site or Gopher server rather than spending the extra money on a Web server.

If you're selling industrial supplies, you may do best on a focused online service like IndustryNet, which connects buyers and sellers of material for industrial companies. (See Appendix for more information about this.)

If you're selling cosmetics, opt for an online service with a high percentage of female subscribers.

You can get demographic information about any online service by simply asking for it. If you're planning on establishing a Net storefront, you can draw customers from specific newsgroups or mailing lists that focus on topics related to your business.

Your location will also affect the amount of promotion you do. If you set up in a mall in an online service, the mall itself will attract lots of browsers. If you're on CompuServe, your mall contract comes with a credit for advertising in the service's glossy monthly magazine, along with some electronic marquee notices. If you set up an individual site on the Net, you'll have to work harder to make people aware of your store by participating in newsgroups and mailing lists, or by sending announcements to Internet magazines. If your store is on the Web, you may have to approach Web mall operators about adding links from your storefront to their store directories.

How much traffic do you expect?

Your location should fully support the kind of traffic you hope to get, or it should be easily expandable to support an increase in traffic. If you expect 10,000 people a day to access your store, make sure your storefront's technology can handle it. There's nothing worse than enticing customers to your store and then having them find the door locked. If in your wildest dreams you expect perhaps 100 people a day to browse your site, you can live with a slower setup.

What makes a store fast? The type of telephone connection to the Net, the type of server hardware you're using, and the amount of other traffic moving through the same link.

A Net connection can occur over everything from a dial-up connection and a modem operating at 9600 bits per second (bps) to a T1, T2, T3, or T4 line. A T1 line delivers data at 1.5 million bits (megabits) per second. A T2 line works at up to 6.3 megabits per second, a T3 transmits at up to 45 megabits per second, and a T4 line screams along at 274 megabits per second. There are also fractional T1 lines that use only part of a T1 channel and operate at 128,000 bits per second and up.

The server that presents your store to the Net can be anything from a $1,500 PC to a $60,000 high-speed Unix workstation. If you rent a server, the cost of the hardware and phone connection is reflected in the rental price you pay.

Even with the fastest server and the fastest connection, access to your server can be slowed by other traffic using the same part of the data highway. For example, you may rent space on a virtual server and share the same connection and hardware with a dozen other stores. That's fine if each store has only a few dozen accesses, or *hits* per day, but it can mean that browsers have slow access or are blocked from entry when the server gets too busy.

And even if your ISP has a fast connection to the Net, the actual speed of that connection is affected by other traffic. We've seen store-fronts connected to the Net via a T1 line that were slower than store-fronts connected via a 56,000-bit-per-second line, all because the T1 connection was in a part of the Net that had a lot of other traffic.

If you're expecting thousands of hits per day, you're better off pay-ing for a dedicated server and Net connection rather than space on a virtual server, whether you buy the server or rent one from an ISP. *(See p. 90.)*

If you're in an online service's mall, the service should provide all the access you need, and reliability shouldn't be much of a problem.

If you rent an FTP site or a virtual Gopher or Web server, on the other hand, make sure the ISP that supports it has a fast, reliable con-nection to the Net. Otherwise, would-be browsers may have trouble connecting to the site or getting information from it. Find out how many hits per day the ISP says it can support on your server, how many simultaneous hits it can support, and how many other stores are sharing the same equipment. Ask for references to other businesses sharing the same equipment or using the same Net or online mall and find out if they've had problems with customers gaining access.

How much can you spend?

Any expenses associated with your electronic storefront are considered marketing expenses, since you're using an online presence to boost your other marketing efforts. An online storefront must fit within your overall marketing budget, and the costs of running such a store can vary widely.

If you buy your own equipment, you should be prepared to invest $50,000–$100,000 on the server and phone link during the first year of operation. If you rent equipment, you'll spend from $250 a month and up. If you rent a virtual server, you may spend as little as $50 per month. FTP sites are even cheaper.

In figuring out the cost to set up a store, however, the cost of the hardware and connection are only the beginning. Here are some other expenses you'll have.

Production costs After you've arranged for the physical storefront, you have to stock it. This includes gathering the information you want to display, designing a server interface or menu system (if your ISP, consultant, or presence provider doesn't provide one), formatting your information for display in the store, and producing any graphics, menus, and buttons you want to provide.

Disk space If you rent a server or virtual server, you'll probably pay a monthly fee for any disk space you use. The charge is usually for a certain number of megabytes or gigabytes per month. Figure out how much information you want to display, what's reasonable in the way of disk space, and what it will cost you.

Maintenance Once the store is up and running, you'll have to pay someone to monitor its activity, make periodic changes to its look or information content, and perhaps work out new links or gateways to other online malls.

Access If you own your own server, you'll have monthly charges for the telephone link between your server and the ISP as well as a service charge from the ISP itself. Pricing for rented servers and virtual servers usually includes any access costs. Some ISPs charge a flat rate, but many others vary charges by the amount of activity your server gets.

Does your provider have a track record?

Anyone with a Unix workstation and a leased line connection to the Net can set up shop as an Internet Service Provider, and there are now hundreds of ISPs around the world. Providing server space or a Net presence has been one of the major growth industries on the Net for a couple of years now. But the quality of your store's presentation and the reliability and speed with which your customers can access it are vital to your business. Don't trust your Net presence to somebody who got into the business yesterday.

At a minimum, your service provider should offer a range of service options for different volume levels, including virtual servers and full servers. If you need help designing your store's look, find an ISP or presence provider that can do it, and get references from other store owners who used that company so you can see just what kind of a job the provider did in designing stores and providing access for others. Finally, shop around. Prices for storefront construction services and Net connections are all over the map. One provider might be trying to charge five times as much as another provider in the same area. Do your homework so you don't end up paying too much.

DESIGNING AN ELECTRONIC STOREFRONT

Whatever type of electronic storefront you end up with, your main goal is the same as in the physical world: your store should be enticing, easy to find, and inviting to visit. The following basic suggestions will improve any type of online store.

Design for accessibility

If you've chosen a location for your store, you've already made a decision that affects the method and ease with which customers can reach it. But whatever type of store you have, your goal is to make it stand out from the others.

Make it visible. If your store is located in a mall, make sure the store name and description are easy to see. A lot of mall directories span more than one screen. If possible, get your name on the top menu or home page, or at the top of the mall department where you are listed. If your store is on the Net, try to place listings about it or links to it (if it's a Web site) on as many other mall sites and directories as possible. A store all by itself is like a book in a library that nobody knows about — people may end up finding it, but only by chance. Spreading notices about your store around the online world or adding Web links magnifies your visibility.

Make it fast. Any time spent waiting online can seem like an eternity, so design your store for maximum presentation speed. This means using information that can be transmitted quickly. Avoid using too many graphics or large typefaces in your descriptions, and make graphics optional.

Be as concise as possible with your department names and descriptions. Use short paragraphs rather than long ones. Subheadings in your information give people visual bookmarks to use as they scan your text.

Make it easy. Shoppers can become frustrated when they have to take too many steps to view your information. Make every piece of information you offer as directly accessible as possible. Rather than having three options on your top menu or home page and having each of them lead to two more options, put all six options on the top menu or home page so people can proceed to them more directly. If possible, make the order form available not only on the top menu, but from within each department.

Also, use a consistent design on each page. If you have a Web site and your home page features navigation buttons to jump to your catalog or order form, for example, put the same buttons on every page in the store — don't force customers to learn a new interface each time they move from one department to another.

Make it clear. One way to steer customers wrong is to use ambiguous or misleading names for menu options or buttons in your store, or to cram information together so it's hard to read. For example, put your price list under "Prices," not under "Sales." Apple's price list on AppleLink is always hard to find because it's stuffed away under the Sales and Marketing department, rather than in the Products department.

If you have a Web site and you're using graphics, make sure the pages make sense without the graphics. Here's one that doesn't:

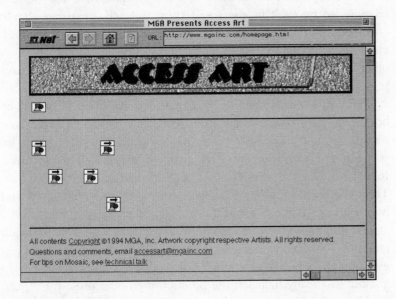

You can't tell anything about this store's contents without downloading six more graphics — a task that could take a couple of minutes if your customer has a 14,400-bps modem connection to the Web. This kind of obscurity just places one more hurdle between the customer and the sale. Don't force a customer to download graphics just to figure out how to navigate through your store or to learn what you're selling. *(See Milne Jewelry's department list on p. 94 to see how you can use text and graphics together for more clarity.)*

Design for customer involvement

There are many examples of poorly designed stores on the Net right now, menus or Web pages that just sit there and wait for the customer to start exploring. But the best guerrilla-owned storefronts use computer technology to add value to the presentation. Your design can use the equivalent of in-store signs, banners, lights, and sirens to draw customers further inside.

Use promotional messages. Your store's top menu or page should have a promotional message that changes frequently. Every online service uses welcome messages that change daily. CompuServe's What's New window greets members every time they connect. Your storefront should have something new and exciting every time a customer returns to it. One of your top menu items could be a "what's new" list of recent changes, so frequent browsers will know instantly what they should check out. The list could contain notices about price cuts, new merchandise, new graphics available, a new customer feedback area, or other features of the store. If customers think your store will always have something new, they'll keep coming back to see what it is.

Think up evocative names for store functions. The 7 UP company boosted its sales tremendously by coming up with "The Uncola" as a new name for its product. You can make shopping fun and engaging for your customers by using evocative names for the options in your store. Instead of a *Place Order* button, you could name the button *I Want This*. The online world is impersonal enough without your adding to it with boring generic names for your store's departments and options.

Use graphics. If your store is on the Web, take advantage of it with graphics. You shouldn't bombard customers with unwanted and unnecessary graphics, but some products just won't sell without a look-see. If a graphic will really help sell the product, then offer one. In fact, you could offer it in several sizes or resolutions so customers can decide how much time they want to spend waiting for the graphic to appear. For example, Grant's Flowers on the Branch Mall has boosted sales by doing something phone-order florists can't do: it lets you see a color photo of each of its arrangements, so you know exactly what you're getting. By putting pictures of his arrangements on the Net, Larry Grant says his store now gets orders from customers in Japan, Australia, Europe, and other places who would never have ordered from him before.

Provide free information. A few folks may wander into your physical store and browse simply out of boredom, but in the online marketplace, most people are looking for information. The more information you can provide in your store, the more likely it is that people will drop by. Your product descriptions and prices are information, but customers want more than price lists. Add value to your store by offering free information about related topics that will help sell your merchandise.

The Racquet Workshop in Clear Lake, Texas, sells tennis equipment, but its Web site also offers weekly tennis news updates, graphics of major tennis stars, tips on playing technique, and the rules of tennis. By giving customers this free information, the Racquet Workshop has become a source of tennis news that also happens to sell equipment. And since its prices are as low as anybody's, the chances are that people stopping by for the free information might pick up a new racquet there when they need one.

Information can also add to your credibility by showing how knowledgeable you are about what you sell. At Milne Jewelry Company's store on the Branch Mall, you can get advice about cleaning and caring for turquoise jewelry as well as a buyer's guide to southwestern jewelry.

Design for buying comfort

Effective marketing is a circle that begins with your message and ends with a satisfied customer. Your online storefront is a ghost that exists only in cyberspace until your customer completes a satisfactory transaction. Customers act as if the store does exist, of course, but they won't really feel comfortable with that assumption until a satisfactory transaction has taken place. It's like buying from a mail-order firm that you've never heard of before — you're a little anxious until that sweater, tie, or commemorative Elvis plate actually arrives at your door.

Design your store and its merchandise to soothe your customers' concerns about the permanence and stability of your business. There are several ways to do this:

Offer a guarantee. Every mail-order firm worth its stamps guarantees satisfaction. There are few services you can offer that will provide more comfort for your customers.

Display your physical address and phone information. If your online store is a branch of a physical store someplace, your customers will feel a lot better knowing that. They'll be more comfortable buying from a company that has an actual building than from someone who's simply Net-selling from their kitchen table.

Host a feedback area. Design a message area for customer questions and comments, or make it clear that you welcome feedback. Buying and selling are always a two-way transaction, and guerrillas always encourage a dialogue that gives the customer more of a stake in the sale. As you collect and respond to questions in your feedback area, pull out the ones that are frequently asked and compile them into a FAQ (Frequently Asked Questions) file customers can browse. This will add to your information offering and cut down on the number of times you have to answer the same questions.

Use a nonthreatening order form. People hate thinking they're locked into something, and a poorly designed order form can give them acute claustrophobia. If possible, put all the ordering information on one screen so customers can review their entire order easily. Offer an easy-to-use Cancel function on the order screen, so customers know they can change their minds, like this:

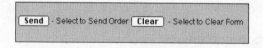

Include a few words about your ordering policy on the form, explaining delivery times, problem resolution, and other store policies to make customers feel more at ease. Finally, offer the option to order via fax or an 800 number for customers who don't want to send a credit card number through cyberspace.

Get some design help

If you use a consultant to help design your store, make sure you get one who has experience with computer interface design and (if it's a Web site) graphics design. A Web page layout can benefit from the same graphics savvy used by an experienced magazine or advertising designer. Any storefront's navigation system will be better if its design is influenced by someone who knows how to make computers easy to use. Ask your ISP, presence provider, or consultant about these types of experience. If nobody on your store construction team has it, find someone who does. If you see a storefront design you particularly like while surfing the Net, contact the owner and find out who helped build it — they can probably do an equally good job for you.

Test your design

Before you go public with your storefront, test the design by accessing the store from different kinds of computers. What looks great on one computer system may not look so great on another. Host a pre-opening period for your friends and associates. Invite them to browse your store and offer any comments or suggestions about its look, feel, and operation.

If possible, ask people to try accessing your store at different times of the day or days of the week, so you can check out the speed of your ISP's Net connection. One way to turn such testing into a promotion of its own is to offer significant discounts or free gifts for testing the service by asking early browsers to record their addresses and names in your feedback area or send them to your e-mailbox.

- -

OPERATING AN ELECTRONIC STOREFRONT

Once your store is up and running, your manner of operating it will greatly contribute to your success or failure.

Be attentive

Customers demand service. Service is the only way to establish your credibility. Remember, customers are entrusting their digital bits and bytes to the black hole of cyberspace until you respond and reassure them that there's an actual human being on the other side of the screen. There are several ways to remain attentive to your customers.

Check for queries and orders frequently. Your level of store traffic will determine just how frequent "frequently" is, but never let twenty-four hours lapse without checking your store for orders or queries. In the first few weeks of operation and after any new promotional efforts, check your store every two hours. If you can't check your online presence this often and you're in a Net mall, try to arrange to have orders faxed directly to you as they come in. Some presence providers offer this option.

Respond quickly. The more quickly you can respond to orders and queries, the more impressed your customers will be and the more quickly they'll come to trust you. Nobody likes doing business with someone whose business is just a part-time hobby. Your attentiveness to your store will convince customers that you're in the business full-time — even if you're not. Unless you're delivering merchandise within a day, send a confirmation message for each order so the buyer knows the order was received and that the goods are on their way.

Check your own service. You can't fix a problem if you don't know you have it, so act like one of your own customers once in a while to make sure your store is working properly. Dial up your online service or the Net and navigate to your store. Browse around and display its information. Send in an order yourself once in a while. Try this at different times of the day and night and on different days to determine whether there are any access problems.

Check out the competition. While you're Net-surfing or mall-cruising, check out some of the other vendors, particularly those in the same type of business as yours, and see what they're doing. They may be trying promotions or store designs you hadn't considered.

Make frequent changes

Guerrillas change their physical stores' signage, displays, and sales approaches constantly to keep them fresh and inviting. The same goes for your online store. Change your promotional message once a week. Offer new, nonproduct information regularly and draw customers' attention to it. Come up with a tip of the day or week for your business, news or trends related to your products, or a quote of the day or week for the general enlightenment of mankind.

The time to encourage the next visit is during the current one. Make your store the kind of place where people know they'll see something new every time they stop by. As you now know, netizens are information hounds, and if your store becomes known as a place where new, useful information appears frequently, they'll become regular visitors.

Promote your store

If all you do is open up an electronic storefront and wait for customers to come in and buy, you could be waiting until your bank balance sinks beneath the waves. There are practical tactics for increasing your store's traffic.

Spread the word. Every day you go online, make a point of promoting your business, not only in replies to queries at your store, but in newsgroups, forums, or mailing lists related to your business. (See Chap-

ter 7 for more information.) Post classified ads in the free areas of forums related to your business, or to online services that allow free ads. Send announcements about your store to print magazines such as *Internet World* and *Online Access. (See Chapter 15 for more information.)*

Ask for referrals. When you respond to customer inquiries, ask them to pass along the information to anyone else who might appreciate it. If your information is useful, people will share it.

Seek fusion marketing partners. Make fusion marketing arrangements with other companies that complement yours. If you sell sportswear, make a fusion arrangement with a store that sells sporting goods: you get a notice about your store on the sporting goods store's site, and they get a notice on your site.

Seek out online malls and business directories and make sure your company is listed in them, if possible. Directories like the Internet Mall or the NCSA Mosaic What's New page will list your store for free; other malls will give you space for your name or a link to your Web site for around $50 a month.

Offer to exchange informational articles with other stores if each of you has something the other could use. People reading your article in another store will see you as an expert on the subject. For example, if you're an ergonomics consultant, your paper on proper furniture adjustments could enhance the information area of an office supplies dealer and win business for you at the same time.

Host a conference or write an article. If you're an active member of a forum, host a conference on a topic that showcases your expertise. *(See Chapter 9 for more information.)*

Hold contests. Come up with a crazy contest that relates to your business, and offer a significant prize for the winner. Put the contest information in your store to attract people, and promote the contest in newsgroups, forums, and via online services when appropriate. For example, CompuServe's What's New window has a Special Events/Contests item that always lists any contests its members or merchants have under way.

Plan to revive interest. Most online store owners report a plunge in interest in their sites a few weeks after the initial store announcement. Everyone checks the site out when it's new, but many never return. Plan a promotion or contest for the second month of your store's life to pull shoppers back in, and announce this upcoming event when your store opens. This way, people who visit the store during its early days will have a reason to come back a few weeks later. If your store opens in September, announce a Halloween contest or Thanksgiving promotion.

Promote your store off-line. Tell your other customers about your new online presence. Put up a PC in your store and invite customers to see your online store. Mention your online store in your print ads and brochures, and give customers a reason to visit it (such as the free information they'll find there). If you're in a small town, your online store may even be newsworthy for the local TV station or newspaper. *(See Chapter 15 for more information.)*

Follow up

The best time to improve your reputation and plant seeds for future sales is when the customer is basking in the glow of satisfaction from the last purchase. After the order is shipped and has had time to arrive or after your service is delivered, follow up with a note thanking the buyer for his or her business. Follow-up notes tell people you care about their satisfaction and not just their money.

Be patient

Most online storefronts ramp up slowly. You may spend weeks or months attracting nothing but tire-kickers before you start making consistent sales. When you set up a storefront, commit yourself to at least a year's operation. Remember, there are millions of people on the Net, and despite your best promotional efforts it may take time for many of them to learn of your store. Also, the Net is changing rapidly and more people have better access to it all the time. Waiting a year will give you a chance to expose your store to a larger and larger pool of prospects as the months go by.

SEVEN STRATEGIES FOR ELECTRONIC STOREFRONTS

In summary, these are the seven top guerrilla strategies for choosing and operating an electronic storefront:

1. Choose the right location. Choose a storefront technology and a location that balances the needs of your budget, your desire for the broadest online market access, and the type of product you sell. The store should be:

- easy to find for as many customers as possible
- capable of displaying your products as well as possible
- able to handle the traffic you anticipate
- within your budgets for time and money

2. Make the store attractive, fun, and easy to navigate. It's a mistake to think that people will flock to your store just for the thrill of shopping online. Your store competes with other online stores as well as with print catalogs and physical stores. It should be inviting, attractive, fun, and easy to browse in. If at all possible, it should add fun or convenience that shoppers can't get when they're away from the computer.

- Work with your consultant or designer to put as much excitement as possible into your store design, from its name to the names of departments or options.
- Use promotional messages to keep the store looking new.
- Make the store easy to navigate.
- Present the information in small, screen-sized chunks rather than having product descriptions spread across several screens. Use evocative descriptions that help readers visualize what your products or services can do for them.
- Offer regular customers a special discount for shopping online.

3. Make the store an information source. Give shoppers some free, useful information about topics related to your products or services, and offer something new regularly. Hardware stores sell most of their products in the course of helping a home owner solve a problem or learn about some aspect of home repair. If your store becomes a reliable source of information, people will buy and they'll keep coming back.

4. Reassure customers about your permanence. Do all you can to allay customer fears about buying online.

- If you have a physical address, display it in your online store and invite people to visit.
- Offer a 100 percent satisfaction guarantee on your merchandise.
- Explain your ordering and refund policy clearly.
- Give people a way to ask questions and get them answered promptly.
- Design a clear order form that gives customers the chance to cancel.

5. Pay attention. Once you've attracted customers, the key to satisfying them is service. Pay close attention to your store's activity.

- Check your store mailbox, feedback area, or ordering system at least every two hours so you can respond to customer requests as quickly as possible.
- Shop the store yourself at different times and on different days to make sure it's working properly.
- Ask friends with different types of computer or Net navigation software to visit the store and report any problems.

6. Tell the world. Promotion is vital in the online marketplace, because your store is invisible unless people know about it.

- Use an e-mail signature that includes your store name and its address.
- Participate in newsgroups and mailing lists whose topics are related to your business, and build a reputation as a good source of information.
- Establish fusion marketing relationships with other store owners.
- Use promotional tools such as marquees, What's New announcements, contests, and links to other Web pages to spread your store's name around and invite people into it.

7. Follow up. Build a relationship with your customers that goes beyond one sale, and don't stop trying to improve your store.

- Follow up each sale with a thank you note via e-mail, and ask people to tell friends about your products or services.
- Prepare monthly or quarterly mailings of store news and send them to your customer list.
- Stay abreast of Net or online service developments and add any new services to your marketing arsenal.
- Continue surfing the online marketplace yourself, watching for ideas you can incorporate into your store to make it better.

6
Classified Ads and Billboards

Day in and day out, advertising is the number-one way for you to promote your business. With advertising, you put your message in front of the public whenever you want, as long as you can afford it. In the physical world, you can place ads on anything from billboards, transit benches, buses, and taxis to newspapers, magazines, and television. The advertising possibilities in the online marketplace are more limited, but the results can be just as exciting.

Advertising should be part of every guerrilla's online marketing arsenal because it contributes to your visibility. Remember, your business is invisible online unless people happen by your storefront or see your company name somewhere else. Advertising helps you spread the word about your business throughout cyberspace.

The two main advertising media in the online market are classified ads and billboards. Most online services and some BBSs have classified ad sections where, just as in a newspaper, you can place a brief ad about your business. Some online services like Prodigy charge a fee for posting a classified ad, but many services offer free ad space for their subscribers. On the Net, several newsgroups are essentially collections of classified ads, and these are free as well.

In a classified ad, you're putting your message before an audience that is already shopping, so you have a leg up on gaining the reader's interest. Many people browse online classifieds just as they browse the backs of newspapers and magazines. Some people are looking for a particular product or service, and others are just window shopping. But classified advertising works, which is why it has made the transition virtually intact from the printed world to the online marketplace. In fact, if you have only one product or service, your classified ad campaign can be your main method of promotion.

Billboards are electronic notices that pop into view on your screen as you use a commercial service or surf the Net. Like television commercials, most online billboards usually don't appear when the customer is thinking about your product. But unlike TV commercials, electronic billboards give your customers a chance to find out more about the product instantly, offering doorways to your online store or to a more detailed message in places where you wouldn't otherwise have them.

CLASSIFIED ADS

Online classified ads can serve two purposes:

- to promote other online presences you have, such as advertising your online store or soliciting subscriptions for your online newsletter
- as the main method by which you sell a particular product or service

Online classified ads are almost as old as online services and bulletin boards. Legions of business consultants, multilevel marketers, and all sorts of retailers have used them for years to sell products effectively. If you have an online store or mall presence, a well-placed classified ad can help you spread the word.

How classified ads work

In the online world a classified advertising section is like a discussion group or bulletin board. The only difference is that the messages contain blatant ads, rather than discussions about a particular topic. An online classified ad section contains a list of messages, each of which has a title. When you browse the section, you scan the titles and then select a particular title to read the message behind it. The details of posting and reading ads are different, depending on whether your ad is on an online service or BBS, or in a newsgroup on the Net.

Ads in online services and BBSs

In most cases, the classified ad area of an online service or BBS has several subsections, just like the classified section in a newspaper or magazine. Here's the main directory of classified ads on CompuServe:

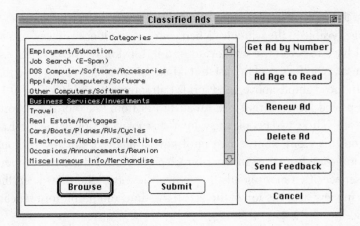

There are several different ad categories, each of which may have its own subcategories. For example, the Business Services/Investments category here has several subcategories under it. Here's the ad list from the Advertising/Promotions subcategory:

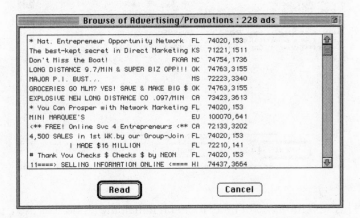

There are 228 ad titles here. Next to the title you can see the CompuServe address and home state of the person posting the ad. Classified areas on other services may show different information, such as the date the ad was posted (see the example of AOL's classified area on p. 36), but the ads always have a title.

Unlike printed classifieds, the ads here aren't sorted alphabetically by title. Instead, they appear on the list in the order in which they were placed. Your brand-new ad will appear at the top of a list when you first post it, but as others are posted, your ad moves down the list until it's no longer visible in the window. When your ad is no longer in view, readers will have to scroll the window to find it. Obviously, the best place for your ad is at the top of the list, but it takes some work to keep it there.

In the example above, the Florida entrepreneur at address 74020,153 has posted four different ads. An advertiser from Oklahoma has posted two ads. These two people are vying for a spot at the top of the list. Each ad on this CompuServe area must have a different title, even though multiple ads from the same person are probably about the same product or service. By reposting ads frequently, these two guerrillas keep their ads in view near the top of the list all the time and profit from repeated exposure.

When someone is attracted by your ad title and wants to read on, they select the ad and open it. Most online classified ads are short and to the point, like this one:

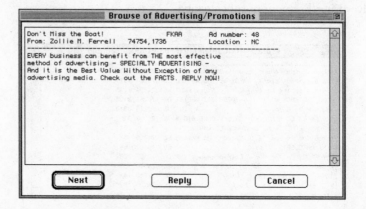

This ad form has a lot more room on it than the author has used, but browsers expect ads to be brief. A lot of people like to browse the classified sections they find online, but they don't want to spend a lot of time reading any one ad.

This ad also makes it easy for customers to respond and get further information. CompuServe and other online services have a convenient Reply button right in the window that displays the ad, and this author asks readers to hit the Reply button to get more information. Other ads ask readers to phone, fax, or send e-mail.

As in printed media, classified ads in online services run for a specific amount of time. Prodigy sells you ad space for a month at a time — $5 for a consumer ad and $20 for a business ad. Even on services that don't charge, your ad will be deleted after a few weeks by the service's administrators. The life of any given ad depends on how active that particular ad area is, and how much space is available for it on the online service's computer. You'll want to check an online classified area every few days to make sure your ad is still there.

Ads in newsgroups

Most newsgroups on the Net prohibit blatant advertising, but some groups are actually set up to contain nothing but ads. Other newsgroups have primarily given themselves over to ads, whether or not the groups' original creators intended that to happen. These groups contain all or mostly commercial ads:

alt.business.misc

biz.misc

misc.entrepreneurs

Any newsgroup with *forsale* in its name is also devoted to ads, but these groups are usually restricted to ads by individuals selling items such as used stereos or ski equipment. If you're advertising in forsale groups, it's best to offer one or two specific pieces of merchandise.

There are lots of forsale groups. There are geographically specific newsgroups like ca.forsale and nj.forsale, and there are groups focused on certain types of merchandise like computer equipment. Before you post an ad to a newsgroup, though, check the group's FAQ (Frequently Asked Questions) message to see if commercial ads are allowed. *(See Appendix for more information.)*

Classified advertising in newsgroups is different from advertising in online services or BBSs in three major ways:

You can place an ad for free. There's no way the Net can charge you to post anything to a newsgroup. All you pay is the online time you spend posting the ad. Because newsgroups are free, the ad-related ones get more activity than fee-based classified sections on Prodigy or elsewhere. Some of the ad-related newsgroups get dozens or hundreds of new postings every day. And while some online services only allow you to post a particular ad to one classified area, you can *cross-post* an ad to several newsgroups on the Net at the same time.

Newsgroup ads aren't classified. The classified sections on online services are divided into different categories so you can choose a category to browse that will contain only ads for certain types of merchandise or services. Any given newsgroup is just one long list of ads, like this:

```
┌─────────────────────────────── nj.forsale ───────────────────────────────┐
  130 articles, 130 unread
   -        Unknown          Complete 286 system for sale.
   -        Mark J. Sarisky  Gear Sale
   -        Dr. Peter Forst… ==> VIDEO PROCESSOR and VIDEO EDITOR for sale <==
   -        shah             PAL palmcorder for sale..
   -        Unknown          Sun i386Dx forsale.
   -        Roger A. Quon    TICKET: Phila --> Detroit $100
   -        Sang T. Lee      Re: FORSALE: HP Scanjet IIcx Color Scanner
   -        Jesse Bunch      Megatek X-Window Accelerator Cards For Sale Cheap!
   -        Abdellatif Marr… ***repost:Dot matrix printers***
   -        Alec Yin         Forsale: SNES games
   -        Joshua M. Burgin For Sale - Desk + Shelving Unit
   ▷ 3      Jason H.         Basic 486 System for sale.
   ▷ 2      on belay         For Sale - Avalanche & K2 boards
   -        Fred Falk        RECORD/CD Expo, Wayne, NJ 10/8
   -        Norman Garfinkle Sears Kenmore Stack Washer/Elec. Dryer for sale in N. NJ
   -        avinash.kachhy   Indian Festive Ornamental Ladies Dress for Sale
   -        131G40000-S.W.N… NJ:  1986 IROC for sale
   -        say,h sabit      ONE WEEK VACATION RENTAL IN FLORIDA
   -        Charles Lesburg  WTB: 19", 20" or 21" monitor for Mac Q700
```

As you can see, this group is a hodgepodge of ads for everything from vacation rentals to cars to clothing to computer equipment. Most people who post ads on forsale newsgroups cross-post, so this sort of chaos is normal. Some newsgroup titles help restrict the type of merchandise sold on that group (misc.forsale.computers.pc-clone is devoted to PC-compatible computers, for example), but once you view any newsgroup, you'll see one long list of ad titles.

The jumble of ads on any newsgroup makes it more difficult for anyone to locate your particular ad, and it makes it all the more important for your ad to have a position on the list and a title that will give it maximum visibility and pulling power. *(See "Marketing with classified ads" on p. 119 for more information.)*

Ads on newsgroups usually last longer. Newsgroups don't have the same time restrictions you'll find in a more formal online classified section. Ads can sometimes remain on a newsgroup for weeks or months. Once items are deleted, they're sometimes placed in an archive file on an FTP server.

As in an online service, the list of messages in a newsgroup is chronological, and when new messages are added to the group, your message moves down the list. Because of this, it's vital to check any ad every few days to make sure it still has good visibility. Unlike with online services, you can post an ad with the same title over and over again on a newsgroup, if you like.

To get an idea of what's out there and who is posting what sorts of ads where, browse the newsgroups yourself. *(See Chapter 7 for more information about browsing newsgroups.)*

MARKETING WITH CLASSIFIED ADS

With thousands of ads in dozens of different places in cyberspace, you're competing fiercely with others for your readers' attention. Your product or service probably isn't unique, and even if it is, you'll still have to get readers interested enough to respond. Here are some ideas for creating classified ads that work.

The title

Your ad title may be the only chance you have to reach a prospect, so make it count. The title must stand out in a list of titles and make the reader want to know more.

- Use 32 characters or fewer if your ad is on an online service, because that's all the space your title will get. It would be a shame if the best part of your title was invisible to most readers.
- Use power words like the ones on p. 74 in Chapter 4 to spark your readers' curiosity.
- Ask a question to position what you're selling as the solution to a problem, such as *Tired of tax problems?* or *Sore back?*
- Be as explicit as possible about what it is you're selling. In the newsgroup example on p. 118, one ad title reads *Gear Sale,* but *gear* could mean anything from transmission parts to hiking equipment to audio components.
- Use capital letters, asterisks, or other emphatic symbols to help key words in your ad title stand out visually from the others. As we explained on p. 72 in Chapter 4, capitals and emphatic symbols are the online equivalent of shouting. They shouldn't be used in normal e-mail or newsgroup messages, but classified ads are the exception.
- Test different ad titles on different classified areas or newsgroups to

see which ones pull the best. For example, ask readers to reply to Dept. P for an ad on Prodigy, Dept. C for an ad on CompuServe, or Dept. B for an ad on the biz.misc newsgroup.

The message

If your ad title has motivated the reader to open your message, then the message should continue that momentum toward the sale. You can use more space than the ad shown on p. 116, but be clear and concise.

- Choose two or three main benefits of your product or service, and then explain each one in a sentence or two.
- Talk to the reader as if it's just the two of you, person to person. Use *you* instead of *people*, and give the message a conversational tone. For example, *Our experts can show you how to eliminate tax problems* sounds a lot better than *ABC Accountants is nationally recognized for its tax expertise.*
- Explain your company's advantage. Your company's competitive advantage — and it should have one or you won't be in business long — is the reason the customer should do business with you. Make sure the customer knows about it, whatever it is.
- Give the reader an extra incentive to respond by offering something free — a list of tips for gardening, your two-page report on tax news, or a discount on the first order of office supplies.
- Be sure to include your e-mail address, server address, phone or fax number, or postal address so people can respond.
- Use different response codes or key words in different ads, so you'll know which ad is pulling the best. For example, you could ask people to send for your free *Tax Guide* in one message and your free *Tax Report* in another.
- Proofread your message and let others read it before you post it. Your employees or coworkers may point out problems with your copy that you, as the author, have missed.

Check the ad's position

Monitor the ad area or newsgroup daily to see how quickly your ad changes position, and then post a new ad when yours is more than two screens from the top of the list. Don't overdo it, though. There's a difference between posting often enough to maintain your visibility and hogging so much space that other users resent you.

Check for replies

You can't respond quickly to customer inquiries if you don't know they're inquiring. Check your classified ad and your response address regularly. If you post an ad on a newsgroup or in the classified ad area of a forum, check the newsgroup or forum at least daily for responses to your message. Rather than sending e-mail to your mailbox or phoning for more information, some newsgroup or forum readers may use the Reply button in their newsreader software. The Reply button posts a new message in reply to your original one.

You can tell when your message has replies, because a number appears next to it, like this:

```
 -        Alec Yin           Forsale: SNES games
 -        Joshua M. Burgin   For Sale - Desk + Shelving Unit
 ▷  3     Jason H.           Basic 486 System for sale.
 ▷  2     on belay           For Sale - Avalanche & K2 boards
 -        Fred Falk          RECORD/CD Expo, Wayne, NJ 10/8
```

Here, the message posted by Jason H. has three replies attached to it.

Respond promptly

If your classified ad promises free information, make sure you've prepared the free information in advance and have it ready to send out quickly. The more quickly you respond to requests, the more readers will come to trust you. If your mailbox is through an ISP, set up a mailbot program that sends out free information automatically when people request it. *(See p. 66 in Chapter 4.)*

- - - - - - - - - - - - - - - - - - - -

ONLINE BILLBOARDS

An online billboard is a service that displays your promotional message to people as they go about their travels in cyberspace. Most billboards pop up without the reader having to request it, but you can also buy a billboard on a Worldwide Web site that describes your product and explains how to get it. Let's look at some different types of billboards and see how they work.

Prodigy billboards

A joint venture of IBM and Sears, Prodigy is the most commercialized of the online services when it comes to providing opportunities to advertise. Ads appear on Prodigy whether you want to see them or not, and Prodigy charges hefty fees for providing such guaranteed visibility.

As you use the Prodigy service, promotional messages usually appear at the bottom of your screen, like this:

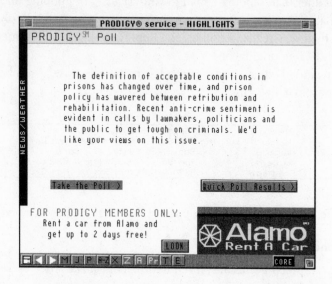

These messages change constantly, and each one costs money. Prodigy sells screen space in *standard advertising units* (SAUs), and it has rates for packages of from five to thirty SAUs in both national and regional markets.

Unlike other online services, Prodigy delivers billboards to different groups of people around the country, depending on the access number they use to dial in. The rates vary by the number of subscribers a billboard will reach and by the type of billboard it is. For example, five SAUs displayed nationally cost $27,500, while a regional edition that reaches fewer than 200,000 subscribers costs $6250. Along with the space rental, you also pay production fees of $2000–$3000 to have the billboard created.

And a choice of billboard audiences is just the beginning on Prodigy. You also have lots of choices about how your ad is displayed and which options the reader has in it. Your billboard might contain a button that takes the reader to an order screen, or to a list of questions and answers, or to your company's online store. Options like this cost extra, both for production and monthly display fees.

Advertising on a Prodigy billboard is expensive, which is why most of the advertisers are major corporations. You can choose a regional audience for a billboard if you're targeting a certain part of the country, but you can't choose when your billboard appears. Alamo's ad for rental cars might pop up when a ten-year-old is cruising the service, for example. Still, the billboards do, on the whole, reach a lot of high-income subscribers.

CompuServe marquees

When you sign up for store space in CompuServe's Electronic Mall, your rental agreement usually includes a certain number of marquees. Marquees are mini-billboards that pop up whenever a customer enters the Electronic Mall itself, or when a customer moves into a certain merchandise category. Here's an example:

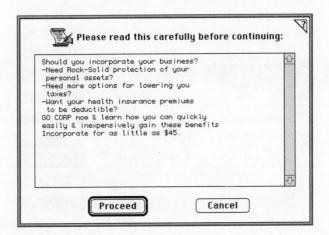

CompuServe marquees don't have graphics, and they can't include a button that takes readers to an order form or more information. And unlike Prodigy's inescapable billboards, the marquees only appear when you enter CompuServe's Electronic Mall. Still, these pop-up messages help you compete for visibility with other mall merchants. Depending on which store rental agreement you sign, you may have enough marquee slots to display a message every week of the year. Electronic Mall rental agreements run from $20,000 to $100,000 per year plus 2 percent of sales made through your online store.

As with Prodigy billboards, CompuServe doesn't give you any control about when your marquee messages appear. Your ad for long-distance phone service might pop up when an AT&T executive is shopping the mall for computer games, for example.

What's New, welcome, and goodbye messages

What's New messages appear as part of the welcome screen subscribers see when they connect to an online service. CompuServe has a separate window containing What's New items. *(See p. 35 in Chapter 3 for an example.)* America Online and Prodigy announce new items on their welcome screens. There's no extra charge for these notices. Here's an example of Prodigy's welcome screen:

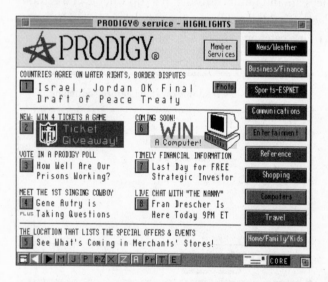

Along with the buttons at the right that take you to various departments, you see eight specific promotions. Options 5 and 7 promote businesses. When you open a new store in the online mall in an online service, a notice about your store appears on the What's New portion of the welcome screen. And when you make a major change to your store or offer a new and exciting service or contest, you should be able to place a message about it on the welcome screen as well. Your online mall marketing representative can help you place your promotional messages on the welcome screen.

On Prodigy and America Online, the sign-off or goodbye screens can also contain promotions. This one from Prodigy is a mini-billboard that carries a charge:

America Online's sign-off screen usually promotes a noncommercial online event like a conference, but as you can see, Prodigy offers products and chances to buy things right up until the moment you disconnect.

Gopher and Web links

If your store is on a Gopher or Web site on the Net, you can use links to your store on other servers as billboards. Like the billboards on Prodigy, each of these links will also be a button or option that browsers can use to quickly navigate right into your store. Here's an example:

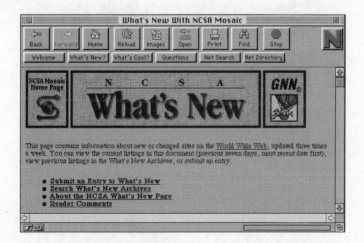

This is the What's New page from NCSA, the National Center for Supercomputing Applications and developer of the Mosaic software that many people use to browse the Worldwide Web. (Mosaic was the first Web browser software, and NCSA gave it away free, so it has more than a million users now.)

The list on NCSA's What's New page is updated every few days. It contains notices for all types of new Web sites, whether they're business, educational, or scientific. You can place a notice for your new Web site here for free by sending it to ncsa-wn@gnn.com. There are also other Web sites and newsgroups where you can announce your store's grand opening.

Since this list is updated frequently, your listing will move or even disappear from the page after a certain number of days or weeks. However, the NCSA What's New page is one of the most active sites on the Web, so any exposure you can get there will be well worth the time it takes to send them an announcement.

On other Net sites that offer a directory of business locations, you may have to pay anywhere from $50 to $300 per month for an announcement or Web link. *(See Appendix for options.)*

Web billboards

Even if you don't have a computer, you can still promote your products or services online by putting up a billboard on a Web site and directing buyers to your fax, phone number, or mailing address. Here's an example:

This Web billboard is located on the Branch Mall. It doesn't allow you to order directly, but it does promote the bookstore's selection, prices, and service and invites you to order via fax, phone, mail, or an e-mail address.

The Web's graphical capabilities also make it possible for you to display color pictures of your wares to attract buyers, like this:

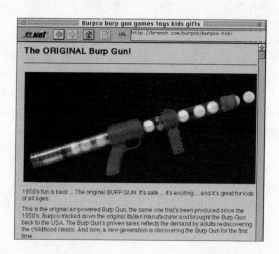

A billboard like this can cost you as little as $30 a month, and it can draw Web surfers to your place of business even if you don't own a computer. People are ordering burp guns solely on the strength of this billboard, having never heard of the company or its catalog before. *(See Appendix for information about finding Internet Presence Providers who rent billboards like this.)*

SEVEN STRATEGIES FOR CLASSIFIED ADS AND BILLBOARDS

Anybody can post an ad or rent a billboard, but only a guerrilla will make the most of it. These seven key strategies make the difference:

1. Use a strong title. Whether you're writing a classified ad title or the heading of a billboard, use a short, enticing title that fires the reader's curiosity and encourages him or her to take the next step.

2. Use people talk. Ad and billboard messages should talk to a specific person, not to the undefinable masses. Write copy that mirrors what you'd say to someone if you were talking to him or her in person.

3. Use power words. Check out the list of power words on p. 74 in Chapter 4 and use them in ad or billboard titles and message copy. They work.

4. Make it easy to respond. If the online service offers a quick button that takes readers to an order or reply form, use it. If not, use e-mail as the response mechanism rather than postal mail, because your prospect is already connected to the computer and can send e-mail quickly and easily. Use a mailbot if you can.

5. Offer something free. Give customers a tangible reason to respond to your message — a limited-time offer, a discount, or free information. Even if a prospect is curious about your product or service, the offer of something free will help push them forward to the next step in the sale.

6. Check your ad regularly. If you post a classified ad in an online service or newsgroup, check its position daily to make sure it's still in a good position to be read. Repost ads when they drop more than two screens down from the top of the list. If you post in a newsgroup or forum, make sure you check your message for any replies attached to it.

7. Code responses to track their effectiveness. Use coded responses to test the effectiveness of different ads or billboards.

7

Forums and Newsgroups

Two of the most important elements in a successful marketing campaign are visibility and credibility. Customers can't buy from you if they don't know who you are, and they won't buy from you if they don't trust you to deliver the goods. Online advertising will give your business visibility, but it can cost money and you don't have much control over who sees your message. Participating in newsgroups and forums lets you communicate directly with the people most likely to be interested in your business, and it lets you do it in a way that gains your company both visibility and credibility. Better still, it costs you nothing but time.

Discussion-group marketing requires subtlety and tact. Rather than boasting about your product or service in a classified ad, you respond to messages posted by others or propose discussion subjects of your own. This may seem like a roundabout way to win customers, but it works, sometimes dramatically.

One netizen we know has an interest in futures trading. He also has some friends in the brokerage business. Surfing the Net one night, he stumbled upon a newsgroup related to futures investments. It was a relatively inactive group, with only seventeen posted messages at the time. One of the messages posed an investment question, and our friend posted a reply with a partial answer. Along with his partial answer, he mentioned a broker friend who would know the whole answer, and added the broker's 800 number.

The next day the broker called to thank our friend, saying his phone had been ringing all morning with calls from people who had read that newsgroup posting. In two days the broker had twenty-three new account leads from that one posting; many of the callers ended up opening accounts.

This futures broker normally spends about $400 to produce a single new account lead, but thanks to a newsgroup posting he neither made nor encouraged, he gained a handful of leads for nothing. By marketing in discussion groups for yourself, you can do even better. Online guerrillas have told us that next to electronic mail, participating in newsgroups and forums is the top tool for generating sales leads.

Your online marketing arsenal should definitely include newsgroup or forum marketing. It takes time and patience to do it right, but it pays off. Let's take a close look at how these groups work and how you can make the most of them.

ABOUT FORUMS

Forums are discussion groups located on commercial online services and some bulletin boards. Sometimes a forum is just one discussion area (scuba diving, for example), and sometimes it's a collection of areas on a handful of related topics. (An aviation forum, for example, might include discussions of ultralights, air shows, and jets.) In addition to discussion areas, forums often contain libraries of files posted by members and conference rooms where members can chat. Sometimes forums have their own classified ad areas as well.

To participate in a forum, you must be a subscriber to the online service or BBS that hosts it. In online services, browsing many forums is an extra-cost option that isn't covered under the basic subscription rate. The additional cost is usually nominal: check your service's pricing policies to find out what it is.

You can usually browse the messages in any forum as a visitor, but you may have to formally join the forum before you can have access to its libraries, conference room, or classified ad area. Not to worry, though. Joining simply means registering your name with the forum, and there's an option to do that whenever you enter a forum.

Navigating in a forum

The Health & Fitness forum on CompuServe shows how a typical forum works. The Forums area is a major feature of CompuServe, as it is in most online services, and you can go to it from the main welcome screen. Once you move to the Forums area, you see dozens of different forums named there.

After selecting Health & Fitness forum, you see a message asking if you want to join by registering your name. This procedure doesn't cost anything, but it helps the forum administrators know exactly how many people are regular members and who they are.

Once you join the forum, you see its main window:

This window has icons for each of the forum's features. You'll find the same basic features in most forums on an online service. Clicking any icon takes you to a different area.

Newsflash is an announcements area where the forum's administrators post news about changes to the forum itself. The administrators use this area to promote new items in the software libraries, or to announce the time and date of a conference on a particular topic. This area also tells you the subject(s) covered by the forum, lists any general rules of behavior in the forum, and tells you who the forum's administrators are and how to reach them. On other online services, this area will have a different name like Forum Information.

Enter Room . . . takes you into the forum's conference room. This is a chat room where members can chat with each other at any time, or where they meet at specific times for a prearranged conference featuring an expert on a particular subject. For example, the Health & Fitness forum might invite an expert on jogging to hold a conference on that subject at a certain time. The Newsflash area would promote this conference so members knew about it in advance. At the appointed time, dozens of members would enter the conference room to listen to the expert field questions from the conference's moderator, or to pose questions themselves.

Who's Here tells you which other forum members are currently browsing the forum. You can page any other members present and invite them into the conference room for a chat.

Browse Libraries shows you a list of the forum's software libraries, like this:

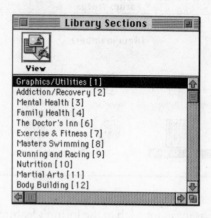

Files stored in this particular forum are grouped into more than the dozen libraries shown here. You can open any library to see a list of its files and download them to your own computer. Typically, these libraries contain programs or articles about forum subjects. On some business-related forums, one library may be devoted to product announcements, résumés, or company information.

Browse Messages takes you to the forum's message boards. This particular forum has seventeen different message boards.

Section	Topics	Msgs
General Discussion [1]	78	182
Addiction/Recovery [2]	89	391
Mental Health [3]	60	292
Family Health [4]	13	18
The Doctor's Inn [6]	27	87
Exercise & Fitness [7]	40	98
Running and Racing [9]	19	48
Nutrition [10]	28	48
Martial Arts [11]	45	222
Body Building [12]	29	128
NETWorking [13]	6	9
Women's Health [15]	13	49
CFS/CFIDS/ME/FMS [16]	103	468
Self Help/Support [17]	6	20

Message Sections — View Topics — Messages since Tue, Jun 21, 1994

Inside any message board are the messages themselves. For example, if we open the General Discussion board, we'll see these messages:

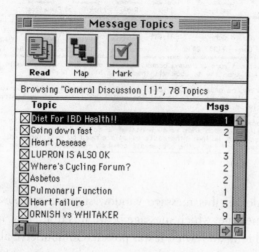

Each message has a title, and the number at the right indicates the number of replies attached to each message. When a message has one or more replies attached to it, the whole group of messages is called a *thread*. With the messages displayed, you can read them online, reply to them, or mark them so they can be downloaded to your own computer. *(See "Reading and posting messages" below for more about this.)*

Waiting Messages is a list of private messages sent to you by other members of this forum. This feature allows forum members to send messages to one another within the forum itself, rather than having to leave the forum and use the online service's general e-mail function.

Reading and posting messages

To read any message or thread online, you open the message board you want and then select the message you want to read. The message opens in a window like this:

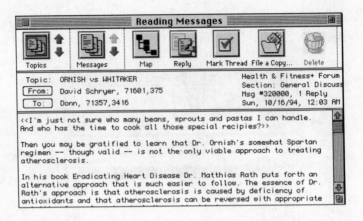

The header in this message window shows the topic name, who posted the message, which message board it is from, how many replies are attached to it, and when it was posted. CompuServe also gives you lots of options for dealing with a message with icons right at the top of the message window. You can move from topic to topic on the board, move from message to message within this thread, see a "map" that shows the current message's location relative to other messages and threads, reply to the message, mark the thread for downloading, file a copy of this particular message on your disk, or delete the message. You can duplicate these functions through menu commands on other services if they're not available in the message window.

If you click the Reply icon, for example, you'll see a blank message form and you can type your response. The message will then be added to this thread. To post a message on a new topic, you use a menu command in the CompuServe software.

Since you could well be paying for each minute you're connected to a forum in CompuServe or another online service, you can mark messages or a thread and download them to your own computer for off-line reading. You probably won't want to download every message you see, so you can choose which ones you want by marking them. The checked box at the left of each message indicates that these messages are marked.

Marking also lets you keep track of which messages you've already read. On this forum, all messages are automatically marked when you first join because you haven't read any of them. Once you've read or downloaded messages, you can unmark them so that the next time you get messages from this area, only the ones you haven't read yet will be downloaded.

Starting your own forum

Online services each have dozens of forums, but if you spend most of your online time on a particular service that doesn't have a forum relating to your business, you might want to start one. To create a new forum, come up with a plan that states the purpose of the forum and its main features (message boards, libraries, conferencing, ads, or whatever), and then propose the forum to the online service's management. The service's management will probably have a specific proposal process you go through to pitch a new forum. Newer online services like eWorld or smaller ones like Delphi or GEnie may welcome new forum ideas, since the variety of discussion groups on a service is one of its major drawing cards. ·

The trick to proposing a new forum is to make it specific enough to draw potential customers for your business, yet general enough to draw a significant portion of the online service's subscriber base. If you sell woodworking tools, you might propose a woodworking forum, but that would probably be too specific for an online service's subscribers at large. However, a handcrafts forum might be general enough, and you could have a woodworking message area where you can gain credibility by answering questions. You might also include a woodworking library and start it off by posting your own articles about carving techniques or advice on how to choose tools.

Running your own online forum gives you more freedom to post your company information (since you make the forum rules), but it also means spending time online every day to monitor the forum's activity and make changes as needed. Like an electronic storefront, your forum should continually offer something new to its members (aside from posted messages) to keep the browsers and members coming back.

ABOUT NEWSGROUPS

A newsgroup is the Net's version of a forum. It's a place where a group of people post and read messages on a particular topic. Unlike forums, newsgroups support only messages, not libraries or conferencing.

But despite this limitation, newsgroups offer a lot of marketing leverage. Nobody has to subscribe to an online service or BBS to join a newsgroup. Your potential audience includes anyone who has access to the Internet and who is interested in the newsgroup's topic. Many newsgroups are followed by thousands of people around the world. And once you have access to the Net, it doesn't cost you a dime to participate in as many newsgroups as you like.

How to access newsgroups

In order to access any newsgroup, your connection to the Net must include a *newsreader*, a program that can access and read the contents of newsgroups. There are programs designed solely for reading newsgroups, such as NewsWatcher, tin, or rn, and there are Web browsers like Netscape that include the ability to participate in newsgroups. If you have a shell account, your ISP will give you the ability to read newsgroups. Online services offer newsgroup access, too.

Every Internet services provider subscribes to a selection of newsgroups, but there are thousands of newsgroups and no ISP has them all. In order to access any particular newsgroup, your ISP must subscribe to it.

To find out which newsgroups you can access, use your newsreader program to display a list of those available on your system. (If you're on an online service, go to the service's Internet area and use the function to read newsgroups.) If you hear about a newsgroup that might help you promote your business but your ISP doesn't subscribe to it, you may be able to get it by asking your ISP's administrators to subscribe to it. If your ISP refuses to subscribe to a newsgroup you need access to, switch your Net account to an ISP that does.

Newsgroup names and categories

There are several types of newsgroups on the Net, but the largest collection of groups is called Usenet. Usenet is divided into eighteen categories, or *hierarchies*. The prefix of a group's name indicates the newsgroup hierarchy. Some of the Usenet hierarchies are:

alt (alternative topics)

biz (business)

comp (computers)

misc (miscellaneous topics)

news (news and discussions about Usenet itself)

rec (recreation)

sci (science)

soc (social topics)

talk (controversial topics)

The suffix of the group's name indicates its subject. For example, news.announce.newgroups contains announcements of new Usenet groups that have been formed, and misc.entrepreneurs focuses on entrepreneurship.

The important thing about group hierarchies is that there are two unofficial classes of groups: mainstream hierarchies and alternative hierarchies. Most ISPs subscribe to all the mainstream hierarchies, which include comp, misc, news, rec, sci, soc, and talk. But ISPs only subscribe to some of the alternative groups, which include the alt and biz hierarchies.

Moderated and unmoderated groups

Like mailing lists, newsgroups can be moderated or unmoderated. An unmoderated group will accept postings from anyone about anything, so it's up to individual members of the group to stay on the topic, and sometimes they don't. When the group doesn't stay on the topic, it becomes littered with off-topic messages and other messages flaming those who can't stay on the topic or generally lamenting the group's deterioration. On the other hand, postings to unmoderated groups are automatic, so they appear on the Net within minutes of your sending them.

A moderated group's postings are all forwarded automatically to the moderator's e-mailbox, where he or she reads them, decides whether or not they're on the topic, and then either posts or discards them. Moderated newsgroups stay on the topic, but it may take a day or more for your message to be posted, since it has to be read and evaluated first.

Joining a newsgroup

Assuming your ISP provides access to the newsgroup you want, joining a group is simple. You just go to your online service's Internet area and display the list of newsgroups, or direct your ISP's newsreader software to list all the available newsgroups. (This usually happens when you start up the newsreader anyway.)

One popular newsreader for Macintosh users is the NewsWatcher program developed by John Norstad at Northwestern University. This program is distributed for free on the Net. When NewsWatcher opens, it displays a list of the newsgroups to which your ISP subscribes, like this:

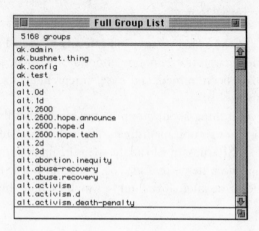

```
▤▤▥▥▥▥▥  Full Group List  ▥▥▥▥▥▥ ▣
  5168 groups
ak.admin                                    ⬆
ak.bushnet.thing
ak.config
ak.test
alt
alt.0d
alt.1d
alt.2600
alt.2600.hope.announce
alt.2600.hope.d
alt.2600.hope.tech
alt.2d
alt.3d
alt.abortion.inequity
alt.abuse-recovery
alt.abuse.recovery
alt.activism
alt.activism.d
alt.activism.death-penalty                  ⬇
                                            ▣
```

This window lists all the groups (5168 of them) to which this particular ISP subscribes. Your newsreader window may well be different, since there are many different newsreader programs. For example, the tin program shows group names in one column and a brief description of each group in another.

Once you see the list of groups, you can view the contents of any group by selecting it. It can take a minute or more for your newsreader to display the messages from a group that contains hundreds or thousands of messages. To speed up your access to certain groups, you can build a personal group list with your newsreader software. When you find a group that interests you, you tell your newsreader that you want to subscribe to it. Once you've subscribed, your newsreader program knows that you always want it to retrieve any new articles that have been posted to that group since you last viewed it. Here's a personal group list:

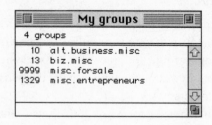

```
▤▤▥▥▥  My groups  ▥▥▥ ▣
  4 groups
  10   alt.business.misc                    ⬆
  13   biz.misc
9999   misc.forsale
1329   misc.entrepreneurs
                                            ⬇
                                            ▣
```

Notice that the group list shows the number of unread messages in each group, so you know whether or not there's much new happening on a group since you last read it.

If you decide you don't want to continue your subscription to a newsgroup, you simply delete its name from your personal group list.

Reading and replying to messages

As in a forum, a newsgroup's messages appear as topics in a list. *(See p. 118 in Chapter 6 for an example.)* You can read any message by selecting it. A message can have one or more replies attached to it. When you have a message open, you can reply to it by choosing a Reply command in your newsreader and then typing your message.

Whenever you read a message, it's automatically marked as having been read. Normally, your newsreader will give you the choice of displaying all the group's messages, or only those you haven't read. When a newsgroup contains hundreds or thousands of messages, it's faster to display only the unread messages. You can mark messages as read without having actually read them by using a command in your newsreader. (Often, you can tell by a message's title that you don't want to read it.)

In most cases, you'll be able to download any new messages to your computer so you can read them off-line at your leisure, instead of having to try to speed-read through dozens of messages while your online connection meter is running.

Finding out about newsgroups

There are thousands of newsgroups on the Net, and your newsreader software will probably provide access to most of them. Only a few of these groups will be suitable for your marketing purposes, though. The trick is to discover which groups they are.

One way to find out what's going on in these groups is trial and error. Browse the list of newsgroups displayed by your newsreader, open up any that look interesting, and read a few messages on it to see if it's a group you might want to participate in regularly. If it looks potentially interesting, subscribe to the group and monitor its activity for a couple of weeks.

Your newsreader software will also notify you about any new groups that appear on the Net. New groups appear every week (if not every day). Most newsreaders automatically display a separate list of groups that have appeared since you last browsed the newsgroup list. You should check any new groups that look interesting, since it's easier to build a reputation on a newsgroup if you are active in it from its beginning.

Another way to find out about newsgroups is by reading an Internet magazine or consulting a directory like *The Internet Yellow Pages*. Directories list newsgroup names and subjects. Internet-related magazines often have articles about new or interesting newsgroups as well.

Finally, you can check the news.announce.newgroups newsgroup on the Net itself for messages announcing groups that have been recently formed.

STARTING A NEWSGROUP

If you can't find a group that suits your marketing purposes, start one of your own. A newsgroup doesn't exist on only one host computer system, and you don't necessarily need permission to create one. Internet access providers like PSI and Netcom sponsor newsgroups about the Net or about their services in particular. Software companies like Oracle and computer companies like Digital Equipment host newsgroups of their own to offer product information and advice. You can do the same.

A newsgroup exists in the storage space provided by every ISP that subscribes to it. New postings to the group are transmitted over the Net and are received by all ISPs subscribing to that group. So a newsgroup's existence and its readership are determined by the number of ISPs who subscribe to that particular group, and by the number of people connected through those various ISPs who participate in that group.

There are two ways to create a Usenet newsgroup:

- Create a group in an alternative hierarchy like alt or biz by simply having your ISP or a consultant set the group up. You then announce that the group exists and invite people to participate.
- Formally propose a new group in one of the mainstream Usenet hierarchies, and then solicit a discussion and a vote about whether it should or shouldn't be created. If your proposal wins, the group is created.

The advantage to having a group in the mainstream hierarchies is that it will be subscribed to by most ISPs, while a group in the alt or biz hierarchies will have more limited distribution.

Starting an alternative newsgroup

To start a newsgroup in an alternative hierarchy, you only need to find a consultant or ISP that knows the Unix commands needed to create one. Once the group exists, you announce the new group by placing a notice in news.announce.newgroups and any other place that seems appropriate. Since an alternative group won't automatically gain subscriptions from different ISPs, you should promote the group by posting announcements to related newsgroups and mailing lists. The more people you can interest in joining your newsgroup, the more they'll request their ISPs to subscribe to that group, and the more ISPs will join.

So, for example, you could set up alt.oldfords to further your reputation as a source of information about restoring antique Ford cars (and thereby attract customers to your parts business). You would certainly want to announce the new group in groups such as alt.autos.antique and alt.autos.rod-n-custom. As members of these groups ask their ISPs to subscribe to alt.oldfords, your group will develop a following.

Starting a mainstream newsgroup

To start a newsgroup in one of Usenet's mainstream hierarchies, you follow a more formal procedure. You propose the group name and discussion topic on news.announce.newgroups (and on any groups specifically related to your topic) and request a discussion about it. The discussion takes place on the newsgroup news.groups. As part of the discussion, you lay out more specific plans for the group, including which topics it will cover, whether or not it will be moderated, and who the moderators will be, if any.

After thirty days of discussion, members of news.groups decide whether the new newsgroup is appropriate. If the new group is deemed appropriate, you come up with an official name and a group charter, or policy for how the group should be used. You then call for an official vote among news.group's members to create the group. The votes are tallied by an independent group called the Usenet Volunteer Votetakers. The voting period lasts twenty-one days, and the results of the vote are posted to news.announce.newgroups.

If the vote goes your way, the group's creation is announced in news.announce.newgroups. As one of the mainstream Usenet groups, your group is automatically subscribed to by most ISPs.

You'll find more details about this procedure in the news.announce.newusers newsgroup, or in a general Internet guide. *(See the Appendix for details.)* If you're connected through an online service, the service may also have some information files that describe the process.

To moderate or not to moderate?

The other big decision you have to make about setting up a group is whether or not you want to moderate it. If the group is focused enough on a particular subject, you may not need to moderate it. Some people selling things tend to *spam* the alt and biz hierarchies (cross-posting their ads to several groups without regard for the ad's relevance in them), but a newsgroup that's tightly focused on a particular topic may be able to tolerate an occasional spam attack. But if your group's topic is fairly general, you may have to moderate it to keep it on the topic that is nearest and dearest to your marketing purposes.

If you decide to moderate a group, remember that it will require your giving the group a lot of your time as you read each contribution and decide whether to post it.

MARKETING IN FORUMS AND NEWSGROUPS

It's not hard to figure out the basic procedures for using forums and newsgroups. With a little research you can find the right groups in which to bolster your online reputation. But actually building a good reputation is another matter. These areas of the online marketplace abound with messages that are never read, or worse, messages that generate hostile responses. Building a positive reputation on a newsgroup or forum takes time, and it requires tact. Here's how guerrillas do it.

Lurk first, post later

Before you post anything to a newsgroup or forum, monitor its activity and read messages on it for at least a week. It takes that long for you to learn the group's etiquette. Some of the points you need to fully understand include:

- what's acceptable and not acceptable in the way of promotional messages
- what's considered an appropriate message length

- which topics are of the most interest to the group's members
- which group members are the most active, and which of them have views similar to yours
- which messages or message titles draw the most replies

Read messages diligently and learn what kinds of information and which methods of expression are regarded the most highly. You'll quickly learn how to become one of the good guys.

Use descriptive topic names

The names you give your postings should arouse curiosity and encourage group members to read your messages. When you reply to a message, your newsreader or forum software automatically suggests *RE: something* as the new message name. It's tempting to let the newsreader suggest a message name for you, but the problem is that lots of people do the same thing. If your message title is *RE: something* and there are six others with the same title, yours won't stand out. Worse yet, it'll be lumped in with all the others. If there are half a dozen messages whose topic names are *RE: Butterflies,* anyone who reads and isn't interested in the first one of them will probably never bother to open the rest of them. Your topic name should explain the main point of your message.

Don't be crass

Whatever you do, don't simply post your marketing message or an ad for your business. This is the surest way to draw lots of flames (poison-pen replies) from all but the ad-related discussion groups and forums, and it may permanently damage your reputation. If you've already made this mistake, an abject apology that includes some useful information or a useful comment about another member's posting may help restore you to the group's good graces.

But this isn't to say that you can't pitch yourself. It's all a matter of doing it properly. Here's a message you might post to a newsgroup about gardening if you wanted to promote your online garden supply business:

```
I've been enjoying the discussion here for awhile,
and would like to ask for some help. I'm in the lawn
and garden supplies business and am looking for useful
information to post on my Web server. I already post
excerpts from articles in Green Thumb News, as well as
a list of seasonal gardening tips for four different
regions of the United States. Does anyone here have
ideas for other selections of information?

Thanks for your help!

George Beasley
------------------------------------------------------
Garden City Online
http://www.gardencity.com, email: info@gardencity.com
The Gardener's Source For Supplies & Info
------------------------------------------------------
```

Rather than a sales pitch, this message acknowledges the group's expertise and then asks for help. This message may provoke further discussion about what constitutes useful gardening information. It may encourage any experts on the group to send articles they've written as potential additions to your Web site. It will definitely put your Web site's name and address before a group likely to be interested in it, and it will almost certainly attract some visitors.

Don't be banal

One mistake newbies make when attempting to join a discussion is to post a message just for the sake of posting one. When America Online first allowed access to newsgroups, a lot of groups had to suffer through messages like *Hi. Is this the Internet?* If you're not sure about how to post a message or whether or not you're in the right newsgroup, check out the news.announce.newusers newsgroup and read its general information messages.

Even if you know you're in the right place and you know how to post a message, don't reply to someone else's comment by simply agreeing with them. Posting a message that repeats someone else's message and says you agree is a waste of time for everybody in a discussion. If you don't have something new to add, keep lurking until you do.

Provide useful information

Each discussion group has its own ideas of what "useful information" is, but you can increase your chances of hitting the mark.

- Don't assume people are interested in your subjective opinions until you've developed a reputation as someone whose opinions matter. Instead, back up your opinions with citations from other sources, or base your comments on actual experience.
- If you come across a short article or a message on another group that you think the current group's members would appreciate seeing, post it (as long as it's not copyrighted), and include some comments of your own about it.
- If you've written an article that you've stored somewhere online and you think the group's members might find it interesting, include some of the article's information in a message and direct members to the article's address. An Internet consultant we know maintains a list of Internet Presence Providers, and she occasionally refers people to it in her newsgroup and mailing list postings. *(See Appendix for the address of this list.)*
- Respond to questions posted by other members if you can offer some constructive advice, but don't claim experience or knowledge you don't have. If you can provide a partial answer, do so, and try to direct people to others who know more. This will show group members that you're not just in the game for yourself.

Use a company signature

Create a signature for your messages that identifies your business and its online address. Customers can't find you if you don't tell them how. *(See "Your signature" in Chapter 4, p. 76.)*

Choose a handful of targets

You only have so much time in a day, and you can only devote so much of it to forums and newsgroups. Don't overdo it. As you're shopping around, look for two or three groups whose topics most closely relate to your business, and focus on those. Establish your presence in one group at a time. Stay away from groups that are so active that you can't keep up with them, or so inactive that nobody ever posts messages in them. You should be able to come up with a short list of forums or newsgroups that match your market. If you try to keep up with more than three active groups, you probably won't be able to keep up with any of them.

Participate frequently

Check every forum or newsgroup for new messages at least every day or two, and try to respond to questions or add helpful comments to the discussions whenever you can. Frequent postings keep you visible, and if you wait too long to respond to a previous message, people won't remember the prior discussion.

Propose a conference in your forum

If you're in a forum on an online service, send a note to the forum's administrator and propose holding a conference. Your pitch to the administrator should include a description of yourself and your experience as well as some noteworthy accomplishments. The pitch should convince the administrator that you know your stuff and that your area of expertise would make for an interesting and popular conference for the forum's other members. *(See Chapter 9 for details.)*

If your pitch is accepted, the administrator will announce your upcoming conference in the forum's What's New area. If your subject is broad enough and you schedule the conference at least two months in advance, you may also be able to get the administrator to propose an announcement about it on the online service's welcome screen or What's New list. *(See Chapter 6).*

SIX STRATEGIES FOR FORUM AND NEWSGROUP MARKETING

Here's a list of key points to remember as you go about promoting your business in forums and newsgroups.

1. Do your homework. Diligently seek out forums and newsgroups that relate to your business as closely as possible. The more closely a discussion group's topic relates to your business, the more likely its members are to become your customers. Lurk on any group for at least a week before you even consider posting a message to it. Make sure you understand the group's culture and etiquette before you join the discussion.

2. Don't waste the group's time. Post messages that are on the topic, and that add to the discussion. Don't simply agree with others, and don't post blatant ads. Back up your opinions with facts.

3. Be helpful. If you see a posting or article someplace else that your group might appreciate (and its author allows it to be reproduced), post it with your comments. Whenever someone posts a question and you can provide all or part of the answer, do so. This is the best way to gain other members' respect.

4. Use a company signature. People can't find you or your online store if they don't know your address. Sign every message with your name, company name, and address.

5. Be attentive. Check your newsgroups and forums every day or two for new messages, and participate in the discussion whenever you have something to add. Frequent postings equal visibility.

6. Be patient. Success doesn't happen overnight. Group members must learn to trust you by the quality of your contributions to the discussion. Some people may not have an interest in your product or service for months, but if you persistently and patiently stay involved, they'll remember you.

8

Bulletin Boards

Bulletin board systems are miniature versions of commercial online services. Rather than catering to hundreds of thousands of subscribers with information and services designed to suit the largest online audience, each BBS serves a smaller slice of cyberspace. BBSs serve individual cities like Houston, subject areas like fishing or boating, or other specific communities such as programmers who use Microsoft languages. BBSs tend to have loyal and active groups of subscribers, so your marketing efforts on them have a good chance of falling on receptive ears.

The trick to BBS marketing is finding one or two boards whose subscribers will be keenly interested in what your business offers. There are about 60,000 BBSs in the United States alone, so you'll have to do some hunting, but you're sure to find a board whose topic fits your marketing purposes like a glove. There are hundreds of different BBS topics, including computer games, Christianity, vacations, politics, home brewing, shortwave radio, reptiles, software development, health, real estate, self-employment, and law enforcement.

When you find one or more boards that match your target market, you can use many of the same guerrilla marketing techniques covered in Chapters 4–7. Most BBSs have e-mail systems, file libraries, and chat systems. Many host one or more forums, and some have conferences and classified ad sections as well.

In this chapter, we'll see which BBS features can support your marketing campaign, how to find a BBS that matches your target audience, how to start your own BBS if you don't find the right one, and how to promote your company's identity and generate sales through the bulletin board of your choice.

MARKETING OPPORTUNITIES ON A BBS

A BBS is like a commercial online service, only smaller. Like an online service, subscribers dial a phone number to reach the BBS, and then use the resources available on the BBS to communicate with each other, play games, read news, download information, or shop. Some BBSs are free, but most charge a subscription fee between $25 and $150 a year.

The main differences between a BBS and a commercial online service are size, features, and access.

- A BBS typically has one or two thousand subscribers.
- A BBS usually has a text-based interface rather than the graphical ones used by most commercial services.
- A BBS has fewer features than an online service.
- A BBS usually has one or two phone numbers you use to access it instead of hundreds of local numbers across the country.

But from a marketing standpoint, you use the same features to pursue your marketing goals on a BBS as you do on an online service. Let's see how these work on a bulletin board.

E-mail Nearly every BBS has electronic mail that allows members to communicate with one another. Many BBSs these days also have mail gateways to the Net, so you can exchange mail with other netizens from your BBS. You normally have to be a registered member or a paid subscriber to a BBS to have a mail account on it.

Forums Most BBSs have one or more forums. These work like the forums on online services, although the interface probably won't be quite as classy. On the other hand, people who join a forum on a subject-specific BBS will be much more likely to stick to the discussion topic and to visit it regularly.

Chat rooms and conferences Chat rooms are online social gatherings that don't stay on a particular topic, so they're not a promising avenue for marketing. However, conferences on topic-specific BBSs are a great place to build an online presence.

File libraries Other than chatting and e-mail, the file libraries are the most popular feature of a BBS. Libraries on topic-specific BBSs are a good place to post useful articles or information that enhance your reputation.

Classified ads Boards that host classified ads have the advantage of letting you zero in on a particular geographic area, or letting you sell highly specific items to a target audience. You can market diving equipment on a divers' BBS. If you live in Los Angeles, you can offer your job skills on a Los Angeles employment board.

HOW TO FIND THE RIGHT BBS

You could spend hundreds of hours and hundreds of dollars dialing all over the country and poking into BBS systems at random before you found even óne that met your marketing needs. But time is more valuable than money to a guerrilla, so here's a shortcut: get a copy of *Boardwatch* magazine. *Boardwatch* is the leading monthly report on the BBS industry. It covers news about BBS technology and general developments in other online communications markets such as the Net and commercial online services. *(See Appendix for contact information.)*

Every month *Boardwatch* lists a couple of hundred BBSs with the name, phone number, and a brief description of each. You can go through the list each month, weed out the BBSs that don't meet your needs, and find others worth checking out. Along with the list, there are individual ads for BBSs throughout each issue, especially in the classified ad section at the back. Each ad offers a more complete description of a BBS, such as the specific features it offers, the number of dial-up connections it has, and what its subscription rate is, if any.

By browsing through just one issue of *Boardwatch*, you should find one or two BBSs that can deliver the subscriber base you're seeking. And if you like what you see in one issue, following the magazine for a few months will produce even more results.

Boardwatch also runs a list of list keepers — BBSs that maintain lists of other BBSs. Each BBS list keeper focuses on a particular selection of BBSs, so you can obtain lists of BBSs that focus on specific topics or geographical areas. For example, several BBS list keepers maintain lists of BBSs that relate to handicapped issues. Another keeps a list of BBSs related to firearms. Some lists are geographic, such as a list of BBSs in the 713 area code. By dialing up the right BBS list keeper, you just might find a dozen or more BBSs that are right up your marketing alley.

If you're an America Online subscriber, the BBS Corner also has a list of BBSs.

EVALUATING A BBS

Once you've put together a list of potential BBS targets, it's time to go online and start exploring. You may find more BBSs that match your marketing target than you can keep up with, so you'll want to zero in on the cream of the crop.

Every time you dial up a BBS, you're asked to log on, just as you would on an online service. Every BBS allows you to log on as a visitor or guest, although you probably won't have access to all of its features unless you actually become a member or subscriber.

If the BBS has a subscription fee, you'll usually be allowed to register anonymously as a guest to check out all the features it offers. If the BBS doesn't have a subscription fee, you'll probably be asked to register by entering your name, address, and phone number in order to see and use all of its features. In either case, you should be able to move far enough into any BBS to evaluate it without having to commit any money to a subscription. When evaluating a BBS's marketing potential, consider the following:

Access

Some BBSs have more than one hundred dial-in lines to give lots of callers access at the same time; others have two or three lines and end up producing a lot of busy signals. If you have trouble connecting with the BBS, other people will probably have trouble too. Look for another board that is easier to connect with.

Most BBSs have local calling numbers, which probably means subscribers will either be local or they won't spend a lot of time in any one calling session. The largest boards offer 800-number access for a flat hourly fee of about $12, or they offer connections through public data networks like SprintNet, which have local dialing numbers in every major city. If several boards have roughly equivalent features and content, choose the one that's easier and cheaper to dial, because it will attract more subscribers.

Finally, find out if the board places a limit on the amount of time a caller can be connected. Some boards manage call-in traffic by limiting a caller to a certain number of minutes per call, or to a certain number of minutes per day. Make sure these restrictions aren't unreasonable: a one-hour limit is reasonable, but a fifteen-minute limit probably isn't.

Features

Check out the BBS's main menu to see what kinds of services it offers. Here's an example:

```
THIS IS THE N.A.C.D. MEMBER'S AREA

Access to this area is limited to Members ONLY.
-------------------------------------
<G>oodbye, <T>ime, <-> Top Menu, <B>ack to Previous Menu



<D>ive Site Reports ... Water Conditions, etc.
<F>orum ... Member's Open Message Area
<E>quipment Forum ... Equipment Ideas, Defect reports, etc.
<L>ibrary ... Assorted Text Files, Articles, etc.
<M>ail ... Electronic Mail to Other Users
<W>anted/For Sale ... Items for Sale or Wanted by Members
<C>ombined read ... Read all boards you have access to

Command:
```

This is a free BBS. In order to see this menu, all you have to do is register as a member by typing your name and address. Notice that this board (for the NACD, the National Association of Cave Divers) has a general forum, an equipment forum, a library, a mail function, and a classified ad area. This is a small BBS focused on a very specific subject, yet you can see it has several features we could use for marketing. We could join one or both of the forums, upload an article to the file library, or run a classified ad. On most BBSs, all forums are moderated.

A BBS doesn't have to have dozens of features or forums in order to suit your marketing purposes. What it needs is a steady and active subscriber base that is interested in the same topic you are.

We can see the features here, but to really find out how active the board is, we'll have to explore beyond the main menu.

File libraries File libraries are a major drawing card for any BBS, so have a look. Do the categories of files look useful? Are there lots of files? Let's look at the file library on the NACD BBS.

```
Listing of Library Files available on the NACD BBS.

When the prompt asks for your choice, please enter the number of the article.
If you choose to download these articles, an error correcting protocol (such as
ZModem) is highly recommended).

 1 - "The Physiologic Basis of Decompression" by Richard Vann, Ph.D.
     This is must reading for those interested in a greater under-
     standing of the physiology of DCS.

 2 - Australian InWater Recompression treatment for DCS. This is
     a description of the Australian method of inwater recompression
     treatment of DCS, includes treatment tables. This is included for
     your information only. Neither the NACD or the SYSOP of this BBS
     recommend or advise the use of this information in the actual
     occurence of a diving accident.
```

This is a small library, with only seventeen files listed. All the files are articles about scuba diving. While the library is small, however, it's potentially very useful to a marketing guerrilla. If you were a travel agent specializing in scuba diving vacations, your article about cave diving in the Aegean Sea might interest subscribers and promote your services. Many boards have file libraries that contain software such as pictures or utility programs, but there's always at least one library category for articles like the ones above.

Forums Look at the board's forum or forums to see if the messages are serious or frivolous. Here's a sample from the NACD BBS:

```
Section has 37 Msgs, #115 to 894
Starting number, <CR>=First:

Msg # From                To                  Subject                 Board Name
----- ------------------  ------------------  ----------------------  ----------------
115   ED SUAREZ           TO ALL TEKNA SCOO   SEA HORSE TECH SYSTE    EQUIPMENT FORUM
237   RONNIE HALL         ALL                 CYKLON 5000 VS ODIN     EQUIPMENT FORUM
289   R SECONN            ALL                 FARALLON SCOOTER        EQUIPMENT FORUM
327   ED SUAREZ           TO ALL              PLUS RATINGS FOR STE    EQUIPMENT FORUM
337   ED SUAREZ           ALL BEUCHAT ALADI   LOW BATTERY WARNING     EQUIPMENT FORUM
349   ED SUAREZ           TO ALL BEUCHAT AL   MORE ALADIN DIAGNOST    EQUIPMENT FORUM
397   ANDREW MESHEL       ED SUAREZ           PLUS RATINGS FOR STE    EQUIPMENT FORUM
402   ED SUAREZ           ANDREW MESHEL       PLUS RATINGS FOR STE    EQUIPMENT FORUM
418   GLENN KIMBLE        ALL                 DRYSUIT WANTED          EQUIPMENT FORUM
558   RONNIE BELL         ALL                 WANTED  DRY SUIT IN     EQUIPMENT FORUM
576   ED SUAREZ           ANDREW MENDELSSOH   USDIVERS M2 WARNING     EQUIPMENT FORUM
583   ANTHONY MARTINEZ    ALL                 DIVE-RITE MODULAR VA    EQUIPMENT FORUM
587   ANDREW MENDELSSOH   ED SUAREZ           USDIVERS M2 WARNING     EQUIPMENT FORUM
588   ANDREW MENDELSSOH   ANTHONY MARTINEZ    DIVE-RITE MODULAR VA    EQUIPMENT FORUM
```

These messages look like elements of a serious discussion, although you can see that some classified ads have crept in, as in message number 558.

This particular BBS shows messages by number, rather than by date. There are thirty-seven messages in all, and half of the ones of this first screen are from the same person. This isn't encouraging. It would be better if there were more messages with more authors.

Another way to judge a forum's activity is by the message dates. This forum doesn't list message dates — we have to open a few messages to see the posting dates inside them. Messages here are numbered in ascending order, so the one with the highest number at the bottom of the list will be the most recent. Forums can have dozens or hundreds of messages, but you can choose an option to display only those posted after a certain date or those above a certain number.

On most BBSs, including our example here, the classified ad section is just another forum. The NACD's Wanted/For Sale forum looks just like the one above.

The Interface

No matter how intriguing a board's subject is, it won't get much action if the BBS software supporting it is difficult to use. The BBS program determines how a board looks and works, and there are more than three dozen commercially available bulletin board programs that BBS operators (or *sysops*) can use when they set up their systems. Some BBS operators write their own software, too. But as you explore the BBS world, you'll start to notice that many boards look and work the same because they're run on the same software.

Still, different BBS operators have different ideas about ease of use. The better BBSs have a Help option or a list of commands that's available everywhere, while other BBSs force you to do more guesswork.

If you're used to a nice graphical interface on a commercial online service or a graphical shell account from an ISP, you'll find many BBSs to be quite primitive in comparison. In some cases like the Guerrilla Marketing Online BBS, you use special software on your computer that gives you a graphical interface to the BBS, just as if you were using Prodigy or AOL.

Once you've explored a handful of boards, you'll have a general sense of how they work. If at this point you still find a board difficult to use, take your marketing attack elsewhere unless the board's topic and subscriber base is so perfect for your purposes that the hassle is worth the trouble.

Activity

Most BBSs have one or two thousand subscribers, but if those subscribers are active on the board and they're receptive to your marketing messages, they can do a lot for your bottom line. However, it's hard to tell just how many subscribers a board has, or how active they are. Some ads you'll find in *Boardwatch* or *BBS* (another bulletin board magazine) may claim a certain subscriber base for a BBS. *Boardwatch* does an annual poll of its readers and features the top ten BBSs in the country in its September issue each year. But most of the time you'll have to do a little detective work to find out just how active a board is.

As you browse a BBS, check the dates of forum messages or the dates when files were uploaded. Look at the variety of names attached to forum messages or uploaded files, and see if there appear to be lots of names that appear over and over. That's the measure of solid activity. A board could have 20,000 subscribers, but it won't do you much good if there are only 10 regulars.

MARKETING ON A BBS

The specific marketing techniques you use are determined by the BBS feature you're using at the time. The fundamental techniques have been covered elsewhere in this book. *(For advice about marketing with e-mail, see Chapter 4. For classified ad strategies, see Chapter 6. For information about marketing in forums, see Chapter 7.)*

On top of this basic advice, here are a few BBS-specific pointers that will help your attack succeed.

Know the policies

Every BBS has policies regarding commercial messages and general behavior. In most cases, these policies are posted in an information file that is automatically displayed when you register, or that you can display from the board's main menu. Read these policies and follow them. The BBS may have a library where you can upload a file describing your business, for example, but you'll find that out a lot more quickly if you read it up front rather than having to stumble into the appropriate library to discover it.

The general information file will also tell you how to contact the board's administrator or sysop. The sysop is the king of the BBS, and what he or she says goes. The sysop can help you make the most of the BBS, and he or she can cancel your account if you step out of line. If you're not sure about whether it's okay to do something, clear it with the sysop first.

Know the board

Even if you've reviewed the board's general rules of behavior, watch what others do on it before posting messages yourself. By reading other forum messages, ads, or library files, you'll quickly get a sense of how to go about promoting your business. Some boards prohibit commercial announcements completely, while others have a special forum or library for them. A board that frowns on blatant commercial announcements doesn't prohibit you from marketing, however. It just requires you to be more subtle about it. *(See Chapter 7.)*

Your marketing campaign should also take the board's capabilities into account. It won't do you much good to promote your Net storefront in a BBS forum if the BBS doesn't provide access to the Net. Instead, you'll have to offer to provide a catalog or information about your services directly through the BBS mail system or one of its libraries.

Tread lightly

A BBS is like a small town. A bad reputation is much easier to get and much harder to get rid of than it is in the relative anonymity of a major online service's forum or a Net newsgroup. Because they have so much more traffic, an online service or newsgroup may have a fairly short memory: you might step over the line with a blatant ad one month and then have the luxury of dealing with a mostly new audience when you try a different approach the following month. But on a BBS, you're more likely to deal with the same group of people month after month. You should be much more careful not to offend anyone.

In the beginning of your campaign, focus on providing useful information by posting nonpromotional articles in the BBS libraries or answering questions in the forums. For example, you might post a forum message alerting other members that you've just uploaded a new article to one of the BBS libraries. In this case, you're just alerting people to some new information, which is a lot different than posting an ad for your business.

Make a commitment

One of the advantages of the smaller subscriber base on a BBS is that with some persistence and a spirit of helpfulness, you can become one of the board's leading lights. Even on an active board, a handful of subscribers usually stand out as key members, people to whom others on the board turn for answers and advice. By making regular visits to a BBS and always trying to post useful information, you can become a respected leader. And if people also know that you offer products or services that can help solve their problems, you'll probably gain lots of customers in the bargain.

SETTING UP YOUR OWN BBS

Marketing on someone else's BBS carries many of the same restrictions you face on an online service or on the Net. You have to conform to the customs and tastes of a user community that was there before you were. If you set up your own BBS, you're the ruler of your own online world. Naturally, you'll want to create a world that many others find attractive and interesting, but you'll have a lot more leeway in terms of promoting your products and services. You can post your company name right on the board's welcome screen, offer a catalog of your products in a library, and even schedule conferences with yourself as the speaker so you can share your wisdom and build your reputation with others.

· Company-sponsored BBSs are a successful part of many marketing campaigns. Computer hardware and software companies have used them for years as a way to communicate with their customers, offering price lists, product descriptions, and technical support. Now, consumer-oriented companies such as bookstores, office supply stores, newspapers, art galleries, and auto buying services are finding that having their own BBS is a good way to expand their market into cyberspace.

For example, Penny Wise Office Products in Edmonton, Maryland, hosts a BBS that callers reach through an 800 number. Once on the BBS, callers can browse its catalog of merchandise and place orders online. Penny Wise has been operating its BBS for four years now, and has many steady customers on it. Combined with the company's online storefronts on CompuServe, America Online, and GEnie, the BBS accounts for 20 percent of Penny Wise's multimillion-dollar annual sales volume.

Even if you don't market products directly, your company BBS can help enhance your reputation. The Raleigh, North Carolina, *News & Observer* newspaper operates a BBS called NandO.net. The BBS provides Internet access for the Raleigh community and also distributes the

News & Observer electronically. NandO.net opened in February, 1993, with five dial-in lines and now has more than a hundred lines due to its popularity. The board also features a children's educational area called Nando Land, and offers online editions of books and articles in such categories as literature, American history, world history, and poetry.

NandO.net supports itself by charging subscribers $20 per month for full Internet access. But by offering lots of free information along with free subscriptions for kids and the handicapped community, the *News & Observer* also enhances its reputation as one of the community's good guys.

What you need to run a BBS

Running a BBS requires investments in hardware, software, and time. On the hardware and software side, you can get started for less than $2000 with an inexpensive PC clone, a 14,400 bps modem, an inexpensive BBS program, and a single phone line. As your BBS grows in popularity, you can add disk storage, more phone lines, faster modems, and a multiplexer that allows several callers to reach the BBS at once. To get an idea of how much it will cost and what it will require, pick up a book about starting and running a BBS. *(See Appendix.)*

On the time side, you have to plan time for designing the board as well as for running it. You'll need several weeks to figure out what you want to put on the board and how the information will be organized. You'll also have to gather the material you'll be offering. When the board is up and running, you'll need a sysop or administrator to take care of it. The sysop monitors the board's activity, takes care of any problems, answers subscriber questions, posts new information, and deletes old information when it's no longer useful. You can do all this yourself, or you can find a consultant to do it for you.

If you do it yourself, you'll find that the major BBS software companies usually offer lots of help. Each of them has its own BBS that stores answers to frequent questions, and you can e-mail the company's technical support staff for help in ironing out specific problems as they arise. If you'd rather hire a consultant, the best way to find one is through a referral. Find a BBS that you like and then contact the sysop or owner. Most successful BBS operators are happy to talk about their experience, and eventually you'll get a reference to a consultant who can help you. *Boardwatch* and *BBS* magazines feature articles about the ins and outs of BBS management, and each summer there's a major trade show called the Online Networking Exposition and BBS Convention (ONE BBS Con) where you'll find a whole convention center filled with BBS experts.

Three keys to BBS success

The three most important goals in choosing BBS hardware and software are accessibility, expandability, and ease of use.

Accessibility Your board is useless if people can't connect with it. Make sure you offer easy telephone access with as many lines as necessary. If you're going for a national audience, get a connection to the Internet so netizens can reach your system via Telnet. Going on the Net expands your promotional opportunities a hundredfold, and it increases your potential audience about a thousandfold. Even if you're not on the Net, offer your paid subscribers an 800- number access option for a flat monthly fee. With a cheaper phone connection, people will feel freer to spend more time on your system.

Expandability Many a BBS operator has suffered from success by choosing a system that became increasingly difficult to expand as membership grew. Some BBS packages place limits on the number of subscribers or the number of dial-in lines. Blue Ridge Express, one of *Boardwatch* magazine's top ten BBSs in 1994, grew from four lines in 1986 to thirty-six lines in 1994. Now Webb Blackman, Blue Ridge Express's operator, is shopping for new BBS software because the package he's using won't handle more than thirty-six simultaneous callers. Moving your BBS off one software package and onto another is a major undertaking that you should avoid if possible.

Usability There are lots of BBSs to choose from, and no matter how unique the information yours offers, people won't call it regularly if it's disorganized and difficult to use. Give careful thought to the board's layout of features. All major features should be visible on the main menu, and callers should be able to navigate back to the main menu from within any feature with one or two steps at the most.

Some BBS programs give your board a graphical user interface with windows, menus, and icons, while others are text only. On the Guerrilla Marketing Online BBS, subscribers get a special software package they use to dial into the board so they can see graphics and menus and navigate more easily. If your BBS has a graphical interface, it will be more attractive to customers who are new in the BBS world, but you'll have to supply your callers with a special access program to run on their computers. A well-designed text BBS isn't as inviting, but it's what veteran BBS prowlers expect, and it's available to any caller. The choice depends on the audience you hope to attract.

What to put on your BBS

Your BBS should be an exciting and attractive place to visit. The specific contents will depend on the product or service you're selling, but the features you offer will affect the amount of effort required to maintain the board. Here are some considerations.

What's your marketing goal? Part of your decision about content will be influenced by the board's purpose. If you want to offer information as a way to enhance your reputation in general (like NandO.net), you'll focus on articles and other information files. On the other hand, if you plan to sell products (like Penny Wise), you'll put up a catalog and descriptions of the merchandise, along with some tips about how to use it.

What would your customers like? Rather than simply posting a catalog of your merchandise, try to post as much helpful information as you can. You can offer buying advice, care and maintenance tips, or pearls of wisdom gained through your years of experience in your field. One way to involve your customers from the beginning is to take a survey in your physical store or through your other customer contact channels and ask people what they'd like to see on a BBS. Offer them some choices, such as libraries of how-to articles, an online catalog, a user advice forum, and so on. If you involve customers in the board's creation, they'll want to check it out once it's up and running.

What's your audience? Your board's content will also be governed by the audience you're seeking. If you want to attract local subscribers, focus on localized information. For example, NandO.net carries lots of information about the state of North Carolina. If you're going for a national audience, you'll want to choose information that will be equally useful and interesting to anyone.

How will you keep callers interested? If you have the lowest prices on your merchandise and you offer speedy delivery, callers will keep coming back to your board. But you can boost caller volume by offering special promotions and collateral information. For example, Penny Wise Office Products features seasonal specials for items such as calendars in the fall, and it has offered lines of ergonomic computer products along with advice for strain-free computer use.

Attracting callers to your BBS

Once you set up your BBS, promote it as widely as possible. Unlike with a storefront in an online mall or on the Net, nobody can stumble across your BBS by accident: they have to know the number and have a desire to call it. Here are three ways to promote your BBS:

Advertise. Take out advertisements in appropriate print media. If you have a BBS that promotes your local store, run ads in the local newspaper or the regional computer newspaper. Run a classified ad in *Boardwatch*, *BBS*, *Online Access*, or (if you have an Internet connection) even *Internet World*. If you have a physical store, put up a sign inviting people to try your BBS. You might even set up a computer in the store that's directly connected to the BBS and invite customers to check it out. If you publish a mail-order catalog, be sure to feature the BBS option prominently, and consider offering a discount for online orders.

Use Promotions. Send announcements about your board to *Boardwatch*, *BBS*, and other magazines that cover the online world. You may get a free mention in the magazine.

Once your board takes off, send out a press release that stresses your board's uniqueness and success. You might generate a full-blown article about it and gain thousands of dollars' worth of free publicity. *Boardwatch* does at least one article a month on individual BBSs. The featured boards are interesting to *Boardwatch* readers because of their contents, rapid growth, or use of BBS technology. Find an angle you can use to turn your BBS into a news story. If yours is the first local BBS or the first one set up by a local business (and it could well be), this will make interesting news for the local newspaper. A press release about your BBS will probably result in an interview and an article.

If your board can be reached via the Net, promote it through mailing lists and newsgroups. A newsgroup called alt.bbs.internet carries messages announcing new bulletin boards.

Use gateways. If you're selling products via your BBS and making money, consider expanding your reach and visibility through an online storefront on America Online, CompuServe, another online service, or a Net mall. These storefronts are expensive, but once you've set up a BBS, the cost is the only extra for you: you've already done all the work to set up the store itself. The rental fee for a mall store buys you a doorway to hundreds of thousands of potential customers. It also expands your opportunity to promote the store through online billboards, marquees, hypertext links, and welcome screen notices.

SIX STRATEGIES FOR BBS MARKETING

As you begin exploring marketing opportunities on BBSs, you'll quickly find yourself knee-deep in details like phone numbers and menu choices. To help you focus on the ultimate goal, remember these key guerrilla strategies.

1. Find the right BBS. If you're marketing on existing BBSs, search diligently for the one whose topic most closely matches your business and expertise, and choose only the best of those you find. Don't participate in more boards than you can handle: it's better to be a key member of one board than to be a marginal player on six of them.

2. Learn the culture. Monitor all the features of a board for a week or so before you start posting things, so you're sure you understand the best way to get your points across. Read the board's information file or send a message to the sysop if you have questions about appropriate behavior.

3. Proceed with caution. If you're going to err, err on the conservative side when posting marketing messages. A BBS is like a small town with a long memory. Protect your reputation as a member of the community.

4. Decide what your board should accomplish. If you're setting up a BBS of your own, decide what goals you want it to achieve, and whether you want to attract a local, regional, or national caller base. The board's capacity and content will depend on your marketing strategy.

5. Maximize access to your BBS. Your audience expands geometrically if you provide an Internet gateway into your BBS, and the cost of doing this is minimal compared with the audience you'll gain. Even if you're not on the Net, offer a flat-rate 800-number connection to put distant callers at ease about the time they spend on your board.

6. Promote your BBS wherever and whenever possible. If your BBS offers information, then promoting it is no sin. Promote your BBS on relevant newsgroups and mailing lists, through advertising, and through the off-line methods covered in Chapter 16.

9

Boosting Your Online Reputation

E-mail, storefronts, online advertising, newsgroups, and forums are the most common ways to promote your business and build an online presence, but they're not the only ones. There are other important strategies for boosting your online reputation by becoming a respected source of information.

For most netizens, cyberspace is like a huge combined encyclopedia and conference center where the collections of articles and topics of discussion change constantly. Anyone in an online service, BBS, or on the Net can contribute an article or add to a discussion, but even the cleverest contributors are soon forgotten unless they contribute regularly and in the most visible areas of the online marketplace.

It's a lot like gaining fame on TV. If you appear on a nationally syndicated television show, you're introduced to millions of viewers across the country. The next day somebody else is on the show and your fifteen minutes of fame is up. Fame is being noticed; enduring fame is being noticed over and over again. Even the national media superstars have promoters who work nonstop to make sure their names aren't forgotten. Whether you gain fame on TV or in cyberspace, your moment in the sun is soon forgotten unless you follow it up with a continuous stream of appearances and noteworthy deeds.

To build an online reputation and maintain it, you have to draw people's attention by providing useful information, and then continue to hold their attention by spreading news about that information and providing more new information. You can do this in forums and newsgroups by becoming a regular participant in the discussion, but your comments are temporary and you have to keep making new ones to stay in the spotlight. If you publish information, you create visibility that lasts for months or years.

In this chapter, we'll see how you can provide information through online conferences and online publications. Becoming a source of online information increases your credibility far more than an advertisement, and publishing new information regularly lets you maintain your good reputation indefinitely.

CONFERENCES

An online conference is the electronic equivalent of a public seminar or speech. An audience gathers to learn from a speaker about a particular topic. By becoming the speaker in an online conference, you get a chance to show people what you know and how it can help them, and to promote your business in the bargain.

The conference takes place in the main conference room of an online service, or in a smaller conferencing area in a particular forum or BBS. A main conference room has space for an audience of as many as a thousand, while a forum conference might host a dozen or two members.

The conference format is questions and answers. A moderator introduces the conference speaker and asks a few general questions to get things rolling, and then members of the audience ask questions of their own. On the computer screen the whole thing looks like a film script, with the names of individuals followed by their comments. *(See p. 42 in Chapter 3 for an example.)*

Conferences are arranged by the administrators of an online service or of a particular forum. A conference typically lasts an hour. Each of the major online services holds several main conferences every week. Forums and BBSs may host conferences once every week or two. There are lots of conferences going on all the time, which means lots of opportunities to put yourself in the spotlight.

Once you schedule a conference, the online service, forum, or BBS administrator promotes it. A few days before the conference, the administrator puts up a notice announcing it on the area's welcome or sign-off screen or on the forum or BBS menu.

As you might expect, it's much more difficult to line up a spot as a general speaker on an online service than it is to speak in a forum or BBS conference, but both types of conferences are well worth arranging. In either case, an hour's work will get you the kind of visibility and credibility that would take weeks to get through participation in a newsgroup, forum, or mailing list.

To arrange a spot in a conference and successfully conduct one, you need the following:

- the confidence that you will make a compelling online speaker
- a conference topic that appeals to a large portion of the online audience
- a description of you, your business, your accomplishments, and your expertise that will convince the administrator that you can provide lots of information in a useful way
- a pitch that targets the right conference slot at the right time
- a plan for conducting the conference that will give the greatest boost to your business

Gaining self-confidence

You won't go far in promoting yourself as an online speaker unless you believe you have what it takes to do it. Most people break out in a sweat at the idea of speaking in public, either because they don't feel they know enough about a particular topic, or because they can't bear the idea of getting up in front of a group. Your campaign to put on a successful online conference must start with the firm belief that you're up to the job. Let's explode a few myths that might be keeping you from believing you'll make a great online speaker.

You're no expert. Sure you are. If you're at all successful in business, you know more about succeeding in business than most people. And the chances are that your specific business has required you to develop expertise that will be interesting and useful to others. Whether you sell flowers or music recordings or you're a highly paid financial consultant, you know more about that subject than almost anyone else. That makes you an expert. If you're planning to break into online conferencing, it's no time for false modesty.

What you know isn't interesting to others. Each of us has special knowledge, but most of us don't think anybody else is interested in it. It isn't the subject that turns people off, it's the packaging. You may think nobody is interested in learning what you know about turquoise jewelry or leatherwork, but it's really a matter of presenting those subjects in the right light. After all, if Stephen Hawking can turn his knowledge of astrophysics into a best-seller called A Brief History of Time, you can find a way to make what you know interesting to lots of people. (In "Choosing a conference topic" on page 166, you'll see how to turn your experience into a likely conference topic.)

You can't speak in front of a crowd. Fear of speaking in public has a lot to do with physically standing before an audience and wondering if you'll freeze up, if your hair is out of place, or if your fly is open. In the online world, you don't have to worry about things like this because your presence is just a string of letters across a computer screen. This relative anonymity puts everyone at ease; it's the reason online chat sessions are so popular. People don't actually have to look at each other when they bare their souls or make indecent proposals. And if you're worried about your typing speed or accuracy and how that will reflect on your electronic persona, relax: most participants in online conferences and chat sessions make typos as a matter of course.

You're not clever enough. You don't have to bombard the audience with pearls of wisdom every second. A lot of online conferencing is just like having a conversation. The conference format helps you with this. At the beginning of the session, the moderator introduces you and asks you a few general questions to get the discussion moving. Naturally, you will have supplied the list of questions, so you'll already know the answers. Once you're through the opening, you move into a question/answer session with the audience. If you've chosen the right conference topic, this should be no different than answering questions for customers in your store or on the phone.

Choosing a conference topic

Once you're convinced you can do a conference, the key to making it happen is selling a topic. You have to find a topic that the forum, BBS, or online service administrators are convinced will be interesting to their members. To do this, approach the problem from two directions: what you know and what topics are likely to sell.

First, start noticing the topics of conferences that are already set up. Check out some of the conferences themselves to see how closely the actual discussion matches the topic, how the conference leader handles things, and what sorts of questions and answers are offered. In the process, you'll get ideas about what makes a good conference topic along with a general sense of how conferences proceed.

After you've done some basic conference reconnaissance, think about your business, the expertise you offer your customers, and how you can package that expertise as a conference topic. A good topic should be:

- broad enough to attract the widest possible audience
- specific enough so that people get some useful insights

- close enough to your business so that conference attendees are motivated to follow up with you later

One good source of topics is major news or achievements. For example, if you're the author of a successful book or the head of a company that has been prominent in the news, you may be able to do a conference about it. Online services feature authors, entertainers, and business leaders all the time. Even if you're not in the media spotlight, you may have a new product or service that's interesting to a group. If your company makes a unique instrument for airplanes, you should be able to interest the members of an aviation forum.

If your products or achievements aren't newsworthy in themselves, turn your expertise into a conference topic. Think about what you know and how you can present it in terms of solving a problem or answering a widely discussed question. If you're in a consumer services business like accounting, insurance, or investment counseling, it should be easy to come up with a conference topic that has broad appeal and yet allows for specific insights. For example, *Planning for your retirement* would interest lots of people, and you could structure the conference so that you offer a handful of useful tips before opening up the discussion for questions.

If your business is consumer merchandise such as toys or hardware, choose a subject area for its interest level. For example, you probably *could* talk about different types of screws and bolts if you're in the hardware business, but you'll be much more likely to interest people with a conference on deck building, house painting, or flooring.

The conference audience and location will also help you focus your topic. If your conference is in a topic-specific forum, you should assume more knowledge in the audience. For example, if you're an investment counselor speaking to an investors' forum, you might choose a topic like *Investing in Derivatives.* But if you're speaking in a main conference on an online service, you'll want to choose a broader topic like *Investment Profits Without Risk.*

When evaluating any prospective topic, put yourself in the audience's shoes. Think about the members of the forum, BBS, or online service, and consider some topics you might want to learn about if you were them. Ask yourself whether you would attend a conference on the topic you're considering. If the answer is no or even maybe, move on to a topic that's more compelling.

Once you've come up with a topic, give it a catchy title. The title of your conference is like the cover of a book or magazine. Nobody will get past it if it doesn't arouse their interest. Some good conference titles raise questions or answer them. If you know everything about diesel mechanics, your audience in an automotive forum will be more interested in a topic like *Why Diesels Won't Die* than in a topic like *Diesel vs. Gasoline Technology*. Other titles promise to solve a problem, like *Writing Successful Advertisements*.

Finally, your topic should have some connection with your business. You may know a lot about fly fishing, for example, but doing a conference on the topic probably won't do much for your auto leasing business.

Describing your qualifications

With a topic in mind, your next challenge is to convince the forum or online service administrators that you are the perfect person to present it. After all, it won't do your cause much good if you propose a great topic like *High-Power Investing* and the powers that be then decide to approach someone else about doing the conference.

When you propose a topic, the information you provide about yourself, your business, and your expertise should convey the sense that you and your subject were made for one another. One or two paragraphs of text ought to do it. Be sure to explain your experience and qualifications, including any key achievements that prove you know the subject.

Let's suppose your conference topic is *Bargain Vacations*. Your qualifications might read:

> For the past fifteen years, Jane Waggener has designed exciting low-cost vacations for hundreds of customers across the United States, making it possible for her clients to visit exotic locales like Latin America, Micronesia, India, Greece, Egypt, Japan, Scandanavia, and the Balkans for as little as $300 per person per week, including airfare.
>
> Jane has spoken about low-cost travel before a variety of community groups, and has contributed to such magazines as Horizons and Travel and Leisure. Her insights about saving on food, lodging, and tours can bring the world within reach for anyone.

The first paragraph offers specific details about Jane's years of experience, her client base, and the vacation destinations she knows about. The second paragraph gives more details about Jane's achievements and the specific areas where she can help people save money. The sketch ends with a little flourish that reinforces the conference topic, along with the idea that anyone can benefit from Jane's expertise.

Keep your qualification sketch down to a couple of paragraphs, but provide as much specific evidence as possible of your experience, its usefulness, and proof that you can share it with others. By itself, having worked in a business for a certain number of years doesn't prove anything: the proof is in the specific achievements and details you provide.

Pitching your conference idea

The final step in arranging a conference is the pitch itself. If you've developed a likely topic and a good information blurb on yourself, the only remaining hurdle between you and success is timing the pitch.

Online conferences are scheduled weeks or months in advance, depending on their size and importance. If you want to be the featured speaker one night on America Online or Prodigy, you'll have to arrange the engagement two or three months in advance, but you can probably set up engagements for smaller conferences a month in advance. The conference administrator can give you information about the amount of lead time for proposing a conference and which specific information is required for the pitch.

The people who schedule conferences are always looking for topics that will generate the most interest from their subscribers or members. To have the best chance of success, your topic should be fresh and timely. Study your online target carefully for several weeks and make notes about the conference topics presented. Don't pitch a topic that's close to one that has just been featured. If the investment forum just had its weekly conference about bonds, wait for a couple of months before pitching your conference about tax-free investing.

You can also increase your chances of success by linking your conference topic with a particular time of year when people will be more interested. If you're in the gardening business, you could propose a conference on spring planting for March. If you're an accountant, you could propose a conference on year-end tax planning for November or early December.

Handling the conference

When it comes time to conduct the conference, make a plan about what you hope to accomplish. List three or four key messages you want to get across in the talk, and then prepare questions for the moderator to ask you that will lead to answers containing those messages. The conference moderator probably won't be intimately familiar with your business or the topic, so he or she will appreciate having a starting point. And from your point of view, answering the questions will allow you to convey your key messages and to focus the audience on your topic. If you offer enough questions, the moderator may start the conference off with a couple and then save the others to jumpstart the discussion if audience questions drop off later on.

The rest of the conference is easy. Just do your best to answer the questions as if you were talking in person to the individuals asking them. When you can't answer a question, don't try to bluff your way through it. Your audience will respect you a lot more if you admit you don't know an answer and offer to find out than if you try to fake it.

At the end of the conference, make sure the audience members know how to reach you for further information. Ask the moderator to wrap things up by announcing your e-mail address, phone or fax number, or postal address.

Post-conference promotion

Guerrillas save time and money by leveraging their work. When you've done the work to devise, pitch, and put on a conference, leverage it as much as possible. After the conference is over, the text record of its proceedings are usually stored somewhere in the forum, BBS, or online service archives. Find out from the conference moderator or forum administrator where the proceedings are stored and then have a look at them. You may be able to use them in other ways.

For example, if you offered some especially brilliant insights during your talk, you can direct other people to the conference record. This is the online equivalent of offering a tape recording of your last speech to customers interested in your views on a particular topic.

You can also reproduce parts of the conference as a separate document. Read the conference proceedings, select a few questions and answers, and then publish them as a Q&A document *(see below)*.

- -
BECOMING AN INFORMATION PROVIDER

Information is the coin of the realm in cyberspace. A quick trip anywhere online will convince you that a lot of the scenery is information:

files, lists, databases, and news. Information is as varied as life itself and as plentiful as the grains of sand on a beach, but everyone who goes online is always looking for more of it.

In a conference you present information at a given time and place, but by publishing electronic documents, you can provide information to a much broader audience indefinitely. By becoming an information provider, you gain visibility as an author and respect as someone who makes useful and lasting contributions to the collective knowledge of the online world.

Through the information you provide, you give people a chance to know you and to understand how your knowledge can help them. And since you're the publisher of the information, you can include a promotional message in every document you produce. You can also store your published information in your online storefront, giving customers another good reason to visit your little corner of the online marketplace.

The main goals in publishing information are to offer something useful to your target audience and to promote your business identity in the process. As long as you achieve these goals, the type of information and the source of the information aren't important. You'll find that you have a lot of options. You can:

- prepare original reports and articles on your field of expertise
- compile information from other sources into one handy location
- publish your own newsletter or electronic magazine

If you don't feel up to doing any of these, your company can sponsor a newsletter, magazine, or directory provided by someone else and gain respect for helping to support it.

Here's how to become an information provider in three simple steps:

1. Decide which information you want to present and how you want to present it.
2. Choose a distribution method and distribute it.
3. Let your target audience know it's there.

Sources of information

Most of us don't think of ourselves as publishers because our ideas about publishing are trapped in a vision of paper and ink. But publishing is based on distributing information, and we do that every day as we answer customer questions, offer advice, and even when we display brochures or catalogs about the things we sell.

The most common hurdle in publishing is writing ability. Most people don't see themselves as professional writers. However, anyone with average writing skills can get a few useful points across. If you can't write, find someone else in your business who can, or hire a professional writer to turn your ideas into print. You might have to spend a few hundred dollars for an article, but you'll end up with a promotional tool you can use for months or years.

Another problem we run into when thinking about publishing is that it's a specialized skill reserved for media people. The beauty of computers and the online marketplace is that anyone can be a publisher. There are millions of documents available on the Net, and most of them were put there by people who never published anything in a traditional newspaper or magazine.

All you really need to start your publishing empire are a few nuggets of truth and a place to put them. As long as the information is useful, your readers will thank you for it.

Often, thinking about a particular type of document can help you come up with ideas for information you can provide. Here are some types of documents that can get you started.

Q&A and tip sheets Think about the advice you've given to customers over the years, and imagine how you could distill it into a short question/answer sheet or a list of tips. These documents are from one to a few pages long, and cover a particular subject related to your business. If your products or services are varied enough, you might build a whole library of Q&As or tips on different subjects.

If you can't come up with ideas on your own, pull some from a brochure or flier you've seen in the course of your business. If you're in the building supplies business and one of your distributors left you a particularly helpful brochure about choosing roofing materials, you might turn it into an article or tip sheet. If you don't want to rewrite such a document substantially to avoid copyright problems, ask the original publisher for permission to reproduce it as is.

Articles An article is a longer document that explains or discusses an issue in greater detail. You might start off with a Q&A or tip sheet and then expand one or more of the tips or answers into a full-blown article. A list of tips about choosing the right scuba gear might be expanded into short articles about choosing a wetsuit, choosing a regulator, and the outs and ins of choosing fins.

Again, if your own insights don't lend themselves to article-length documents, get permission to reprint or excerpt from articles you've read elsewhere. You may have access to a trade or industry publication whose articles could help your customers, and you'll win a lot of friends if you share those articles with them.

Newsletters and zines If you're really ambitious, you can publish a regular newsletter or electronic magazine (called a *zine*). These documents feature collections of articles, lists, or anything else you want to put in them. Newsletters are text-only documents focused on a particular topic. Zines began as short newsletters for the Generation X crowd on such esoteric topics as "Cult of the Dead Cow" or "Holy Temple of Mass Consumption," but they now encompass more mainstream topics as well. Some publishers include graphics in their zines and distribute them on their FTP or Web sites or bulletin boards rather than via e-mail.

The information in a newsletter or zine can be your original creation, or you can simply compile and edit information from various sources. The Edupage newsletter is a summary of high-tech news compiled and distributed three times a week by Educom, a consortium of colleges and universities. Edupage's editors read a variety of newspapers and magazines and then write up one-paragraph summaries of technology stories. At the end of each summary, Edupage adds the publication, date, and page number of the original article for those who want to read more.

If you can't come up with information on your own, compile articles you've seen elsewhere (as long as you summarize them or get permission to reproduce them). You can even solicit contributions from other members of a forum or newsgroup that discusses the same topic.

There are hundreds of newsletters and zines available on the Net, and you'll learn about them and see them in your travels. To see a collection of zines, check the alt.zines newsgroup. Look at other electronic publications to get ideas about what yours might look like.

Lists and directories Another type of document is a list or directory. Dozens of guerrillas on the Net have already compiled directories of resources available there. People appreciate the service because it can be so difficult to locate resources in the Net's vast reaches. If you're in the travel business, for example, you might prepare and maintain a directory of Internet locations that offer international weather reports. If you're in the auto parts business, you might offer a list of forums, news-groups, and mailing lists related to automobiles. You could also offer a glossary of terms relating to your business.

The beautiful thing about a list or directory is that you don't have to be a writer to produce one. All you have to do is compile the information and revise it regularly to keep it up-to-date.

Don't forget the promo. Whatever type of document you publish, don't forget to include a short paragraph about your business. The whole point of offering the information is to increase your visibility, and that won't happen if you don't mention your company someplace. Just remember that the information, not your company plug, is what builds your reputation.

The promotional paragraph is like the "brought to you by" message at the beginning of a TV program or on the title page of an advertising supplement in a magazine. The paragraph should be in the document, but it shouldn't be so prominent that it overwhelms the document's information content. Most publishers run a simple notice at the beginning or end of the document, like this:

```
****************************************************************
***************
Edupage, a summary of news items on information technology, is provided
three times each week as a service by Educom -- a consortium of leading
colleges and universities seeking to transform education through the use of
information technology.

****************************************************************
***************
```

Distributing information

Once you've prepared information, you'll want to make it as easy as possible for the widest possible audience to get it. There are many ways to display and present information online.

Electronic mail You can mention the document in newsgroups, forums, and mailing lists and then suggest that people request it via e-mail. You then mail the document to them, or set up a mailbot to do it for you. This helps you build a list of interested prospects that you can use for other mailings in the future.

Newsgroups and forums If you have short lists or articles no longer than a page, you can post them to relevant newsgroups, forums, and mailing lists. If the information piece is longer, upload it to the appropriate forum library.

Servers and Web sites If you have an electronic storefront, the obvious place to store your documents is in your store. Then when you promote the information and tell people where to get it, you bring them into the store as well.

Mailing lists If you produce a regular electronic newsletter or zine, distribute it to a mailing list of subscribers and place copies of it on your electronic storefront, if you have one. *(See "Promoting your information" on p. 176 for information on finding subscribers.)*

Sponsoring an information provider

There's no substitute for the credibility and visibility you get from producing and distributing your own information online. But if you really can't spare the time to become a publisher yourself, you can gain some visibility by sponsoring someone else. By choosing a well-known information provider and offering to sponsor him or her, you can bask in the reflected glow of that publication. Here's an example:

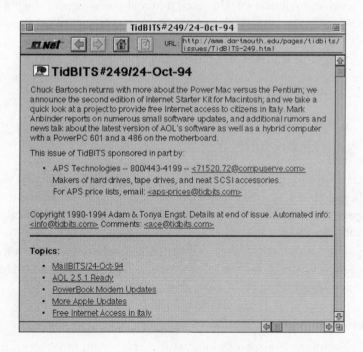

Tidbits is a well-known newsletter on the Net published by Adam and Tonya Engst. As you can see, it's published on a Web site, which gives Adam and Tonya more publishing power by allowing them to incorporate graphics and provide hypertext links to products and companies they mention in each issue.

Notice the sponsorship message below the introductory paragraph in this example. APS Technologies sponsors Tidbits, and because this is a Web site you can navigate right to the APS's company information or price list with a click of your mouse button. Through a sponsorship arrangement like this, APS gets some credit for helping to produce a useful Net resource, and it gains a highly visible location for displaying its name, contact information, and key marketing messages.

Sponsoring an information provider is simple once you find one worth sponsoring. Scour the Net for informative newsletters or zines on a subject that's related to your business. Look for a document that's published on a regular schedule and that has a good following. When you find one, contact the publisher and suggest a sponsorship. In the simplest terms, this amounts to paying for advertising space at the top of the provider's publication. However, it may also mean giving the publication space on your electronic storefront, trading your products or services to the provider in exchange for the sponsorship space, or offering your products to the publication's subscribers at a discount.

If you don't find a publication related to your business, consider sponsoring the creation of one. Here are some possible scenarios:

- Come up with a great idea for a newsletter, find a writer to put it together, then distribute it through your online storefront or through e-mail.
- If you're an active participant in a newsgroup or forum related to your business, look for other knowledgeable and regular participants of the group and approach one of them about producing the publication with your sponsorship.
- Contact a writer for a magazine related to your business or the author of one or more online articles you read and liked, and approach him or her about doing a newsletter on a related subject area.

Promoting your information

Once you create or sponsor information, you'll want to let other netizens know how and where to get it. You promote your information through the same online methods you use to promote your business. In some cases, you'll want to send a copy of the publication or document or post it on a forum or newsgroup. At other times, it will be better to tell people where to get a copy. Here are some specific strategies.

E-mail Send a copy of your Q&A, tip sheet, or brief article via e-mail to your previous customers with a note saying you thought they'd be interested. If you have a broader e-mailing list of prospects, send them an announcement saying the publication is now available and what it offers, and then tell them how to get a copy.

Newsgroups and forums Post the document itself only if it's highly relevant to the discussion. If you've placed a copy of the document in a forum library, it's acceptable to put a notice about your having done that in the forum itself. Otherwise, find a way to mention your document and its location in the course of the discussion. If you've just completed an article about the care and feeding of gecko lizards, for example, watch for questions about this topic on reptile-related newsgroups or forums. Respond to the questions when they appear, and mention your article and how to get it as part of your reply.

Signatures If you're publishing a newsletter or zine, add the publication name and its subscription information to your e-mail signature.

Storefronts If you have an online storefront, set up a library for your documents and promote it as one of your store's departments.

Conferences Ask the moderator to include information about your online publications and how to get them when he or she introduces you. Also, find a way to work your publication's name into the conference. You might suggest that someone read your publication for more detailed information when you answer a question from the audience.

FIVE STRATEGIES FOR MARKETING WITH INFORMATION

To sum things up for this chapter, here are five key guerrilla strategies for promoting your business with online information:

1. Choose an audience and serve it. The magazine graveyard is filled with publications that either aimed at an audience that wasn't there, offered perfectly good information to the wrong audience, or offered bad information to the right one. Don't make the same mistakes. Your business has customers and prospects, and they're your target audience. Whenever you propose a conference topic or produce an online publication or document, make sure the information is aimed squarely at the needs of your audience.

2. Tell the truth and don't steal. People get a good feeling about you when you offer them good information. Satisfied readers frequently spread the word or even forward your publication to others. Unfortunately, netizens will seize on your mistakes like hungry barracuda and tell all their friends about them as well. In fact, they may even parody your publication and post the parody in more places than the original! Make sure any information you publish is accurate and that you have the right to publish it. If you're caught in a lie, an error, or a violation of someone's copyright, your mistake may well shine brighter and live longer than any good you've done.

3. Recycle information. One of the most wonderful things about computers is the ease with which you can edit and recycle things you've written in the past. Create an article or Q&A document from the transcript of your last conference. Turn your Q&A document or tip sheet into a series of articles. Summarize insights from your favorite newsgroup or forum. Without the right packaging, information is no more than a jumble of words. With the right packaging, you can present the same information in many different ways to serve many different purposes.

4. Keep the presses rolling. One good document deserves another; one good conference should lead to the next. If you've started to build your reputation as an information source, the only way to maintain it is to keep producing. Citizens of the online marketplace have an insatiable appetite for information, so you can be sure of a ready audience for your next talk or document. The frequency of your publications depends on the type of documents you produce, your distribution method, and your ability to produce them of course, but you should plan from the beginning to produce a collection of documents. Think in terms of a monthly, bimonthly, or quarterly tip sheet or newsletter, or an ongoing series of articles.

5. Tell the world. Nobody will know what you've done unless you tell them. Use your forum and newsgroup contacts, e-mail address lists, storefront, conferences, and any other means you can think of to promote and distribute your online documents.

10

Seventy-five Online
Guerrilla Marketing Weapons

The online marketplace has vast possibilities for the savvy guerrilla, but it's a jungle out there. Every week, there are thousands of new people joining the fray. The year 1995 alone will probably see 10 million new people join the online marketplace. Every week, hundreds of entrepreneurs will increase the ranks of your competition.

You now know the geography and strategies for your attack. In this chapter, we'll look at seventy-five marketing weapons you can and should use. Your competitors don't even know about most of these, and those that do aren't using very many of them, or aren't using them to their best advantage. Your mission is to understand and use as many of the following seventy-five weapons as effectively as possible.

1. Name In cyberspace, most customers will first hear about your business by its name. Choose a name that both explains what your business is and sets your business apart from others. You can't rely on your personality or your storefront location to distinguish you from the crowd, so your name should help do it. Vague, generic, or ambiguous names can cost you time and money. One Internet consultant spent a lot of time trying to defend his right to the name *Internet Presence, Inc.* This name didn't suit his business purpose any better than a lot of other names, and it was very much like other names out there. It did nothing to distinguish this business from some others. And while the consultant spent a lot of time arguing over whether he had a trademark on this name, his competitors were busy making money.

2. Product/service niche A unique niche or position for your business is crucial online. You might be able to distinguish your business by its physical appearance or location off-line, but these assets disappear in cyberspace. Your unique position in the market is the best way to distinguish yourself from a horde of competitors. This position can be built from the quality of your service, your expertise, your selection, your price, or lots of other possible advantages, but you must have at least one. Find a new niche and fill it, or fill a successful niche better than anyone else.

3. Online business plan Your online efforts should be guided by a business plan that projects your expenses, effort, and earnings at least a year in advance. The business plan also includes your online marketing plan. (*See Chapter 12.*) You can't chart your progress if you don't have a plan. Your projections should be based on diligent research and a realistic understanding of how the online market works for businesses like yours.

4. Identity Decide exactly what sort of identity you want your business to have, and then make sure everything you do online promotes it. Your identity is reflected in the style of your announcements, the design of your electronic storefront, your participation in discussion groups, your e-mail signature, your attitude about service, and in countless other ways. Your business identity transcends any particular advertisement, storefront, or other online effort you make. It should distinguish you among your competition. Everything you do online contributes to your identity.

5. Theme A theme is a sentence or phrase that defines your business. Avis Rent A Car uses *We Try Harder.* Kentucky Fried Chicken uses *Finger Lickin' Good.* Pick a theme that crystallizes your main business advantage. If your theme is short enough, make it part of your e-mail signature.

6. Credibility When people believe what you say, they trust you and buy from you. You earn credibility through service, honesty, and sincere efforts to be helpful. You also earn it through consistency, so don't change your marketing plan in midstream.

7. Reputation Your reputation is the market's awareness of your business identity. Do all you can to promote and protect it in everything you do, from your store's decor to the clarity of your advertisements and discussion group postings. A bad reputation spreads quickly online and is incredibly hard to repair. A good reputation inspires confidence and makes it easier to win business.

8. E-mail signature Develop an informative signature and use it to sign all your e-mail messages and discussion group postings. If you're involved in several discussion groups, create a different signature for maximum impact on each group. Using a signature is like leaving a business card wherever you go in cyberspace. Every guerrilla has one or more of them.

9. Logo A well-designed, evocative logo can help distinguish your business from others on a Web page. Your logo should convey your business identity. Grant's Flowers on the Branch Mall uses a flower logo, and the logo makes this store stand out from its competitors that are identified only by name. A good online logo is small enough that it can be displayed quickly when customers download it.

10. Package The way you package your online presence says a lot about you. Whether you're posting an article or a forum message or you're designing a storefront, make sure your packaging is attractive, clear, and well-organized. Choose a storefront design that works equally well on any type of computer, and format your articles, newsletters, and e-mail messages so they look good on any screen. Proofread everything before you put it online.

11. Pricing Choose prices for your products or services that match your business identity. If part of your identity is your expertise, quality, or superior service, charging a little extra for it shows that you think the advantage is worth it. Tiffany's isn't known for its bargain prices. If your store offers the same products and service as others, then selling at a lower price will give people a reason to buy from you.

12. Decor In an online storefront, the decor is everything from the name you choose to the presentation and organization of your catalog, price list, order form, and other information. It includes the colors and graphics on your Web site, the number of menu pages in your store, and the names you give various options. The decor should complement your business identity, but it has to do so within the limitations of cyberspace. Choose a storefront designer who has experience in graphic design and in computer interfaces to create the best decor for your chosen battleground.

13. Hours and days of operation The online market operates twenty-four hours a day, seven days a week, all over the world. So should your business. Cybernauts expect quick responses to their queries and orders, so make sure you oblige them. Check for incoming orders or questions several times a day, and at least once a day on weekends and holidays. They don't celebrate President's Day in Australia. Your ability to respond more quickly than your competitors will give people a reason to trust you and will lead to more business in the future.

14. Locations Every store is equally invisible on the Net. Multiplying your locations increases your visibility. Your online presence should have as many locations as you can afford. Each Web or Gopher link you add to your online store is another doorway into it from a different part of the Net. If you link your BBS to the Internet, you add access for 20 million potential customers. If your mall store on an online service is generating a profit, consider opening up on another online service. And even if you don't have a storefront, you can be in many different places yourself by participating in newsgroups and forums, by publishing information and storing it in many places, and by holding conferences.

15. Access Give people access to your products in as many ways as possible. Use as many storefronts and links as possible to allow customers with different access methods to patronize your company no matter what. If you have a Web storefront, it's not too much trouble to offer access to it via Gopher for those who aren't on the Web.

16. Neatness Neatness conveys a sense of reliability and competence. It helps give customers the confidence to buy from you. Check all your online messages, displays, publications, and discussion group contributions for proper spelling, grammar, and formatting before sending them out into cyberspace.

17. Order form Ordering online can make customers nervous. Your order form should help put them at ease. Make the form clear and compact. If possible, design it to fit on one or two screen pages. Put the Cancel or Clear button in an obvious place so customers don't feel trapped. State your guarantee, delivery policy, and return policy right on the form.

18. Guarantee Help ease natural reluctance to order online by offering an ironclad guarantee on everything you sell. Make sure you explain the guarantee prominently in your promotional literature.

19. Ordering options Some buyers are skittish about ordering online, so make sure you offer a phone or mail option. Every purchase option you can offer removes a barrier to sales. Penny Wise Office Products has storefronts on CompuServe, GEnie, and America Online, its own BBS, plus 800 phone and fax order lines.

20. Payment options Give customers as many payment options as possible, including credit cards, CODs, purchase orders, checks, and even an in-house credit plan.

21. Service Customers are gambling on you until you earn their trust through service. Respond to every customer request as if your business future depends on it; it probably does. If you're too busy to check your online store for incoming orders every couple of hours, get someone to do it for you. If you're not computer literate, set up your storefront in an online mall that will receive your orders and fax them to you.

22. Convenience Online shopping's main advantage is convenience, so make sure you maximize this advantage as you promote and sell your business. Think about what you can offer online to improve the shopping experience for your customers. Maybe you can offer a wealth of information that's difficult to get off-line. Maybe you can offer instant pictures of your products. Think about unique online possibilities, and make sure you use them.

23. Speed Online shoppers expect speedy responses. Strive to make your service and delivery schedules as fast as or faster than those of your competitors. Some companies are slow to answer questions or submit proposals, and a faster response often gets the sale. Ask friends to visit your storefront and report any problems with response time or access. Change ISPs if you have continuing problems.

24. Bandwidth Bandwidth limits your ability to transmit and receive information online. If you were in an auto race, you'd want to have the fastest car. Buy the most bandwidth that you can afford. Get a fast computer, the fastest modem, and the ISP with the fastest and most reliable access. While your competition is waiting for a screen to scroll or getting a busy signal at their ISP, you can be promoting your business.

25. Customer recourse Develop a consistent policy for handling dissatisfied customers, and explain it clearly in advance. Your policy will put potential customers at ease and will help convert unhappy customers into repeat buyers.

26. Follow-up Treat customers like people and they'll come back to you again and again. Send e-mail thank you notes after each purchase, and let your customers know when you have new products or services.

27. Stationery Display your online address prominently on your business cards, brochures, letterhead, invoices, packing lists, and other documents. Customers will know they have an online option for communicating and doing business with you, and even those who aren't online will respect you for being there.

28. Online advertising Advertising also increases your visibility in cyberspace. Buy space on Web pages, billboards, marquees, welcome screens, and sign-off screens. Post notices on What's New sites and newsgroups that cover new Net features and Web sites. Post classified ads on related forums and newsgroups.

29. Mailbots If you have an account with an ISP, set up a mailbot to automatically distribute your information when people ask for it. The mailbot boosts your service reputation by sending out information instantly, and it gets you out of the e-mailroom so you can focus on more important tasks.

30. Print advertising Buy print or classified ads in magazines about the online world. Use your online address in regular print ads and billboards, too.

31. Brochures Prepare electronic brochures describing your products or services and have them ready to send via e-mail when prospects ask for more information. Again, use a mailbot for automatic responses to queries.

32. Free information Netizens are information hounds. By offering free, helpful information on a subject related to your business, you enhance your reputation and encourage people to visit your online store or to contact you. Your offer of free information can spark the beginning of profitable customer relationships.

33. Catalog It's easy and very inexpensive to put your catalog online. You can reach far more customers with an online catalog than you could afford to reach if you had to print and mail it. You can create text catalogs on Gopher sites, or use color pictures, sounds, and even video on FTP or Web sites.

34. Newsletters and zines Publish an online newsletter or zine (online magazine) on a topic related to your business. You can write the material yourself or collect it from other sources. Your subscribers will appreciate the information and many will become customers. Mail printed copies of your publication to existing customers as a way to stay in touch.

35. Directories Compile a list or directory and maintain it. You'll gain respect as a source of useful information and your business will get extra visibility in the bargain.

36. Research studies Conduct a survey on a topic related to your business. Post the survey on newsgroups, forums, or mailing lists where you participate regularly, and publish the results when you're done.

37. Books and articles Publish your own online or print articles or books to increase your credibility as an expert. Use a ghostwriter if necessary.

38. Reprints Save your ads, billboard or marquee copy, articles, conference transcripts, newsletters, zines, and newsgroup postings and recycle them as informational aids for your customers.

39. Conferences Hold conferences about your area of business expertise. Conferences give you a chance to establish a bond with dozens or hundreds of people at once, and to show them how your experience can help them.

40. Conference archives Research the archives of other conferences to find out how others present them, and re-use information from archives of your own conferences. It's not hard to turn a conference archive into a Q&A document.

41. Column in a publication Contribute a free article or column to a publication in exchange for including your business name and address. Many newsletters, magazines, and newspapers are looking for material, and you can increase your visibility and build your reputation by helping to provide it. If you can't write the article yourself, find a ghostwriter; the fee you pay will be worth it.

42. Samples Send out free excerpts from an article or newsletter you've published, or post them on relevant newsgroups, forums, and mailing lists. If you're publishing good information, it will lead to subscribers and customers. Most electronic newsletter and zine publishers offer free samples of previous issues.

43. Demonstrations If you're in a service business, offer to show prospective customers how you work by performing a partial service. One netizen pitches his scholarship consulting services by offering to create a free list of potential scholarships for every interested client.

44. Gift certificates Offer gift certificates for your products or services so your customers can introduce your business to other people.

45. Audiovisual aids Use the Web or other means to distribute graphics and sounds to round out your presentation. Points made to the eye and ear are 68 percent more effective than points to the ear only. You could even use an FTP site to distribute a short digitized video about your products or services.

46. Advertising specialties Notices in cyberspace are ephemeral, but by printing your name on mouse pads, floppy disk cases, or other computer gear and giving it away, you can keep your online presence in view when the computer's off.

47. Classified ads You can run classified ads for free on dozens of online services, forums, BBSs, and newsgroups. These ads work just as well online as they do in newspapers and magazines. Try different ads and different locations, and use response codes to see which ads work the best.

48. Magazine inserts It's remarkably inexpensive to have postcard-sized ads blown into magazines or included in a magazine's delivery envelope. Most magazines about the online world offer this service at least once a year. *CompuServe* magazine has inserts like this each month.

Inserts are a great way to pull in online business from off-line customers by offering a killer price on a particular product or by promoting a contest or service.

49. Direct-mail postcards Use direct-mail postcards to announce your new online presence, or to announce special promotions. You may encourage an infrequent online traveler to log on and take a look at what you're offering.

50. Club/association memberships Join online and off-line business associations and clubs to make friendships through which you can help spread the word about your business. Some of the best business referrals come from owners of other businesses.

51. Community involvement Become a part of the community represented by your customer base. Participate regularly in forums, newsgroups, and mailing lists and add your expertise to the pool of knowledge. Your involvement boosts your credibility as a source of information and shows potential customers that you're not just in it for the money.

52. Co-marketing and tie-ins Establish co-marketing agreements with other businesses that complement yours. By joining together, you can share the costs of Web pages, billboards, and other online marketing venues. Arrange to display another company's promotional information on your Web, Gopher, or FTP site if they'll do the same with yours. Plug another company in newsgroups, forums, and conferences if they'll plug yours.

53. Directory listings Seek out online directories of businesses and make sure yours is listed in them. Many directory listings are free, and others are inexpensive.

54. Public relations Make your business newsworthy and tell the media about it. You'll gain free public exposure and the kind of credibility no advertising can buy. If yours is the first online store of its kind, that's news, and most Internet magazines will print it if you send them an announcement. If your store is the first online business in your city or community, that's news, and your local newspaper will print it if you send them an announcement. You may even make it into the technology pages of *Newsweek* or *Time* if you send an announcement about a unique Net site or service. Look for a news angle in your business and then tell the media about it.

55. Publicity contacts The easiest way to generate media stories about your business is to make personal contacts. Research local and regional newspapers, radio and TV stations, and magazines or newsletters related to your business. Find out who the reporters, editors, and producers are who cover your business. Get to know the ones in your area over lunch or coffee. Use these contacts when you put out an announcement about your company.

56. Testimonials One satisfied customer is worth three salespeople. Ask your customers for comments on your products or services, and then use these comments in ads, publicity announcements, and other promotional efforts.

57. Sponsorships Sponsor an online publication, newsgroup, forum, or mailing list. Sponsorships boost your reputation as a member of the online community. You'll also have the chance to display your company name again and again before hundreds or thousands of people.

58. Contests Holding a contest brings customers into your online storefront and adds visibility to your name. A contest can also become a promotional opportunity when you put a notice about it on a mall's home page or on the What's New board on an online service. If the contest is clever enough, it may even make news in magazines about the online world.

59. Special events Grand opening, pre-opening, and seasonal events all help to create and maintain an atmosphere of excitement and fun around your business. Schedule a pre-opening tour of your electronic storefront, and plan special events every couple of months to rekindle customer interest.

60. Human bonds People buy from people they like and trust. Do everything you can to make each transaction as human as possible. Use personable language in your messages and ads. Show genuine interest in people's questions and problems. Follow up to ensure full satisfaction.

61. Word of mouth Friends telling friends is a tried-and-true method of expanding your customer base. E-mail makes it easy to spread the word. Ask your satisfied customers to pass on their experiences or your promotional message to others who may be interested.

62. Satisfied customers Satisfied customers will expand your visibility and your credibility. They're proof that you mean what you say and that you'll deliver on your promises. With proper service and follow-up, you'll not only create satisfied customers, you'll know exactly who they are.

63. Market research Ask questions about a new product or service you're planning. This is a good way to promote your business in discussion groups without blatantly advertising. You'll get valuable advice and curious readers will want to know more about you.

64. Competitive research A lot of the people selling in cyberspace these days don't really have a clue about how it works. Formal research into your business, markets, and the demographics of the online battlegrounds will pay off in a better understanding of cyberspace. The better you know your market and your customers, the more likely you'll be to keep them. And by researching your competition, you'll know exactly how to stay ahead of them.

65. Discussion group archives You probably didn't join a discussion group or forum at its founding. Most discussion group messages are put in archives when they get old, but these can be a gold mine of information about participants, their interests, and most important, their e-mail addresses.

66. Server logs If you have an online storefront, your presence provider should maintain a log that shows how many people access your store each day and who they are. Study the log regularly. It helps you gauge the impact of your marketing efforts and find out who is responding to them.

67. Customer mailing list As you gain customers, store their e-mail addresses for later use. E-mail is the surest way to inform people about your company, and your existing customers are your best source of future sales and referrals. Keep the e-mail addresses of your customers and stay in touch with them regularly.

68. Marketing savvy Most of the people doing business online today know little or nothing about marketing. Your marketing savvy is a powerful competitive weapon, and you should do all you can to increase it. The Appendix lists dozens of resources you can use to boost your understanding of the online world, consumer attitudes, and proven marketing techniques.

69. Realistic expectations People who think online marketing is magic end up sitting around and waiting for the magic to happen. It usually doesn't. Guerrillas make their own magic through hard work and savvy. Don't expect your computer to do your marketing for you; you still have to do it yourself. If you approach the cyberspace market realistically, you'll do what it takes to succeed there.

70. Curiosity All guerrillas are willing to go the extra mile, but the most successful guerrillas never stop looking for new tools, tactics, and strategies. Become a student of the online world. Make a point of exploring new battlegrounds you haven't seen. Follow up on interesting news stories in online or BBS magazines and see if you can add new methods to your marketing repertoire.

71. Enthusiasm Convey enthusiasm about your products or services in every message and advertisement. Excitement is contagious, and it leads to sales.

72. Imagination Most online marketers are so concerned with doing things properly that they stick to proven forms and methods. But cyberspace technology is advancing by leaps and bounds. By breaking out of the mold a little, you can gain a lot of attention. Add a voice greeting to your Web storefront, or try some short video clips to liven up your presentation.

73. Humor A little comic relief can make your messages or storefront more attractive and exciting. The online world can be intimidating for newbies, and veteran cybernauts often take themselves a little too seriously. Take some of the pressure off your contacts by injecting a little tasteful humor in your discussions, group postings, catalog, ads, or other online messages.

74. Confidence The online marketplace is still very new, but a lot of businesspeople achieve marginal results there because that's all they strive for. Pursue the online market with the confidence that you will succeed there, and you will. Pursue it as a marginal option that won't mean much to your business, and it won't.

75. Competitiveness This is simply your drive, your willingness to devote as much time as you can to using these weapons. If you put in twice as much effort as your competitors, you'll be twice as far ahead in the race to profits.

Out of all these weapons, sixty require only your time and the commitment to use them. Only half a dozen require a significant investment in dollars. Guerrillas know that commitment and imagination can triumph in an attack, so use as much of both as you can.

THE TEN MOST IMPORTANT WEAPONS

You should use as many of the seventy-five weapons as well as you can, but there are ten that stand out as fundamentally important to your success.

1. Community involvement
2. Identity
3. Competitiveness
4. Credibility

5. Free information
6. Confidence
7. E-mail signature
8. Convenience
9. Satisfied customers
10. Service

Why are these so important? Confidence and competitiveness are vital traits you'll need in order to press your attack. Credibility and identity give customers a reason to do business with you. Community involvement, free information, and your e-mail signature are the vital tools for creating visibility. Convenience, service, and satisfied customers will give you a reputation that brings more customers to you and keeps them returning again and again.

But before you tear off onto the infobahn with these weapons in hand, remember this: each of these seventy-five weapons, and each of the ten most important ones in particular, is a two-edged sword. Use it well and you'll gain customers and profits; use it badly and your online business will fail. Strive for excellence, aggressiveness, and consistency in your use of these weapons and the online marketplace will reward you.

- -
BUILDING YOUR MARKETING ARSENAL

Most of your competitors will use fewer than ten of the weapons we've covered, and few will use more than half of the ten most important ones. Before you begin planning the details of your attack, you should know which of these weapons you plan to use, and how you plan to use it. To get started, look back over the list and assign each weapon to one of three categories:

A: You're using this weapon now or you plan to use it immediately, and you know exactly how you'll use it.
B: You're using this weapon now or you plan to use it immediately, but you're not using it as well as you could, or you don't know how you'll use it.
C: You have no plans to use this weapon.

Your goal, of course, is to move as many weapons as possible into Category A. Certainly there should be more weapons in Category A than in either of the other two.

Look at each weapon in Category B and plan to implement it in a specific way as quickly as possible. As for Category C, you may think you have no need for these weapons, but in time you'll need them to maintain your advantage over your competition. The online marketplace is relatively new right now, but your competitors will catch on quickly and you'll need all the weapons you can muster to stay a step ahead of them.

Recognize, too, that your list of weapons may change. There are seventy-five weapons listed here, but improvements in online access and presentation technology, changes in the makeup of the online audience, and good old ingenuity will surely reveal others as time goes by. Stay alert for new ideas and implement them when you can.

With our online battle lines clearly drawn and our weapons at the ready, we're almost ready to begin planning and pressing the attack. Before we do, however, let's look at some key strategies for success as an online guerrilla.

11

Twelve Strategies for Online Success

Even if you're a diligent student of guerrilla marketing techniques, the online marketplace has its own rules and limits that change how those techniques are applied. In your transformation from guerrilla marketer to online guerrilla marketer, you'll need to adapt your strategies to online battlegrounds.

If you're not familiar with guerrilla marketing techniques, you can learn the basic strategies here, but you'll find a more comprehensive discussion in *Guerrilla Marketing*, the basic text for guerrillas everywhere.

THE ONLINE MARKETPLACE IS ANOTHER COUNTRY

Think of the online marketplace as a foreign country. Netizens and cybernauts are people just like you, but the online marketplace isn't just like the familiar, physical world. Computers and online communications enforce different rules for social interaction and for selling. Guerrillas understand and play by these rules. Just as patting a child on the head conveys affection in America but is considered an insult in Asia, some of the techniques you use for face-to-face marketing can do more harm than good in the online world.

Many a marketer has blundered into the online marketplace with direct e-mail appeals or newsgroup advertising blitzes, and all of them have felt the sting of the online community. Canter and Siegel's spam attack is only the most famous example. These two lawyers posted ads on thousands of newsgroups and generated so much hate mail that their ISP closed their account. But dozens of other companies have found their e-mailboxes stuffed with multimegabyte files of garbage or hundreds of poison pen letters because they posted an ad on the wrong newsgroup or sent out direct e-mail appeals without the recipients' permission.

As a guerrilla, your goal is to market as aggressively and effectively as possible without ruffling any feathers. The more you understand the unique characteristics of the online marketplace, the more easily you'll be able to adapt your strategies for success in it. Before we examine the twelve strategies for success as an electronic guerrilla, it is important to know what makes the electronic marketplace so different from the physical world.

Everybody and everything is invisible

When we go out shopping in the physical world, we see stores, products, and people. Our shopping experience and buying habits are influenced by light, sound, color, or the presence or absence of a crowd. Your store can stand out from others by its window display, sign, size, location, or the crowd you draw. When you market in the online world, none of these advantages work for you.

The online marketplace is like a huge, dark exposition hall. The hall contains millions of people and thousands of exhibition booths. There are thousands of signs, banners, and billboards, and billions of pages of information. The trouble is that it's totally dark, and you have to know exactly how and where to reach any person, booth, or document page in order to see what it offers.

Every business is equally visible and invisible in cyberspace. The Web site that costs Digital Equipment or Silicon Graphics thousands of dollars to maintain is no more visible than the virtual Gopher or Web site you rent for a couple of hundred dollars a month. For large businesses and small, success online comes from making the invisible visible.

If you had a booth in a totally dark exhibition hall and you wanted to draw customers into it, you'd have to reach out to them and tell them were it was and how to get there. You couldn't just put up a big sign, because nobody could see it in the darkness. You'd have to find a way to deliver your message to specific groups of people or individuals. You might hire a team of agents to go out among the people and pass the word. Guerrillas do this all the time at trade shows. Rather than waiting and hoping for the crowd to pass by their booths, they hire people to stand at key places around the exhibit hall and pass out handbills. Instead of letting a booth and one sign be their only presence, they expand their presence by distributing their message in many places.

It follows that to gain an effective level of visibility in the online marketplace, you have to distribute your message widely. Rather than buying just one ad or billboard, you post several little signs in various locations where your customers are likely to see them. Rather than putting up a larger or more elaborate storefront to improve your credibility, you distribute useful information and build a reputation for expertise and service.

The darkness of cyberspace is the great equalizer; it gives you as much of a chance for success as your largest competitors. In many ways, it provides the ultimate guerrilla battleground. Company size and financial resources mean very little; guerrilla savvy and competitiveness will carry the day.

Everything is ephemeral

You can hand out circulars, brochures, samples, business cards, or advertising specialties in the physical world and they'll serve as constant reminders of your identity or message. Leave them on a desk, and they convey your message every time somebody looks that way. But in cyberspace even the cleverest message or the most inviting storefront is no more than an electronic ghost. Every message disappears as soon as the customer moves along or logs off.

Every marketing effort is somewhat temporary because it only remains in the prospect's mind for so long, but messages are even more fleeting in cyberspace. Your marketing efforts must compensate by appearing in more online locations and with greater frequency. You can't rely on a printed brochure to present your message over and over. You'll have to make sure your electronic brochure gets around in the online world.

Things change quickly

In an online world where you can build a new store in a matter of days or change the store's departments with a few keystrokes, the terrain shifts rapidly. Every week dozens of new businesses invade cyberspace, and every month many of those businesses modify their selection of wares or their presentation.

Netizens expect change. Guerrillas satisfy those expectations by regularly offering something new. Your online marketing strategies should incorporate new attractions. Use special promotions, regular publications of new information, publicity announcements, contests, or other means to rekindle interest. The only things you won't want to change are your company name and address.

Shopping is research

In the physical world, we shop and buy things for several reasons. We visit shopping malls with no other goals in mind than to get out of the house, to be among people, and to be entertained. Sometimes the crowd's enthusiasm for a store or product will transform us from lookers into buyers. We're swept up in the prevailing mood.

When you're shopping online, the only prevailing mood is your own. Shopping in cyberspace is a matter of one person and one computer. There may be hundreds of other people visiting the same online store or shopping mall at the same time we are, but we never see them and we're typically not influenced by them. (Although we may be more tempted to buy an item that's listed as a best-seller.)

We're not even influenced by a store's salespeople when we shop online, because we never interact directly with them. We're far less influenced by the appearance of an online storefront, because it's the information on the screen that affects us, not the atmosphere in which that information is presented. We can't feel, smell, or taste anything online.

We don't go online to experience a crowded mall or some holiday decorations; we go online to explore a world of information. If what shoppers want is to expand their realms of knowledge, then you have to offer compelling information to get their attention. Online shoppers may still be intrigued by a promotion for some product or service they didn't have in mind at all when they logged on that day, but you'd better have a good presentation to make that happen. You have to put the right messages in the right places at exactly the right times.

Online guerrillas recognize that information is the major drawing card for their businesses. You could get by with simply posting a catalog of your products and prices, but unless your selection is vastly better or your prices are clearly lower than in competing stores, catalog information alone isn't enough to draw customers in. Teach people something new, and you'll distinguish your store from your competition. Information is what people seek, and the more of it you provide and the better you are at providing it, the more customers you'll have.

There's only so much bandwidth

No matter what we do online, our experience is limited by bandwidth. Bandwidth dictates the amount of information we can receive through our computer during a given period of time, and there's only so much of it to go around. Bandwidth is affected by all these variables:

- the speed of your online connection
- the speed and display capability of your computer screen

- the speed with which you can read and comprehend information
- the cost of your online connection
- the amount of money you have to spend on your connection

A person with a 9600 bps modem connection to America Online can take in more information in five minutes than another person with a 2400 bps connection. The person with the slower connection will wait longer for graphics to appear, longer for his or her commands to take effect. A person with only $10 a month to spend in his online activities has much less bandwidth than a university student who enjoys a free connection to the Net.

A limited budget or limited speed means limited access. Bandwidth is time, and unless you have a free connection to the online world, bandwidth is also money. Nobody likes to waste it.

The most effective online messages are those that don't waste the recipient's time or money. Spam artists invite the wrath of the Net community because they waste bandwidth. Marketers who send out mass e-mailings arouse anger and resentment because their recipients have to waste bandwidth reading and deleting the message. Some recipients who get mail through Internet mail gateways from an online service actually have to pay to receive junk mail. Even participants in forums or newsgroups get testy when a message is longer than it should be, or when a signature takes up more screen space than normal.

Every marketing effort you make online should be designed to make the best use of bandwidth.

Most contacts are made through writing

In your physical store you have a lot of marketing allies that help make the sale. Customers can pick up, feel, smell, and taste the merchandise. They can talk directly to a salesperson. They can even hear testimonials from other satisfied customers.

In cyberspace, your marketing message must be carried through written words. You may be able to help it along with pictures or sounds if you're marketing on the Web, but words do the real selling.

We've known many terrific salespeople who could sell anything face to face, but who couldn't put two sentences together if you asked them to write down a pitch. In the online marketplace, written words are the coin of the realm. Being able to express yourself clearly, effectively, and concisely in writing is essential in cyberspace. If you can't do it, find someone who can.

It's not magic

Despite all the hype surrounding the information highway and the technical allure of cruising through cyberspace, there's nothing magical about the online marketplace. While the Internet does link some 30 million people, few if any of them are suddenly seized with a desire to buy things simply because they've gone online.

The online marketplace is a different place from the local shopping mall, to be sure. It lets you reach customers you could never reach before, and it lets you do business at times and in places that were off-limits before. But marketing is work, and computers don't do it for you. Guerrillas know that online or off, their success always depends on hard work, dedication, and savvy.

THE TWELVE STRATEGIES FOR ONLINE SUCCESS

Knowing that cyberspace is different from other marketing venues and being able to operate effectively in it are two different things. Knowing how the online world operates will keep you from making serious marketing mistakes. The following twelve strategies will help you adopt the attitudes and skills necessary to succeed and profit in cyberspace:

1. Know how to express yourself

Being able to get your message across in writing is the primary strategy for online success. Effective writing makes or breaks every other strategy you apply. Not knowing how to write online is like trying to sell cars in Japan without being able to speak Japanese. Without the ability to get your message across, you might as well have no message at all.

The most important aspects of writing are clarity, precision, and economy. In promotional writing, it also helps to have a personal voice.

Clarity is important because you're not there to answer questions if your message is muddled. Prospects may be able to send you an e-mail message if they need further information, but your messages should be written so as to minimize general questions. Ideally, the only question your prospect should have is "When can I get it?"

Precision is saying exactly what you want in exactly the right way.

Check your messages for spelling, grammar, and punctuation mistakes. If people think you don't care about how your messages look, they'll wonder if you care about the rest of your business.

Economy is important because time costs money in cyberspace. Few people will wade through line after line of gibberish in order to decipher your point. As in print advertising, words are at a premium. Many netizens pay by the hour for online access, and if they're attracted to your message, they'll want to get the facts as quickly as possible.

And ads aren't the only place to be concise. Descriptions of your product or service, order forms, e-mail replies, newsgroup postings, and anything else that you post in cyberspace should be carefully crafted to deliver the most information in the least amount of time. Strive to make learning about your product, ordering, or just contacting your company as easy and efficient as you can.

A personal voice makes it clear that there's a person behind the message. Unless you're giving a conference, you're talking to one person at a time. Your e-mail and newsgroup postings are being read by individuals, not by a crowd, so communicate with that one person. Say, "You'll be amazed. . . ." instead of "Our customers are amazed." Say, "We've come up with a new. . ." instead of "Acme Manufacturing is pleased to announce. . ."

Take the time to hone your writing skills. Test your messages on others before posting them online. If you're no wordsmith yourself, find one to help create and maintain your online presence.

2. Know the terrain

You can't hope to win the battle for online customers if you don't know the battlefields. You wouldn't choose a store location by picking an address off a map. Don't even think about launching an online marketing program without knowing the territory firsthand.

So check out the marketplace yourself. Join several online information services and poke around. Most of the online services have trial offers that give you a few hours of free connect time. It won't cost you much, if anything, to do some basic battlefield reconnaissance. Seek out some BBSs and newsgroups related to your business and monitor them for a few days or weeks to see what's going on there. Visit some online storefronts and see how they work.

Learn your way around each battlefield. Find out who is selling on these battlefields now, what they're selling, and how they're selling it.

Check out the stores in online shopping malls, and see how merchandise or services are described and sold. Find out whether or not each battlefield has access to the Net, and what sort of access it has. Check out the advertising and promotional opportunities on each online service. Look for holes in the marketplace that your product or service can fill. Check out the classified ads.

If you're planning to focus on an online service as your primary battlefield, get some statistics about it. Contact the service's mall marketing representative and ask for a subscriber profile that includes demographics about the service's user community. Any potential marketer on a service is entitled to such information, and it can help you zero in on a particular audience. For example, GEnie boasts a high percentage of satisfied customers, with 44 percent of its user base having been subscribers for two years. Prodigy boasts the most affluent user base, with a median household income of $60,529. America Online has the largest subscriber base, with more than 2 million users.

Check out the forums on each online service, as well as the newsgroups and mailing lists on the Internet. Look for ones that relate to your business and think about how you might participate. If there isn't one, you may want to start one yourself. Forums, newsgroups, and mailing lists are the closest thing to clubs in cyberspace — it's there that you'll build the personal relationships that will establish your online reputation and expand your visibility.

Millions of cybernauts use bulletin boards. There are thousands of bulletin boards covering every subject from job opportunities in Toronto to nutrition in Third World countries. Check magazines like *Boardwatch* and *BBS* for the names of and access information for bulletin boards. The names usually give you a clue about each board's subject. If the name doesn't help, a few minutes on any board will tell you what subject it covers. Many BBSs are now on the Internet, so you may be able to reach them via the Net instead of dialing a direct phone number.

Find out what's permitted on each battlefield. Many online battlefields prohibit commercial announcements, so you'll have to get your message across in other ways. ISPs, online services, and BBSs usually have acceptable use policies that prohibit mass e-mailings or newsgroup postings. Violating those policies can cost you your account and your access.

Even if something is permitted, it may not be effective. Unsolicited e-mail messages in small numbers aren't specifically illegal, but they're frowned upon. Unless your mail recipients already know you, you may alienate them before they even read what you have to say. One California maker of computer accessories sent out 3000 promotional e-mail messages and got flamed by about 100 recipients. On the other hand, the mailing generated $30,000 worth of orders!

Sometimes just having an Internet address and responding to queries by mail pays off handsomely. The Future Fantasy Bookstore, a small independent shop in Palo Alto, California, has averaged 20 orders per day on the Internet since publicizing its Internet address, and it hasn't ruffled any feathers in the process.

3. Fight on one battlefield at a time

Nobody starts a war by attacking on all fronts at once. Choose the single most promising battlefield and establish your advantage on that one before expanding your attack. If you plan to market mainly through online services, pick the most promising one for your business and then map out a strategy for it. (See Chapter 12.) You can always expand your attack after you've solidified your position on the first battlefield.

4. Drill for battle

You wouldn't enter a real battle without knowing how to operate weapons, maintain supply lines, or deploy troops. Don't enter the online market-place without knowing how to navigate and use its features. Whether you're opening up your own Internet storefront, joining a forum, or publishing information, you'll need to know the mechanics of exchanging information and contacting customers, including:

- how to connect with the Internet or your targeted online service
- how to determine the cost of your online presence, and how to connect in the least expensive ways
- how to get help with any aspect of using a particular network, bulletin board, or commercial service
- how to read, send, file, and forward electronic mail
- how to join an Internet mailing list, and how to stay abreast of new ones as they appear
- how to participate in a forum or newsgroup
- how to establish and maintain an online storefront
- how to post a display ad, if your chosen battlefield offers them
- how to post a classified ad, if your chosen battlefield offers them

- how to place news and promotional announcements on an online service
- how to contact a commercial service's marketing staff
- how to contact a forum administrator or BBS's sysop
- how to determine the peak usage times on the service or network you've chosen, and how to find out if and when it's shut down for maintenance

Think of these mechanics as basics of online business. They're the electronic equivalent of understanding how to turn on the lights or set the alarm in a physical storefront. You just can't do business without knowing them.

5. Be aggressive

The Internet is no place for wallflowers. At in-person gatherings, shy people can always hope a customer or prospect will waltz up and say hello, but that's not going to happen on the Internet. Your ability to meet people, locate prospects, provide information, and make sales depends entirely on your aggressiveness.

You have to be the one to post messages in discussion groups, send e-mail, and respond to queries. Nobody is going to choose your mailbox out of thirty million and favor you with their attention. Few people will stumble upon your electronic storefront without having been told where it is.

Marketing is visibility, and the only way to gain visibility is to earn it. So don't just browse the Internet; get involved. When you're not putting in your two cents' worth, you're invisible.

6. Establish a presence

Nobody will patronize your business if they don't know who you are or where you are. Your online presence may begin with an e-mail address or a storefront, but that's only the beginning. As you pursue your marketing plan, you will develop and expand your presence by getting your name and address, your identity, and your message in front of as many people as often as possible.

Most of your future customers won't be shopping when they hear of you. Instead, they'll be seeking information or trying to solve a problem. Remember, information is the key commodity on the information highway. Although your electronic storefront or e-mailbox may be your key *sales* presence, the *information* presence and reputation you develop is what will bring customers to that storefront or mailbox.

Your product or service is the solution to a problem. Don't be afraid to offer your solution. The key to sales is finding people with that problem (or making them aware that they have it), and then letting them know that your product is the solution. Don't be afraid to mention your product or service, but be sure to do it in a helpful and informative way.

Choose a good user or screen name, one that reinforces your business identity.

Establish your store name. If you have an established business name that's well-known, use the same one on the information highway. If not, this is your chance to pick one that promotes what you sell. For example, *Penny Wise Office Products* is a name that conveys the type of business as well as its competitive advantage.

Participate in forums. Target forums whose members are the most likely prospects for your business, and then become an active source of information on them. Don't use the forum just to post messages about your product or service — many forums specifically prohibit commercial messages. Instead, check the posted messages for information requests or problems and then respond to those you can be helpful with. If you've chosen the proper screen or user name and you include it in a sig at the end of each message, this will pitch your business every time you provide a helpful answer. *(See Chapter 7 for more information.)*

Start a forum. Commercial online services have dozens of product- or vendor-specific forums set up by companies like Microsoft, Lotus, or Novell to provide information and online support for their customers. But a number of companies are discovering that they can polish their online presence by sponsoring more general discussion groups as well. For example, Performance Systems International, an ISP, sponsors an Internet discussion group relating to the commercialization and privatization of the Internet. Although PSI doesn't directly promote its own products and services through the forum, anyone active in this forum knows that PSI is the sponsor. PSI gains a reputation as a source of information, and when customers shop for Internet services, they remember that PSI is one of the Internet's good guys.

Since there are limitless possibilities in establishing special interest forums, you should be able to find a venue that helps you promote your business. If your company sells motorcycle accessories, for example, you could build credibility by starting a motorcycle special interest forum on a service that doesn't have one, or by starting a newsgroup or mailing list on the Net. *(See Chapter 7 for more information.)*

Hold conferences. By sharing your expertise with an audience, you'll build credibility and visibility with a lot of people at the same time. *(See Chapter 9 for more information.)*

Publishing online. Your published tip sheets, articles, newsletters, and other documents help increase your credibility over an extended period of time. You can combine information from other sources or create your own material. As long as the publication has your company name on it and it contains useful information, it will add to your visibility.

Get mentioned in print-magazine articles. Your business may be newsworthy enough for you to become the subject of an article in the online service's subscriber magazine, or even in a business-related article in a magazine like *Home Office Computing, Online Access,* or *Internet World.* Start checking these magazines every month for stories that use other business sources, and develop a pitch for an article that includes you as a source. *(See Chapter 16 for more information.)*

7. Be attentive

Internet users are accustomed to quick responses. Somebody requesting information via snail mail might wait days or weeks for a catalog, but Internet users expect responses within twenty-four hours. Whatever battlefields you've chosen, make sure you check them regularly for opportunities and queries. Respond to all requests immediately. If you only check a target newsgroup every few days, you may miss the opportunity to respond to a comment. And your customers will wait a long time for answers to their questions if you don't check your e-mail to discover they've asked them.

If you have an electronic storefront, the store is open twenty-four hours a day whether you like it or not. Many netizens make their connections after dark when telephone and online service rates are lower. Customers in many foreign countries will reach your store in the middle of the night even if they're connecting in the middle of the day.

Naturally, you'll want to sleep sometime, and if you're a small business you may not want to staff your store day and night. But that's the beauty of the Internet: you can receive orders without being connected yourself. Your store should offer enough information to conclude most sales, or to allow people to post electronic questions. If you're properly attentive to your store and your e-mail box, you'll be able to answer any questions within a few hours. If your store is in an electronic mall, ask the mall administrator about faxing orders to you so you don't have to go online to check for them yourself.

8. Be curious

Although you'll probably focus on one particular battlefield at first, don't ignore the rest of the marketplace. Make a habit of setting aside an hour or so every few days to watch for trends or other areas of activity that might expand your efforts. New discussion groups or mailing lists, new forums, and new BBSs are all places you might strike next.

Check the What's New or welcome screen on your online service every time it's updated. Don't just glance at the headlines on the board; check out the actual events or locations being promoted. Every company that gets a notice on the What's New or welcome screen is your competitor, because you're all competing for visibility. Browse shopping malls regularly to find out what the competition is doing, and think about how you can do better.

9. Make personal contacts

Internet pros can quickly tell the difference between those on the sidelines and those in the thick of the action. Since one key to effective marketing is establishing personal contacts, make sure you're not just on the Internet sidelines. Make every contact count, and keep up relationships through frequent contact.

Use e-mail. As you establish connections with others who are interested in your business or other common subjects, add them to your address list and make sure they get copies of other mail or forum postings you think would be helpful. There are thousands of "phantom forums" that don't have an established presence on the Internet, but exist through a selected group of recipients who get copies of one another's messages.

Join forums and newsgroups. When you find forums or newsgroups that present opportunities, become a regular on them. Respond to as many queries as you can, as long as you can be helpful. Even if helping someone directs them to another business or product, your referral will build the kind of trust that will eventually lead to sales.

As you develop online relationships with others, build the human side of the relationship. When you provide information or answer questions, include a few personal details that help people distinguish you from the hundreds or thousands of other people sending mail or posting messages. Most netizens read and respond to many messages every day; make yours stand out.

10. Be patient

As with any marketing effort, patience is essential. Once you put your toe in the water with a forum or online store, stick it out for several months. If you've chosen your battlegrounds wisely and you're sincerely trying to be helpful, your name recognition and reputation as a good source of information will spread throughout the Internet like a ripple in a lake. But it's a big lake, and your reputation will spread slowly. Most businesses that set up online storefronts go through several weeks of browsing before they start making continuous sales.

Just because the world isn't beating a path to your door the way you expect, it doesn't mean that things won't work out in the long run. You may end up with referrals from forum members or e-mail correspondents you originally helped months before. Some referrals will come from across the country or across the world, and from people you've never had personal contact with.

Cyberspace is a changing world, but your marketing plan isn't one of the things that should change. Too many changes there mean wasted time and money. Witness the 1994 debut and retreat of MecklerWeb, a Worldwide Web site for business-to-business commerce. After touting the site's construction for months in its *Internet World* magazine, Mecklermedia Corporation changed its mind and turned the site into a technology advertising vehicle after only two weeks of operation. All the promotional work and momentum that had built for the new enterprise were lost.

Once you establish a plan for your attack, stick with it. If your storefront's opening rates a notice on the What's New page on your online service or on the Web, don't just sit back and wait for miracles to happen after the messages have stopped appearing. Think of a new angle or promotion that will put you back on the What's New page soon.

If you're participating in a forum and you don't get any leads from it, stick it out for several months at least. You can't expect people to storm your electronic storefront the first time you mention that you have one, and even if they do, they probably won't buy right away. The biggest cost is in preparing for battle and starting the attack. The incremental cost of maintaining an attack is so low that there's no reason not to do it.

11. Be consistent

Once you've established a certain presence on the Internet, don't switch horses in midstream. The information you put out, and the way you put it out, establishes your online identity, so strive for consistency. This not only includes becoming a regular feature on a forum or in someone's e-mailbox, but it means you'll want to provide the same kind of information in the same tone.

Consistency is important in any marketing effort, but it's more important in cyberspace than it is in face-to-face contact. When someone can see you, part of their comfort comes from your physical presence. In the online world, however, you're an electronic ghost — you could be gone tomorrow unless you continually reassure people that you're still there. Consistency builds trust, and trust is essential to doing business online.

12. Follow up

As leads and sales proceed from your efforts, make sure you follow up with a personal note of thanks via e-mail. Stay in touch with each customer to make sure their experience with your product or service is a positive one.

Following up not only tells the customer that you care, it provides opportunities for you to mention new products or services and to ask for referrals. A brief mention of a new product in a follow-up note might foster a new sale, or it might be forwarded by your customer to someone else. E-mail is so easy to read and forward that you could end up with half a dozen new customers for each one you thank.

PART III

Managing
Your Attack

12

Planning the Attack

You now know what your options are for your online marketing attack. The next step is to prepare for battle. Your battle plan, or online marketing plan, is a detailed blueprint of your attack. Creating the plan will help focus and refine your thinking about what you hope to accomplish online, how you hope to accomplish it, how much it will cost, and how long it will take. Once you've finished the plan, you'll have a set of step-by-step marching orders to follow that will keep you on track. And as your attack proceeds, you'll be able to compare your results with your initial projections and make adjustments as necessary.

Your online marketing plan will become part of your overall marketing plan. It has six parts:

1. a mission statement that uniquely defines your business
2. a set of goals you hope to achieve with the plan
3. a list of resources you'll need to carry out the plan
4. a list of targets you'll attack
5. a set of weapons and tactics you'll use to attack each target
6. a calendar that guides you through battle

If you already have a basic marketing plan for your business, you have a head start with the mission statement and goals. As you'll see, though, even these areas will need some modification for the online battles ahead.

THE MISSION STATEMENT

Your business mission statement is a sentence (two at most) that describes your reason for being in business and why you'll succeed. The quick answer to this is "To make a profit," but if that's your only goal, you'll probably fail.

Businesses succeed because they provide things people want at prices they're willing to pay, prices that are high enough to produce a profit. Profits may well follow from providing useful goods or services to satisfied customers, but if your focus is only on profits, you'll have a hard time putting enough energy into the products or services to achieve the customer satisfaction that will produce them.

To create a detailed mission statement, start by writing down phrases that describe your business, its reason for success, and its competitive advantages. You should end up with a dozen or two phrases that explain why you'll win in the online market and how you're different from the other guys. When you're finished, look over what you've written and boil it all down to its essence.

Why your business should succeed

Your business should succeed because you fill a unique need, or because you fill a common need better than your competition. The mission statement in your online marketing plan must include reasons why people will want to buy from you in cyberspace. You may already have a mission statement that works for you in the off-line world, but some competitive advantages like your store's size or your sales staff mean nothing online. The following are some competitive advantages that might apply in cyberspace:

Location Your online location may bring you customers you couldn't reach before. The online market makes buying convenient by allowing sales from all over the world at any time. A businessman in Scotland can order a suitcase from the ASU store on CompuServe rather than having to travel to Edinburgh to shop. A product manager in Buenos Aires can browse an American sporting goods catalog and order via the Internet.

Convenience You may also have chosen an online location because your local customers spend a lot of time there. Pizza Hut has established an online store that lets anyone order a pizza as long as they're near a Pizza Hut franchise. The idea developed in Santa Cruz, California, where students at the University of California campus spend a lot of time cruising the Internet. Pizza Hut's marketers figure that a lot of those college students get hungry, and its Net storefront is an easy way to satisfy that hunger. Faced with the choice of ordering from Pizza Hut online and having to get up and use the phone to call Domino's, many students take the Pizza Hut option. If you have a restaurant, you can do what the Country Fare restaurant in Palo Alto, California, does: distribute a weekly menu to your customers via e-mail so they can find out what's cooking without having to call or visit.

Added value Your online business may offer faster service, lower prices, or quicker access to information than people could get off-line, or from your online competitors. Penny Wise Office Products offers additional discounts to its customers who regularly order online. Book Stacks Unlimited lets customers search and order from its database of 270,000 books.

Uniqueness Your online business may be the only one of its kind. The Racquet Workshop is currently the only tennis shop in cyberspace. Of course, the online market is more crowded every day, so uniqueness becomes harder and harder to come by, but you can still carve out a niche for yourself through specialization. As bookstores have popped up on the Net, some have begun to specialize in specific genres. You might, for example, open the only Net bookstore that specializes in cookbooks.

Visibility All the major hamburger chains sell the same product, but their market share has a lot to do with visibility. McDonald's, Burger King, and Wendy's spend millions on advertising to fight for visibility. There are hundreds of Internet gurus, but guys like Mike Bauer of The Internet Group and Michael Strangelove of Strangelove Enterprises rise above the others by participating actively in discussion groups and by publishing online newsletters and tip sheets.

Credibility People buy securities through Charles Schwab instead of Al's Discount Stocks because Charles Schwab has more credibility. The company has been recognized as a leader in the discount brokerage business for many years. You can gain higher credibility than your online competition by offering reliable service and valuable information for your customers.

Service Your key business advantage may be service. Jiffy Lube and Oil Changers have built large franchises on the simple idea that people don't want to spend an hour or more waiting for an oil change at a gas station or dealership. Since netizens expect speed in all their transactions, your company might use a mailbot for instant responses to information requests.

Pricing Discounting has been a major competitive force for over a hundred years, and competition for the price-leader mantle is fierce these days. Still, it's a mantle worth having. If you're in a business where shoppers can easily compare your prices with those for identical merchandise elsewhere, then you'd better be ready to back up your low-price claims with a guarantee. Price guarantees are a hot sales button in many retail businesses. But if you're selling something harder to come by, your prices must only be perceived as low. For example, you might sell art posters or hot sauces on the Net for prices identical to what customers would pay in a store, but they're perceived as low because there are few other companies in the same business.

Quality If you can't compete on price, justify your higher prices by offering better quality in the products or services you sell. Nobody buys stock from Merrill Lynch because they're the price leaders, but because they offer investment expertise. Ace and True Value hardware stores can seldom compete on price with Home Depot or other warehouse chains, so they emphasize their superior expertise and service. Your online business can exude quality through superior presentation, service, and by providing more information than the other guys.

Selection It's far easier to offer a large selection of merchandise online because cyberspace is much cheaper than physical space. You can store a whole electronic catalog in disk space that can be accessed by thousands yet costs only $1 a month. Online bookstores, office supply shops, florists, and other businesses compete by offering a broader selection of goods than their competition.

Building your mission statement

Once you've written down all the phrases you can think of that distinguish your business from its competition and provide concrete reasons for your anticipated success, it's time to distill them.

Look over the list and prioritize the phrases in order of importance. At the top of the list, put the phrases that convey clear, unassailable advantages. If yours is the only auto repair BBS in the Cleveland area, that's an advantage that isn't likely to be challenged. But if your Net storefront has the largest selection of floral arrangements or it's the only one selling vacuum cleaners, your advantage could erode any day. When you choose a territory, be prepared to defend it.

By prioritizing the phrases you wrote down, you'll probably find that only the top two or three make it into your mission statement. That's fine, as long as they're phrases you can successfully defend over time. Your final mission statement should be primarily based on one of the competitive traits above. It should state what you sell, to whom you sell it, and why you're the best. The following examples emphasize the competitive traits outlined above:

> *WrenchNet is Cleveland's one-stop online source of foreign and domestic auto parts and auto repair advice.* (This BBS stresses location, convenience, and expertise.)

Infotime Research is the only company specializing in fast and reliable patent, trademark, and licensing searches for the aerospace and biotechnology industries. (This company touts its uniqueness, service, and expertise.)

Gaming Technology is the world leader in design, installation, and maintenance of electronic lottery systems for government and charitable institutions. (This statement implies visibility, quality, and credibility.)

Bonus Bookmart offers the largest selection of books on the Internet with the lowest prices in the world. (This company claims the low-price crown and stresses selection.)

InstaPix's online graphics service delivers professional-quality image files to art directors and graphic artists within minutes. (This stresses quality and the added value of the Net's speedy delivery system.)

Each of these statements stakes out a business niche that gives the company a competitive edge in its market. Your mission statement should describe real traits of your business that set it apart from the crowd.

The reality check

When you finalize your mission statement, make sure it's one you can live up to. It may sound great to say your company is the largest supplier of fruit baskets in cyberspace, but you have to be able to support that statement with deeds. If you have competitors who already occupy the niche you'd like to occupy, your mission statement should provide compelling reasons why you think you can win it. For example, *WinCo will become the leading online vendor of window coverings by offering a superior selection and color graphic samples on its Web server while guaranteeing the lowest prices.*

SETTING GOALS

It's difficult to plan for an outcome if you don't know what outcome you want. Your goals spell out exactly what you hope to achieve with your online marketing plan. The more specific you can be, the more detailed your plan. You may start out with a general goal like "Develop a large, solid base of satisfied customers," but your goal statements should ultimately be much more specific.

Different goals lead to different expectations

To get started, write down every realistic goal that occurs to you. Maybe you want to develop a profitable business from scratch in the online marketplace. Maybe you want to have the first and biggest online yacht brokerage in Canada. Maybe you're going online to increase your mail-order or in-store sales by going after customers with a different medium. Maybe you're trying to improve your credibility with your off-line customers by offering an online option. Maybe you just want to gain online experience to prepare for the future.

Each of these goals leads logically to different expectations. If your only goal is to gain experience, you'll probably meet it whether your business succeeds or not. If you want to be the biggest business of your type, you'll have to measure success against your competitors. Set a goal worth reaching for, but not one that creates unrealistic expectations, and leverage your strengths. Compaq didn't set out to sell more personal computers than IBM; it set out to capture the market for portable computers because it had a superior design. It was only after Compaq established its leadership in portable computers that it began to set its sights higher. If you set your sights too high or expect an online presence to deliver value that your products or services don't have, you'll be disappointed.

Focusing your goals

General goals like *bigger, biggest,* or *best* are fine, but it's hard to aim for them because they're difficult to measure. Lots of companies are flopping around in cyberspace because their goals aren't focused enough. One way to make your goals more specific is to relate them to your business as it is today.

Picture your business after a year of online marketing, and come up with a realistic idea of where you think you'll be. Will your online storefront be large enough to support a new employee to take care of it? Will your art gallery in Petaluma develop customers in Europe and Japan who represent 10 percent of your sales? Will your metal-stamping company gain five new accounts among the *Fortune* 1000 or develop three steady customers in Mexico? These are goals you can shoot for.

If your online marketing plan is only part of your business, think about your goals in terms of their impact on your overall business. How many customers will you gain online? How many new leads per week will your consulting business generate? How will your online sales stack up against sales from your other marketing efforts? How many international customers do you hope to gain online?

If your online marketing attack represents the launch of a whole new business, think about when you'll return your investment. Will your efforts pay for themselves at the end of a year? Six months?

Your income projection

Once you've listed your goals, translate them into dollars and cents. Make a spreadsheet that projects your anticipated monthly income for each month for a year or two following your first attack.

Most online businesses generate little or no income in their first month or two of operation. Don't expect big sales right away. The biggest reason small businesses fail is undercapitalization: they don't have the money to keep running until they start turning a profit. By projecting no sales in the first couple of months, you can plan to have the money on hand to keep going. And if your sales do happen to take off right away, so much the better.

By thinking through your income projections for the first year or two, you'll have a much clearer view of exactly what you hope to achieve. Your experience online will soon tell you whether or not your goals are realistic. If you think carefully when setting goals and do everything you can to achieve them, you may surprise yourself.

ALLOCATING RESOURCES

Your next task is to decide how much money and time you can commit to achieving your goals. If you're already following an off-line marketing plan, your online attack is an extension of it. You may be justifiably excited about the possibilities of online marketing, but whatever you do, *don't abandon or compromise your other marketing efforts.* Unless you do all your business or generate all your leads online, think about your online attack as an enhancement of, not a replacement for, what you're doing successfully already.

Think about the different resources you'll need to commit to your online efforts. These resources will be in addition to those you spend off-line. You should think about your available resources before you choose the specific battlegrounds, weapons, and tactics you'll use, because you need to be realistic about how much you can commit to your online attack. Time is just as much of a resource as money, and if your online plan is undercapitalized in either area, it will fail. So make some hard-nosed decisions about what you can afford before you commit yourself.

Money

Whether you set up a storefront on the Web or simply get an account on America Online, your efforts will cost some money. Come up with a total figure you can spend to start up your online effort, and then another figure to maintain it each month. Once you have some figures, do your homework and research both startup costs and monthly maintenance costs for various online options. Here are some expenses to consider.

Equipment If you don't have a computer now, or the one you have can't reasonably be devoted to your online marketing attack, you'll have to buy another one. Figure on the cost of the computer, a modem, bulletin board software and related equipment (if you're starting a BBS), and furniture and space for them.

Online access This can include setup charges for an online account, setup charges for a new phone line to link your computer with your ISP, and monthly phone and ISP access charges.

An online presence If you're planning to set up a storefront or purchase advertising space, decide how much you can commit to design, production, and maintenance.

Salaries or fees If you're paying one of your employees to manage your online attack, figure the cost of the time he or she will spend on it. If you'll be using a consultant, include a project fee to get started and then perhaps an hourly or monthly fee for as-needed work later on.

Using the same spreadsheet you created for your income projections, make new categories for each monthly expense, and then divide your total monthly dollar commitment among them as necessary. When you're finished, you'll have a good picture of how you think your business will proceed financially and when you'll begin turning a profit, like this:

	Jan	Feb	Mar	Apr	May	Jun
Sales	$0	$0	$0	$500	$1000	$2000
Equipment	$1500	$0	$0	$0	$0	$0
ISP fees	$150	$100	$75	$75	$75	$75
Consultant Fees	$1500	$1500	$250	$150	$150	$150
Phone charges	$200	$150	$125	$125	$125	$125
Personnel costs	$400	$400	$200	$200	$200	$200
Total Expenses	$3750	$2150	$650	$550	$550	$550
Cash Flow	-$3750	-$5900	-$6550	-$6600	-$6150	-$4700

In this model, most of the costs are in the first two months, and the march toward profitability begins three months after the attack is launched. If the income figures change, the cash flow figures at the bottom will reflect the impact on your business. You'll know in advance just what the online enterprise has cost you every step of the way. You'll also have a yardstick against which to measure your actual results.

Time

Computers are great, but they don't run themselves. It takes time to create an online presence, and time doesn't materialize out of thin air. We wish we had a buck for every software package a small-business owner bought and never used because he or she didn't have the time to learn it. Everyone thinks they'll somehow find the time to do new things, but time is a finite resource, and you can't get more of it without spending less of it on something else.

We'll get into the details of making a calendar later in this chapter, but for now it's important to realize that preparing for and pressing your online attack will require regular attention. Your online store or mailbox will operate twenty-four hours a day, but somebody has to make the online contacts, participate in discussion groups, check for orders in the e-mailbox, or monitor the position of your classified ads in forums. You or one of your employees will have to spend at least some time on these activities every day.

The amount of time you'll need depends on how you'll attack the online market and how far along you are on the learning curve right now.

- If you're new to computers, plan on spending time every day for a few weeks just getting comfortable with one.
- If you're just learning the ropes of cyberspace, you'll need an hour a day for a month or so to read some of the books recommended in the Appendix.
- If you're exploring your online marketing options, you'll need at least an hour a day to check out the various battlefields, get familiar with the terrain, and decide where and how you'll attack.
- Once you have an idea of how you want to proceed with your plan, you'll have to continue your daily commitment for a few more weeks researching the best options for the attack. You may meet with consultants, review service contracts from ISPs, plan a storefront's design, or prepare your e-mail signature and other marketing materials.
- After you launch your attack, you'll spend from a half an hour to an hour a day maintaining it, and another hour or two per week on top of that keeping up with online developments and exploring further marketing options.

We're not listing all these time expenditures to scare you off, but to make you realize that planning and launching an online marketing attack requires a serious commitment. One of the key strategies for guerrilla marketing online is to build a presence by becoming a regular member of the online communities that represent your target market. The only way to do this is to spend the time it takes to participate in discussion groups, read and send e-mail, and pursue the other strategies in this book. It's not really any different from getting started with an off-line business: there's a lot of up-front time and money to be spent before you settle into a profitable and workable schedule.

Look over the time estimates listed above and ask yourself if you or an employee can make this commitment. If the answer is no, change your online marketing plans and reduce your expectations. If you don't have the time to maintain a storefront, maybe you can start with an e-mail address and listings in a few online directories. If your storefront is in a mall, maybe you can have the mall's administrator fax you orders so you don't have to spend time checking for them.

Every cutback you make in your attack will result in lower customer volume and visibility, but it's better to do a few things really well than to do a lot of things badly. If you have the time and money necessary to pursue your plan to its fullest, you'll find that the results will be worth it.

CHOOSING TARGETS

When you know how much time and money you have to devote to your attack, you can start focusing on the right battlegrounds. Compare your available resources with the resources required to attack on each front and then make the best match. Each of the battlefields covered in Chapters 4–8 has its own time and cost requirements.

To match your resources with the requirements for battle, list each of the battlefields in one column on a piece of paper, and create two columns to the left for time and money. Then enter your realistic estimates for the resources you'll need for each battlefield. The specific resources you'll need to commit depend on several variables such as your ISP's charges, the number of discussion groups or mailing lists you participate in and how active they are, and the type of Net storefront you have. Here's a quick survey of key battlefields to help get you started, along with some tips for saving money or time with each one.

E-mail

An e-mail address that reaches the entire Net will cost you less than $10 a month. It will require anywhere from a few seconds to an hour or two a day to check your mailbox and read and respond to your mail. If you're doing direct e-mail solicitations, you'll spend time creating the message you send out and compiling the list of addresses to which you send them.

You can save mail-checking time by setting up your mail program to go online and check it automatically several times a day. Then all you have to do is read what comes in: you save the time you'd spend waiting to connect and download mail each time. If you send out a lot of information, a mailbot can handle that chore for you.

Mailing lists

Participating in a mailing list may cost you extra money if your e-mail provider charges to receive mail through its Internet gateway. Currently, for example, CompuServe charges by the message to pull your mail off the Internet. Even if your Net mail is free, you'll spend from five minutes to half an hour a day reading the traffic from the list and sending appropriate messages of your own when you want to add something to the discussion.

If you start your own mailing list and moderate it, you'll spend from an hour to two hours a day evaluating messages for it.

To save time and money with mailing list subscriptions, see if there's a digest option you can use. Some lists let you set a digest option that delivers the list's traffic compiled into one long message, rather than pummeling your mailbox with dozens of separate messages each day.

An online storefront

It will cost anywhere from $500 on up to design and construct an online storefront, depending on where you locate it and how elaborate it is. The best way to determine the cost is to check out some other storefronts in online services and on the Net, settle on a basic store design, and then contact the owners or mall operators to find out their fees for building and maintaining it. *(Check the Appendix for a list of mall operators.)* An Internet presence consultant can also help give you an idea of the cost.

To this basic construction cost, add the cost of your time or the salaries or consulting fees of others to prepare the material you'll want to put in the store. Finally, you'll have to spend time checking the store or your e-mail address for orders and processing them.

You can eliminate having to check for orders if your mall operator will fax them to you, but you'll still spend time and money periodically to redecorate your store or add new merchandise.

Classified ads and business directory listings

Classified ads or business directory listings may cost $30 to $50 a month, but they're free in lots of places on the Net. The only other costs are the time you spend crafting and posting the ads and spending a few minutes a day checking your e-mail for replies.

Billboards or display ads

These cost $75 a month or so for a Web page ad up to $55,000 a month for thirty billboards on Prodigy. Many Web malls charge by the year and require payment in advance. In addition, you'll pay anywhere from nothing (for a CompuServe marquee) to $30,000 (for a series of Prodigy billboards) to have an ad designed for you. Your time investment depends on whether you design the billboard or ad yourself, and on what sort of response mechanism the billboard has. If you set it up so people can reply to a mailbot, the only messages you'll have to respond to yourself will be orders.

Forums or newsgroups

You'll spend five to fifteen minutes a day reading and responding to traffic on a typical forum or newsgroup. Access to newsgroups is included in the basic fee you pay for Net access, but online services charge a premium of a dollar or more an hour for access to many forums. You may also have to pay long-distance telephone charges to reach some BBSs. Take your costs per newsgroup or forum and multiply them by the number of forums or newsgroups in which you plan to participate.

If you host your own moderated newsgroup, you'll spend an hour or two a day reading messages and deciding whether or not to post them.

Your own bulletin board

From $5,000 to $20,000 isn't an unreasonable amount to plan for a computer, modems, software, and some design consulting for a two- or four-line BBS. You can do it for less if you figure out everything for yourself, but that will require several extra weeks of your time.

Once the BBS is up and running, you'll spend from an hour a day on up maintaining it, responding to subscriber inquiries, and so on. The most active BBSs need two or more full-time people to maintain them.

Choosing battles you can win

Once you've eliminated battlefield options you can't afford, you'll probably still have several choices. At that point, think about each option and look for the best fit with your product or service. E-mail is an obvious choice, because you'll want an online address where you can be reached. Beyond e-mail, we can divide the battlegrounds into active and passive ones.

Active battlegrounds require your constant attention. These include discussion groups and bulletin boards. Passive battlegrounds hang around in cyberspace delivering your message. These include storefronts, billboards, and classified ads. If you sell a service, the only way to gain customers is to show and tell people about it. You can offer copies of your newsletter or tips on income tax filing on a storefront, but you'll get more visibility and build a reputation more quickly by adding your wisdom to discussion groups. If you sell a product or products, a bill-board, Web page, or storefront catalog will give customers a better chance to check it out.

Since you'll have a finite amount of time to devote to online market-ing, think hard about where you can spend it most effectively. If you're not good at writing, you may do better by working with a consultant to prepare terrific copy for your classified ad, storefront, or monthly news-letter than by trying to get your point across in newsgroups or forums.

As you travel through cyberspace, your battlefield reconnaissance will help you decide which battles are the ones you can win. When you've decided, write down the battlefields you plan to attack in the order of their importance.

CHOOSING WEAPONS

With your list of battlefields in hand, it's time to choose the weapons you'll use to attack them. Refer to the list of weapons in Chapter 10 and think ahead to the actual attack and how you'll proceed.

Before you can attack, you'll need some basic tools such as a com-puter, an online account, and basic training as a cyberspace warrior. Don't forget to plan time to acquire and master these.

Underneath each battlefield, note the guerrilla weapons you'll need for success. If you plan to participate in mailing lists or newsgroups, you'll need an e-mail signature ready to go before you do. If you're going to use a storefront, you'll need a design for it and you'll have to gather the material you want to display. Write down all the weapons you can prepare in advance. You shouldn't have to scramble to create a weapon during the heat of battle. Here are some weapons you should have at the ready:

- your business name
- e-mail signatures
- press releases
- information packages you'll mail out on request
- one or more cover letters you'll attach to information you mail out on request
- information you'll publish online
- mailbots
- your company logo

- classified ad copy
- a storefront design
- a catalog
- billboard designs
- a list of target discussion groups or BBSs
- a BBS design
- stationery
- an order form
- samples

As you envision each battle and list the weapons and tactics you'll use, you'll see the battle plan taking shape. Next to each weapon, write down an estimate for the time you'll need to prepare it. Include the basic tools like Internet training and an account. If you find it hard to estimate times, break each weapon down into component tasks like this:

WEAPON	TIME
Internet account	2 weeks
Internet navigation training	1 week
E-mail signatures	3 days
Logo design	4 weeks
Add online info to stationery	3 weeks
Write press release	1 week
Mail press release	2 days
Classified ad	1 week
Storefront layout	1 week
Storefront contents (text, photos)	3 weeks
Storefront software design	3 weeks
Select target forums/newsgroups	4 weeks
Lurk on forums/newsgroups	2 weeks
Storefront activation	2 weeks

When you're finished, you should have a very good idea of how long it will take to prepare each weapon. You'll need this information when you prepare your attack calendar.

MAKING AN ATTACK CALENDAR

Just as a spreadsheet helps you plan your cash flow, a calendar helps you plan your time. Your online marketing attack will have two parts: the preparation phase and the actual attack. The preparation calendar will give you a clear idea of the amount of time per day and the number of weeks it will take you to prepare your attack. It will also help you decide just when to launch your attack. The attack calendar will provide daily marching orders for battle.

Visualizing the attack

By now, your head is spinning with weapons, tactics, strategies, and battlegrounds. Here's how to calm the storm. Think ahead to Day One of your online attack and visualize what you'd like to have happen on that day. Plan the ultimate launch to your marketing attack and then prepare accordingly.

Ideally, you'll want every netizen in your target market to know about your business and to be curious enough to ask you for more information or to visit your store. And if your plans succeed, you'll want to be ready to make sales. How will you make all that happen on Day One? Like the general of a guerrilla army, you'll have to prepare.

Listing preparation tasks

The preparation phase can be broken down into specific tasks. Make a list of activities in the following categories:

Basic training You'll need an online account and an ability to maneuver in cyberspace. Starting from today, start scheduling time to buy a basic Internet guide and read it, buy computer and modem and learn them if necessary, find the right online service or ISP, and get an account. Train your employees, too.

Reconnaissance Schedule time to start surfing the Net or online service and locating the forums or discussion groups you'll want to join. Find out how and where to place classified ads, who to contact about pitching a conference, and how to get listed on the welcome or What's New screen. Learn exactly where your battlefields are and how to participate in them before you launch.

Another part of reconnaissance is locating online business directories and relevant print magazines. Find out where to send a directory listing or announcement, and how much advance notice they'll need so the notice or article appears on your launch date.

Weapons As you conduct reconnaissance, make some time to prepare the weapons you'll need on the day of the attack. Some of these can be prepared a day or two before the attack, and others have to be readied a month or more in advance. For example, to arrange for a magazine article or directory listings that appear on or near the day of your attack, you'll have to prepare announcements and listings well in advance, and send them soon enough so they'll appear when you want. Magazines like *Internet World* or *Boardwatch* usually need six weeks or two months' advance notice if they're to include your announcement in news sections, and they'll need three months or more to prepare a full-blown article if that's what you're shooting for.

If you're opening a storefront, you'll need to plan its design, layout, and order form, collect its contents, and get them to your presence provider or mall operator. You'll need a few days to write classified ads and prepare e-mail signatures or to set up a mailbot.

Drilling for battle Hone your weapons and sharpen your skills before you launch the attack. Start lurking in newsgroups or forums so you'll know exactly how they operate. Try out your storefront design from different computers and make sure it works. Test your mailbot. Train your employees on how to handle online transactions so they can do it quickly and efficiently.

Making the preparation calendar

Using a weekly or monthly planner (or better yet, a project management program if you have one), start from today and schedule your preparation tasks according to the time you have available. At this point, don't work toward a specific launch date, just schedule out the tasks over a period you think is reasonable and then see what sort of launch date that leads to.

Rather than choosing general blocks of days or weeks for each part of your preparation, schedule specific tasks for each day. This will help you discipline yourself to get it done. Set up milestones for progress that include deadlines for having certain research completed or weapons finished. If you're working with others on your attack, assign specific responsibilities to each person on the team.

When you're finished, you'll have a detailed calendar of events that spells out what's being prepared when, who's responsible for it, how much time they'll spend each day, and when each task is due to be completed, like this:

June Marketing Tasks

Sunday	Monday	Tuesday	Wednesday	Thursday	Friday	Saturday
				1 Activate SLIP account (Jeff)	2 Basic Net training (all)	3
4	5 Begin store layout (Jeff & Lisa)	6 Build newsgroup list (Odette)	7 Review store layout (all)	8	9 **Store layout due**	10
11	12 Assemble Store Contents (Lisa), E-mail Sigs (Jeff)	13	14 Review E-mail Sigs (all)	15	16 **Final E-mail Sigs due**	17
18	19 Classified Ad #1 (Odette)	20 Prepare news announcement (Lisa)	21	22 **Newsgroup list due**	23 Begin newsgroup lurking (Jeff)	24
25	26 **Classified Ad #1 due**	27	28 **News announcement due**	29	30 **Store contents to designer**	

When to attack

The beginning of your attack comes at the end of your preparation phase, but setting a specific attack date means striking a delicate balance between readiness and opportunity. If you're like most people who learn about online marketing, you'll probably want to begin your attack as soon as possible. You'll have a target date in mind when you'd like to launch your online presence, and ripeness, as Shakespeare said, is all. Grant's Flowers opened its storefront just before Valentine's Day and cashed in on orders for that occasion during its first two weeks in operation. If you're opening a tax information center or promoting your accounting services, January or February would be much better launch times than June or July.

But while a season or event can give you a marketing boost, you can't allow your marketing plan to be driven totally by a deadline. The armies that succeed are the ones that are well-prepared, and rushing off into battle for the sake of a deadline will do more harm than good. Many a Web storefront has been mentioned in *Newsweek* or *Internet World* before it was really ready for the attention such announcements brought, and customers ended up frustrated. Don't pull the trigger on your attack before you've seen for yourself that everything you need is up and running.

Your preparation calendar will help you plan a reasonable time frame in which to prepare your attack. If the attack date is crucial, you can juggle the schedule a little or assign more people to the job so it gets done more quickly, or delay some secondary battle preparations while you concentrate on the main event. Use your calendar as a guide and it will keep you moving steadily forward.

Scheduling the attack

Starting with Day One of your attack, schedule specific tasks for each day on your calendar. Begin with your attack on the most strategic of the battlefields you've chosen, and plan to spend some time every day maneuvering in that battlefield. Allow a week or two to get used to your attack schedule on the first battlefield before attacking the second most strategic battlefield. If you're using newsgroups or forums as a battlefield, choose the most important one first and establish a presence and a regular schedule of activities there before moving onto the next newsgroup or forum.

The important things about your attack schedule are:

- pressing the attack every day (several times a day if you're checking an e-mailbox or storefront)
- expanding the attack from one battlefield to another in an orderly way

Don't make the mistake of assuming you'll work all these activities into your day or week somehow. If you do, the chances are you won't get them done. Instead, make them a regular part of your day as you would other crucial business activities. Here's a strategy guide to help you schedule activities based on frequency:

Daily: Check your e-mail, storefront, and discussion group activity. Respond the same day to any queries or orders. Mail order confirmations and post discussion group contributions. Check the positions of classified ads.

Weekly: Check the activity log from your storefront. Review the responses to different classified ads and modify your ads or choose new targets if necessary. Add news or promotional items to your storefront. Cruise the Net to scout your competition and look for new battlefields.

Monthly: Read monthly online magazines. Look for publicity angles

August Attack Schedule

Sunday	Monday	Tuesday	Wednesday	Thursday	Friday	Saturday
		1 **D-Day: AOL ad, mailing list presence**	2 Check ad position, e-mail, mailing list	3 Check ad, e-mail, mailing list	4 Post newsgroup ads, check AOL ad, mailing list	5 Check ads, e-mail
6 Check ads, e-mail	7 Check all ads, mailing list	8 Check all ads, mailing list	9 AOL forum, check e-mail, new AOL ad	10 Check all ads, forum, mailing list	11 Check all ads, forum, mailing list	12 Check ads, e-mail
13 Check ads, e-mail	14 Check all ads, forum, mailing list	15 Post article and announcement, check all	16 Check all	17 Check all, prepare forum survey	18 Review AOL ad results, check all	19 Check ads, e-mail
20 Check ads, e-mail	21 Review newsgroup ad results, check all	22 Post new newsgroup ad, check all	23 Check all	24 Post survey on forum	25 Check all	26 Check ads, e-mail
27 Check ads, e-mail	28 Check all	29 Check all	30 Check all	31 Check all		

for your business. Create new information documents (Q&As, articles, etc.), publish them, and let others know about them. Locate new media outlets for publicity. Seek out new Web links or directory listings. Search for fusion marketing arrangements. Research newsgroup archives for past comments related to your business.

Quarterly: Run a new promotion for your store. Add a new department to your store. Prepare an informational article or brochure and e-mail it to your existing customers. Plan a direct-mail campaign.

Your monthly attack schedule should look something like the one at the top of this page.

The first battlegrounds for this attack are a classified ad on America Online and participation in a mailing list. August 1 is D Day here.

As the month progresses, our attacker maintains the initial attack and expands on new fronts. He checks the position of the AOL classified ad, posts ads in newsgroups that carry them, checks his e-mailbox for responses, begins participating in a forum, uploads an article to the forum library and posts an announcement about it, plans a survey for the forum and then posts the results, and evaluates his ad responses.

The events are spread out so the attacker becomes comfortable with the first ones before adding others. Eventually, routine matters like checking e-mail or noting the position of a classified ad won't have to appear on the calendar anymore. Notice that the calendar lists active tactics as well as passive ones, such as reviewing the results from the ads on AOL and the newsgroups. And when specific postings are planned (such as the survey on the twenty-fourth), the calendar includes the task of preparing such postings in plenty of time to get them ready (in this case, on the seventeenth).

Prepare a calendar like this for at least the first two months of your online attack, longer if you plan to roll onto major battlefields more gradually. Eventually, you'll use the calendar only for planning new marketing pushes, and all the checking and evaluating will become part of your daily routine.

13

Secrets of a Successful Attack

Guerrillas know that being the best doesn't mean you have to be the biggest. Your online competitors may have more money or more time to buy more weapons or operate on more battlefields than you. But you can still outmaneuver them with superior market savvy, strategy, and tactics.

WHAT CUSTOMERS WANT

Your first mission is to gain the best possible understanding of your online customers. People shop and buy online for different reasons than they buy off-line, but most of your competitors don't know that. Many companies take their existing products and marketing strategies and transfer them untouched into cyberspace.

But there are specific reasons shoppers go online. Your attack should leverage these reasons to their fullest potential. Here are some reasons for online shopping that you can turn into competitive advantages for your business:

Safety Crime is Topic A among many Americans, and the situation isn't likely to change soon. In a January, 1994, *Information Week* survey, 73 percent of the respondents said they didn't feel safe in a shopping mall. They'll feel much safer shopping from their PC at home, provided your shopping and buying processes reassure them.

We explained some ways to increase buyer comfort in your online storefront on page 105 in Chapter 5, but here are some more ways to make cyberspace feel safer for your customers.

- Include your telephone number in your e-mail signature, ad, or storefront information. Most customers feel better talking to someone about their order.
- Say how long you've been doing business. Businesses often use *Since 1970* or *Established in 1947* to reassure customers about their permanence, and you can do the same online. If you've been marketing or

selling online for more than a year or two, that makes you a cyber-space old-timer as well.

- Offer to provide references from satisfied customers, or include a few testimonial phrases in your marketing information. Mail-order catalogs use testimonials to reassure their customers, and you can, too.

Convenience It's a lot easier to pull a chair up to the old PC and shop from the den than it is to get in the car, fight traffic, burn up some gas, find a parking space, and plunge into a crowd. Your attack should emphasize this convenience. Remind your customers about the difference. You might even offer a "Winter Driving Safety Special" or a "Fuel Efficiency Special" to emphasize the convenience and economy of shopping at home.

Service The *Information Week* survey showed that about 62 percent of its 500 consumer respondents left shopping mall stores without buying because they couldn't find sales help. Holiday times are particularly tough for finding service. Your customers can avoid long checkout lines, crowds, and shopworn merchandise by buying from you. In your storefront, have a department or option labeled *Sales Help* or *May I Help You?* to answer frequent questions. Remind customers that they can order twenty-four hours a day, seven days a week without waiting in line.

Information The *Information Week* survey also showed that nearly eight out of ten consumers felt that the salespeople in stores weren't knowledgeable enough. Information can be your key advantage in the online marketplace, so make sure you use it. A store salesperson would have to hunt for the product's brochure, and catalog salespeople don't always have a lot of information about their products. You can satisfy even the most research-minded consumer by providing all the information anyone could want about your products. AutoVantage Online, the car-buying service with storefronts on Prodigy, CompuServe, and America Online, offers used-car pricing information as well as detailed new-car prices. AutoVantage customers can get pricing information in seconds without having to endure a sales pitch.

In a storefront or online catalog, post the prices, model numbers, size, weight, color, and other specifications of everything you sell. Organize information into logical departments like *Color Choices, Specifications,* and *Purchase Options* so customers don't have to hunt for the information they need. Include collateral information like product reviews, user tips, and Q&A sheets. If you're marketing from an e-mail address, offer to send free information about your products, or reports or guides about your service. This kind of information is difficult or impossible to get quickly outside of cyberspace.

Price Your online presence has the lowest overhead in the business world. Pass some of the savings on to your customers, and make sure they know you're doing it. Offer discounts for online orders, or set up a sales club for regular customers that gives them an extra 5 or 10 percent off all online orders. The Shoppers' Advantage service on CompuServe and America Online promotes savings of 10 to 50 percent for shopping online. AutoVantage On-line offers big discounts on car sales and leases for subscribers on America Online, Prodigy, and CompuServe. Both these services have been paying hefty storefront fees for years because discounting works. Offering a lower price is a powerful incentive that helps overcome any discomfort customers have when buying online.

ORGANIZE FOR BATTLE

Every trip through the online marketplace brings an assault of information. Names, addresses, and ideas fly at you wherever you go. E-mail messages and addresses, newsgroup postings, server and document addresses, appear on the screen one minute and are gone the next. Unless you make an effort to capture and organize this information, you'll spend a lot of time backtracking to recall it later. That reference to a directory of consultants that you suddenly want to locate will be buried among hundreds of newsgroup postings, and you'll have to dig through them to find it. The article you posted to several forums now needs to be updated, but you can't remember all the places where you posted it. You'll save yourself a lot of time and frustration if you know exactly how to lay your hands on anything you've read or published in the past. Here are some things to organize:

Discussion group messages People have a way of mentioning other Net sites, articles, directories, or consultants that you may need in the future, but you'll never remember how to find them if you don't save the information when you first see it. Copy and save any interesting messages. Either copy the whole message into a word processing document or copy the important information out of the message and into a file on your disk. Set up a series of word processing documents that categorize information with names like Net sites, Directories, Consultants, and

Reports, and then copy whole messages into them. Or use a database program to clip and save important references in different categories.

E-mail messages Create a series of directories or separate mailboxes in which to store incoming mail. Like a stack of organizer trays on your physical desk, these will help you retain and organize messages according to content. Use one mailbox to store messages that need an immediate response (and then respond to them as soon as you're done collecting your mail). Use another mailbox to store messages you'll follow up on later. Create individual mailboxes or directories for replies to different newsgroup postings you made. If you conduct a survey, for example, store the replies in a mailbox called Survey Replies.

An electronic Rolodex Starting from Day One, build a database file of online contacts. These are the people you contact or who contact you each day. In each database record, list the person's name, company name, e-mail or URL address, and a note about who they are and why they're important. Every contact is a potential customer or source of valuable information, and it's easy to forget these contacts as they float by in the cyberstream. If you don't want to set up a special database file by yourself, there are several different "contact manager" programs such as Sidekick, ACT, and Now Contact that are already set up specifically for information like this.

Publication logs Whenever you put up information online, whether it's a newsgroup posting, a classified ad, an uploaded file in a forum library, or a catalog on your storefront, keep a record of what it is, where you posted it, and when you posted it. It's easy to publish a document in several different places on the Net and then forget where you put it. Then when the document needs to be revised or replaced, you can't remember exactly where all the copies are.

Bookmarks, group lists, and hot lists When you find a particularly useful newsgroup, forum, FTP site, or other online location, use your search utility or browsing software to add it to a list of favorite places. Every online service lets you create a list of favorite places. Every Web browser has a hot-list or bookmark function where you can store URLs for Web sites you visit frequently. Newsreader software lets you create a custom list of groups you like reading. Search utilities like Veronica, Archie, and Anarchie let you store addresses of favorite sites or resources. When you visit a site that looks interesting, add it to your list so you can return to it easily later.

When you're in doubt about whether a reference is worth saving, save it anyway. It's better to save too much and end up with a lot of stuff you don't need than it is to consign one important piece of information to the vast darkness of cyberspace. You can always do a semiannual housecleaning on your hard disk to get rid of information you really don't need.

FOLLOW UP RIGHT AWAY

It's easy to get caught up in the hustle and bustle of online activity, flitting from one discussion group to another and prowling the Web. References to new sites, ideas for new marketing arenas, thoughts about an ongoing discussion and other visions dance through our heads in an unceasing chorus line. But if you let such visions dance out of view, they may be gone forever. Act on your impulses as quickly as you can.

Check out new resources. When someone mentions a new Net resource or Web site and it sounds interesting, check it out right away, before you log off for the day.

Respond to discussion group postings. Hardly a day will go by when you don't have an idea or comment about something you read in one of the newsgroups you're following. But unless you respond immediately, the moment is lost and the opportunity is missed. If you don't respond to a message within a day or two, the discussion has moved on to another topic and your point falls on deaf ears. If you have something useful to say, say it that day.

Follow up with prospects. It's incredible that people with e-mail addresses take days or weeks to respond to queries, but they do. Service separates the pros from the amateurs, so make sure you're identified with the pros. When a prospect is looking for information, he may ask several sources. If you get that information out the fastest, or if you're the only one who sends it, you're the one who will get the business. Use mailbots whenever possible, and follow up within an hour of any specific request for information that you receive via e-mail or your storefront.

Follow up after the sale. Make a sale and you make a sale. Establish a relationship and you're well on your way to repeat business and a lot of referrals. Your follow-up should include a thank you, and you can sweeten it by offering some helpful information about the product or service. If you sell a bracelet through your jewelry store, follow up via e-mail with a thank you note and some advice about cleaning it.

Thank people for references. If you get a referral from anyone else, be sure to send a thank you note via e-mail. An honest appreciation for favors past may lead to more favors in the future.

INVOLVE THE CUSTOMER

It's so easy to flit through cyberspace that it takes an extra effort to build customer relationships. Yet relationships are what lead to sales, repeat sales, and profits. You build relationships by:

- giving customers an emotional stake in your business (arousing curiosity, empathy, or excitement)
- by multiplying the number of times they contact you
- by increasing the quality of each contact

The following are some proven ways to build customer involvement:

Surveys

Newspapers survey their readers periodically about which features they like or don't like. Manufacturers ask all sorts of questions on their mail-in warranty cards. People love to give their opinions, so ask them about your business.

Introduce the survey by explaining that you're going to make some changes or additions to your product line or services. This way, people know something new is in the works. Explain what you're doing now, and invite people to check out your storefront if you have one. Ask people for advice about your approach, or for suggestions about new products or services they'd like to see. If you have some changes in mind, mention them and ask people what they think.

At the end of the survey, announce that the results will appear the following month. Offer to send them to anyone who requests them, or post them in a newsgroup or in your storefront. And when you send the results, mention how you used them to change your business. People will want to see the changes for themselves.

If you're asking for advice on a newsgroup or forum, follow these guidelines:

- Announce who you are, why you're taking the survey, where else you're doing the survey (if you're posting it to several groups), how you'll use the results, and when you'll post the results. Running a blind survey makes people suspicious and cuts down your response rate, so reassure them that you're not simply trolling for e-mail addresses to be used in a spam attack.

- Post the survey results promptly. Comment on the results and invite others to comment. This holds up your end of the survey bargain, and also keeps the group involved in your business.
- Explain which of the changes you've made to your business.
- Thank everyone for participating.

Contests

If you run a contest with a good prize, people will want to find out if they've won. When you launch a new product or service, run a contest to choose a name for it. Give one of the newly named products away to the winner. You can even combine a contest with a survey, soliciting names for the product first and then posting a survey to choose the best one. Give each voter an incentive to participate by offering a small discount or a giveaway item such as a tip sheet or a buyer's guide.

Contests get people involved with your business, and they also increase your visibility. If you run the contest on an online service or BBS, you'll be able to announce it on the What's New list. If the contest is wild enough, it might even make the welcome screen or a magazine column devoted to online happenings.

Limited offers

Offer something extra to the first ten, twenty, or fifty people who respond to your e-mail message or visit your storefront. It's easy enough to count responses by monitoring the server log or by just counting the replies in your mailbox. Holding a race to see who can respond first will make visiting your business a higher priority for online browsers.

Teasers

Instead of spilling all the beans about your product or service in a newsgroup posting, billboard, or classified ad, tell just enough of the story to get prospects interested in knowing more. PR companies and marketing departments frequently do this sort of thing before trade shows. They know their exhibition booth will be competing for attention with hundreds of other booths, so they get people involved by whetting their curiosity, curiosity that can only be satisfied by a visit to the booth.

Members of forums and discussion groups love getting the inside story. In the weeks before a MacWorld computer show a few years ago, one computer company teased readers on a CompuServe forum by telling them about some of its new Macintosh PowerBook products. The company hinted that it had one revolutionary product that would only be unveiled at the show. The booth was jammed.

The trick to doing this online is to offer just enough information. Give too little information and readers won't be curious; give too much and you won't get a chance to explain further. The makeup of your teaser depends a lot on the product or service you're offering.

If you're offering a service, get people involved with teaser notices like this:

You're paying too much income tax, and we can prove it. Send for our free tax guide.

People love to get something for nothing, and your brochure or demo lets you show exactly what you can do.

If you're selling a product, the teaser might explain what problem the product solves, or what benefits it provides, without saying what the product is. Apple Computer's first ads for the Macintosh were about breaking the bonds of conformity, not about computers. People flocked to Apple dealers to see what the machine actually looked like. Television ads featuring rocks and trees drove auto buyers into Infiniti showrooms to see the actual car when the line was introduced.

Mailing list subscriptions

E-mail is the best way to maintain an ongoing relationship with your customers, but sending unsolicited e-mail is a good way to generate flames and lose your online account. If just one person complains to your ISP about an unsolicited e-mailing, you'll be warned that further complaints will cost you your access. Do it again and you'll be hunting for a new ISP.

But that doesn't mean you can't build a mailing list. You just have to convince people that you'll be sending out information worth having, and then get their permission to send it. When you mention your newsletter, article series, directory, or other publication in a discussion group posting, tell people how they can subscribe and how often they'll receive mailings. Most people don't want their mailbox stuffed with product announcement messages every day, but they don't mind receiving a mailing once a month or so. Your listing of new yachts for sale, reviews of hot new books, or a list of quarterly investment tips may find a welcome audience, and it gives you a way to establish ongoing contact with your market. (But don't forget: offer to remove people from your mailing list if they don't find the information useful.)

If you have a storefront, include an option to subscribe to your mailing list on your home page or top menu, and then under the option explain the frequency and content of the mailings at the top of the subscription form.

EXPAND YOUR STRENGTHS AND CUT YOUR LOSSES

Time, money, and bandwidth are finite. Make the most of yours. Come up with a reasonable testing period for each battlefield you attack, and then evaluate it regularly. If you've given a particular battlefield a shot and it's not producing results, then devote that part of your resource budget to another one. Here are some guidelines for what's reasonable for each of the main battlefields:

Classified ads Try a classified ad for a week or two and see what happens. If it doesn't ring any bells, try a different ad or a different location. If you spend fifteen minutes a day checking classified ads that aren't bringing in queries or customers, that's fifteen minutes you might be better off spending in a discussion group.

Discussion groups Spend at least a month actively participating in a discussion group. We'll be surprised if you don't generate at least a few leads this way. In evaluating a discussion group, factor in the information it provides as well as customer leads. Joining the Inet-Marketing mailing list may not bring you any customers for your online shoe store, but it's a treasure trove of marketing war stories and news about online marketing technology.

Storefronts and BBSs When you commit to setting up a storefront or BBS, commit for a year. The work you'll put in to establish the server deserves a chance to be rewarded. Many storefronts report initial spurts of interest followed by a drop-off. Use promotions, new information, and other weapons to revive interest.

Publications If you decide to publish a newsletter, give it time to build readers. Figure at least a year to develop a loyal subscriber base. Even if you never develop a base, distributing the newsletter and announcing it give your business good exposure. You may end up keeping the publication just as a reason to keep putting your name out there.

DON'T OVERLOOK THE BASICS

It's easy to get carried away by the potential of online computing. Computers are pretty reliable, so we assume that once we set things up on a computer, they'll continue to work flawlessly forever after. The online world can also be so absorbing that we can start overlooking other basic aspects of our business. We end up chasing the techno-butterfly that might bring us profits instead of gathering the crop at our feet that surely will. Don't let this happen to you.

Check your weapons. There's a big difference between using weapons and using them well.

Is your mailbot working? Could you be using it to distribute three different information kits instead of one? Remember, mailbots can respond to different e-mail messages by sending out different files, so you can use one mailbot to respond to different groups of prospects.

Are your e-mail messages and signature formatted so they look good on any screen? The most carefully designed signature may turn into garbage on certain screens, and most people find it annoying to have to reformat messages to read them easily.

Are your discussion group postings generating positive responses from others? If you're not adding useful, provocative posts to a discussion group, your reputation is headed in the wrong direction. It's okay to be controversial, but if everyone else on the group vehemently disagrees with your message, you can quickly get a reputation as an unproductive member of the discussion.

Is access to your storefront fast and reliable? Is your order form clear enough so that orders can be processed without delay? You can set up a great storefront, but if people can't reach it or one of its features isn't working, it can be doing you more harm than good.

Maintain your other marketing efforts. Don't let your online marketing attack interfere with your other marketing efforts. If you're using your fax machine's telephone line to access the Internet, you may be reducing access for customers who want to fax orders to you. If your best receptionist or telephone operator is busy answering e-mail, you're no longer putting your best foot forward on the phone. Think carefully about which of your resources can best be deployed in each portion of your overall marketing plan.

Back up your data. This is a chore most computer users love to hate, but it's vital. The addresses, messages, hot lists, and other data you gather during your online attack are as valuable to you as the customer list in your filing cabinet. And don't think that having printouts of your records gives you an adequate margin of safety — imagine what it would be like to have to type all that data back into your PC. Back up your computer's disk to save not only your data, but the software you use to go online. If you don't, a disk failure will force you to install and set up your software all over again and rebuild your contact database. All disks fail eventually, and such a failure can derail your attack for weeks or months if you're not prepared.

Your marketing attack will take guts, grit, savvy, and determination, but if you're willing to use these traits you will succeed. You'll be helped in your initial attack by the excitement of striking out onto new battlefields. But as the attack wears on, you'll need to maintain the momentum. In the next chapter, we'll see how to keep the ball rolling.

14

Sustaining the Attack

You'll spend a lot of time and energy preparing your initial salvos into the online marketplace. The first days of your attack will be charged with excitement and anticipation. You'll probably be rewarded for these efforts with a lot of attention at first as your fellow cybernauts get to know you and your business. But as the weeks go on, the surge of attention may subside.

At this point, you'll realize that online marketing requires the same patient and persistent effort to bring sales that off-line marketing requires. Cyberspace isn't a magical cure for all your sales ills, and it can be discouraging when that reality strikes. You may become a less frequent visitor to the newsgroup that you once prowled daily. You may spend less time surfing the Net for new opportunities and ideas, or thinking of ways to spruce up your storefront.

Apathy is a dangerous thing in any marketing effort, but it's especially dangerous in cyberspace. When you have a physical store, a print advertising campaign, or a mail-order catalog, you can get away with a little apathy now and then. On those days when you're feeling lazy, your storefront, ad, or catalog are still out there carrying some of the marketing load. But apathy online means that your classified ads lose their positions on forums, you drop from sight in your target discussion groups, and your storefront loses its appeal. In short, the presence you worked so hard to create begins to crumble like a sandcastle at high tide.

In the online marketplace, you have to keep up your marketing attack, day in and day out. Your attack must continually build your online presence and draw customers to your business. Maintaining your online presence requires two things: keeping your key messages in front of your online market and maintaining your enthusiasm.

You won't be able to accomplish the first objective if you lose your zeal for cyberspace, so let's attack the apathy front first.

MAINTAINING YOUR ENTHUSIASM

Probably the hardest part about maintaining your attack is retaining that initial excitement and enthusiasm for your online efforts. As you settle into a routine of posting messages, checking mail, and monitoring your storefront, the new and exciting quickly becomes ordinary. But success over the long haul means keeping your key messages in the marketplace, continually searching for new markets, and finding new approaches to existing markets. And doing these things requires you to remain enthusiastic and committed to your marketing attack. Here's how to keep up your excitement level.

Tune in to online news

Apathy comes from hopelessness. Hope comes from new ideas. Every day in cyberspace brings new businesses, new discussion groups and conferences, and new ideas for marketing online. But you won't know about any of these unless you tune in to a source of news for your online market.

- If you're marketing primarily on an online service, check the What's New area every day, and follow up on new stores, promotions, services, and conferences.
- Subscribe to the Net-happenings and Internet Mall mailing lists for the latest on Net commerce and capabilities. Even if you're marketing primarily via one of the online services or a BBS, you'll get new ideas about improving your presence from knowing what people are doing throughout cyberspace.
- Check out the Guerrilla Marketing Online BBS for the latest marketing news, secrets, and war stories.
- Participate in at least one marketing-related discussion group or mailing list, such as Inet-Marketing, IMALL-CHAT, or HTMARCOM. This is where the online marketing pros hang out. You'll always find a lively discussion going on about the best ways to get your messages across and attract customers. Recent topics on Inet-Marketing included the pros and cons of marketing via unsolicited e-mail, technologies for secure credit card transactions on the Net, critiques of new Web storefronts, sources of information for international marketing, the future of America Online, and tips for choosing an Internet presence provider.

Read all about it

Subscribe to one major online magazine or newspaper and read it. Publications like *Internet World, Boardwatch,* and *Online Access* aren't the most up-to-date sources of news, but they do offer in-depth coverage of online services, new sales tools or information resources, and general trends in the evolution of cyberspace. You'll learn about new Web browsers, new ways to protect credit card information online, and what's going on with CompuServe, Prodigy, America Online, Delphi, and other services. By the time you read this, there may be a monthly or even weekly print publication devoted specifically to online marketing and sales. Every issue will give you new techniques to try and resources to check out.

Business or marketing publications give you a broader view of how online activities fit into the overall picture for other businesses. Magazines like *Adweek* or *Sales & Marketing Management* cover online advertising and marketing trends. *Adweek* just did a special report about online advertising and how some of the country's largest ad agencies are planning campaigns for today's Net and tomorrow's interactive television. Reports like this show you how the pros are attacking the online market.

Publications like the *Wall Street Journal, Business Week, Fortune, Barron's, Forbes, Inc,* and *ASAP* regularly tell you how America's most successful companies are jockeying for position in the online market. They report on mergers and strategic alliances between telephone companies, cable TV companies, and other firms that are shaping the future of cyberspace. The *Wall Street Journal* has been staying on top of Microsoft's plans to offer an online service, to include Web browsing capabilities in the next version of Microsoft Word, and to deliver software for interactive television systems. *Business Week* did a mid-1994 special issue on the information revolution that included articles on everything from how the Internet works to how online technology is changing every aspect of business.

Computer magazines are another information frontier to explore. Cruise your local newsstand every month and browse major magazines like *PC Computing, MacWorld,* and *Computer Shopper.* You can skim through these and zero in on articles about modems, communications software, and the Internet.

Whether or not you find something you can use in every issue of every magazine you read, you'll be staying on top of a changing land-scape. Guerrillas know that understanding changing weapons and bat-tlefields and taking advantage of them is the path to continuing victory.

KEEPING YOUR MESSAGES IN THE MARKETPLACE

The pace of change in the online market makes it a challenge to continue your attack. You must promote your identity with a consistent set of key messages you developed when you made your online market-ing plan. But you also have to find new ways to package those messages so they don't grow stale. It's like consumer products marketing. Soap and cereal haven't changed all that much over the past few years, but marketers are constantly changing their packaging. Storekeepers shift the same products into new displays to maintain buyer interest. Those boxes of Cheerios that sat on a low shelf for weeks suddenly begin flying out the door when piled in a pyramid at the end of an aisle. Sales of Tide jump a little every time Procter & Gamble changes the box.

In cyberspace, your soap and cereal is the information you post about your business. Whether it's a discussion group message, a classified ad, a storefront or a billboard, every bit of information you put out is an ad for your business. But information grows stale much more quickly in cyber-space than it does in print, so you have to keep changing the package. When you run the same ad once a week in your local newspaper and keep it up for three or six months, your consistency promotes an image of stability. Try the same thing in cyberspace and netizens will wonder if you're still in business.

The key to maintaining your identity is to find new packages and locations for your messages and products without changing your basic pitch. Here are three strategies:

- Repackage your messages to maintain your visibility with the same audience without boring them.
- Repackage your products to penetrate new markets.
- Find new locations for your messages to expand your market.

Repackaging your message

When you're putting your messages before the same audience again and again, you need to find creative ways to keep the readers' attention. Like a diamond whose facets reflect light in hundreds of ways, your basic message can be refocused to renew interest. All you have to do is turn the jewel a little. The trick is to think about your product's various features and benefits and turn each one into a message that enhances your basic theme.

Tide has had the same basic package design for decades. That familiar orange box is such a fixture in the detergent section at the market that Procter & Gamble would be nuts to abandon it. But while people want the familiarity of Tide, they don't want to feel they're being left in the dark ages of detergent technology. So Procter & Gamble continually freshens the box's appearance by changing its size or shape, putting new banners on the front, or promoting new benefits. Tide's fundamental message is that it cleans clothes better than other brands, but the brand's managers have found hundreds of ways to say that over the years so the product remains a best-seller. A hundred years ago, dirt was dirt and soap was soap. Thanks to Tide and other detergents, we now have ground-in dirt, greasy dirt, dozens of different stains, and an army of enzymes and other cleaning agents with which to fight them.

You can do the same thing with your online product or service. Suppose your product is a book about vacationing in New Zealand. Your basic message is that your book is the ultimate guide to travel in New Zealand. You participate in the rec.travel newsgroup as a means of promoting the book. In that one newsgroup, you could post separate messages oriented around travel costs, the South Pacific, long air flights, aboriginal cultures, forgotten outposts of the British Empire, vacations in the Southern Hemisphere, and exotic destinations where people speak English. You're still selling the same book, but you're pitching its many benefits in different ways.

One sure way to repackage your message is to align it with a current event. Every day, the newspapers carry at least one story related to your business, and your opinions about the subject make a suitable topic for discussion. If you're an investment counselor, rising interest rates give you an ongoing topic against which to frame your message about maintaining investment value over time. If you sell sporting goods, the 1994 baseball and hockey strikes would have made a lively topic. By following the news regularly, you'll have an unending source of discussion topics that can give you fresh entrees into your discussion group.

Freshly packaged messages work in an online storefront, too. Your tip of the day or week can change. You can offer a specific feature like news updates or the latest tips on using your product that keeps people coming back. You can even run topic-related specials. A report on rising auto thefts leads naturally to a Crime Buster Special on auto alarm systems. A news item about cuts in Social Security leads naturally to a pitch for investment services.

Don't forget your existing customers, either. Even though customers know your business and what it can do for them, they need to be reminded that you're still around. Stay in touch with a quarterly e-mailing. Send out tip sheets or news updates related to a topic in the media. Send out e-mail greetings for holidays. Every message helps to maintain your visibility.

The lesson for online guerrillas is clear. Once you've worked hard to establish your online presence with a key message, build on it through repackaging.

Tailoring your product for new markets

While you're refocusing your message to maintain visibility and excitement within one market, think about repackaging your product for new markets. Dave Asprey of the West American T-Shirt Company had been wholesaling custom T-shirts to local stores and street vendors in San Diego for four months when he decided to go online. He came up with a great T-shirt for coffee drinkers and posted a notice about it on the alt.drugs.caffeine newsgroup.

Dave got more orders for that shirt in two months than he'd had for all his other shirts in six months of off-line marketing efforts, so he expanded from there. His T-shirt line now includes creating custom shirts for other newsgroups, and he's listed his name in a coffee vendor's resource list on the Worldwide Web.

Dave is lucky to be selling a product that can quickly be changed to suit different markets, but no matter what your business, you can find ways to expand your market by creatively tailoring your product to suit it. Again, think of the different benefits your product or service offers and you'll see how it can serve different markets. With thousands of discussion groups and forums in cyberspace, you can target many different market segments.

Suppose you have a book about exercise. You might start out by joining a forum on health and fitness, but you could expand into specific forums on various forms of exercise or various sports. Last time we looked, there were dozens of Usenet newsgroups on different sports, including scuba, skiing, skydiving, skating, golf, and triathlon. Athletes of all kinds need to maintain their strength through exercise, so your book can help all of them.

To help jog your thinking about new markets, save a copy of the Usenet newsgroup list from your newsreader, or consult a directory like Harley Hahn and Rick Stout's *The Internet Yellow Pages*. Browse the selection of forums on your online service. Check out lists of BBSs in *Boardwatch*. You'll see dozens of new markets you can attack.

Seeking new locations

Even if you have just one product, one key message, and one key market, you can still increase your visibility by finding new places to post your message.

- If you have an online storefront, look for new directories, Web sites, and Gopher directories where you can list your business. Half a dozen new Web browsers have come into use during the past year, and each of them points users to a different home page directory. If you don't have a link on as many of those home pages as possible, you're missing lots of customers.
- Whatever your business, develop a publicity angle for it and seek media targets where you can pitch it. *CompuServe* magazine does articles about its online merchants, services, and subscribers in every issue. *Internet World* and other online magazines have news sections and columns that announce new businesses. *(See Chapter 16 for more on publicity campaigns.)*
- If you're planning a conference, leverage your effort by changing the title and focusing on two or three markets instead of one. Your conference on low-cost remodeling will probably be welcome on several home improvement forums on different BBSs and online services. All you have to do is find them and target them with your pitch. You can also speak at industry conferences and trade shows to build your reputation.

WHY YOU SHOULD MAINTAIN THE ATTACK

We've said that it takes visibility to market your products online, and it takes constant effort to maintain constant visibility. Here are some more reasons why it's important to maintain your attack:

The market is growing. Estimates are that one way or another, everyone in the country will be online by the year 2003. The Internet at least doubles in size every year, and with companies like Microsoft building Internet access into their products in 1995, the growth rate will be much faster than that. Making a short strike on the battlefield guarantees that you'll miss the real bulge in growth.

The market is changing. Within the next five years, new technologies like interactive television will expand your opportunities for online marketing. You won't be able to exploit these new weapons and battlegrounds unless you stay in the fight.

Your competition is growing. Although serious online marketing has been going on for at least ten years now, we're only at the beginning of the curve. In August 1994, a new Web site called Hot Hot Hot began selling spicy foods. By October, there were three such sites. Dave Taylor's Internet Mall listing of online businesses gains four new entries every day. Most of the largest companies in America are still holding off on their marketing efforts, but eventually they'll all go online in some fashion, making it a very crowded marketplace indeed. Your continuing efforts will help keep you ahead of the pack.

People forget. Information seen online one day is forgotten the next, so it's important to keep putting your messages out there to remind everyone. In just one online journey, a typical netizen comes across hundreds of pieces of information. The only way that netizen will remember yours is by seeing it every day or two.

It's a good way to keep your existing customers. Even if all your customers are satisfied, they'll forget about you if you don't stay in touch. Make sure they know you're alive and well by maintaining your presence.

You've made an investment. Any effort and money you put into launching your attack is an investment. Continue your marketing effort and it will pay off; stop your efforts and you've lost it. Most online businesses report that it takes at least three months to start making consistent sales. Don't quit before your efforts have a chance to work.

With the right attitude, the right weapons, the right battlefields, and a little guerrilla creativity, you can sustain your attack indefinitely. In the next chapter, we'll see how you can use online resources to improve your other marketing efforts.

Using Online Information

Cyberspace is a great place to spread the word about your business, but it's also the world's largest library. With a little time, you can get the same competitive information that major corporations pay big bucks for without spending a dime. In some cases you'll spend a few dollars to access commercial databases, but in every case the information you'll gain can mean a lot to your bottom line. You'll discover new international markets or suppliers, spot the latest business or economic trends, and find out what customers are saying about you or your competition. And because you're a guerrilla, you'll be able to act on that information much more quickly than your larger competitors.

In this chapter, you'll learn how to tap the power of online information. We'll classify some different types of information and show you how to zero in on them. We'll see how to use Internet navigation and search tools to find information. And we'll get a sampling of just what's out there in cyberspace. The amount of information is so vast that we can only scratch the surface here, but you'll learn enough to discover more for yourself.

CLASSIFYING ONLINE INFORMATION

Unless you're playing a game online, everything you see on your screen is information. That's part of the problem when it comes to finding what you want. There's so much information that it takes some digging to locate any of it. Here are four broad classes of information that will help your business:

- reports and statistics that help you understand markets or trends
- customer and supplier contacts that expand your market or lower your costs
- inside intelligence and market insights about your competitors, your associates, and your own company
- professional advice about marketing, finance, taxes, law, management, and other areas of business

First, we'll look at each category in general. Then we'll see exactly how and where to locate the information you need.

Reports and statistics

Reports and statistics help you spot likely markets and learn more about your competitors. There are thousands of reports from government agencies, statistics compiled by government and private bureaus, and articles that help you understand everything from export laws to crop conditions.

Looking for the best place to test-market your new fruit drink? Check out the Department of Agriculture's database of economic and consumer statistics and see which state consumes the most fruit juice. Thinking about exporting personal computers to Albania? Find out about regulations and tax laws from the Department of Commerce's report on international business practices.

You'll find information like this in each of the major galaxies of cyberspace: the Internet, online services, and BBSs. Here's a rundown.

The Internet Of the three information galaxies, the Net offers the most data, and all of it is available for free. It's also the only place where you'll find research studies and reports from many educational and scientific institutions. Here's a sample of what you'll find:

- directories of consultants
- trademarks and patents
- SEC filings
- census figures
- international status reports
- Internet names and addresses
- crime statistics
- federal and international laws
- government reports and publications
- zip codes
- economic and agricultural statistics
- results of public opinion polls
- export guidelines
- Small Business Administration industry profiles
- demographics

The list goes on and on.

Online services CompuServe, America Online, Prodigy, Delphi, GEnie, and other commercial services all have selections of information databases. Here are some examples:

- abstracts from more than 50,000 publications
- company and industry reports from major brokerage houses and research firms
- archives from major international newspapers
- a directory of 80 million telephone numbers in the United States
- a listing of all books currently in print
- financial information on European and international companies
- current and historic stock, commodity, and mutual fund prices
- legal articles

Along with the Big Five services listed above, there are online services geared for specific businesses and professions. Lexis is a database of law citations and legal articles. Specialized services like this offer more detailed selections of data for higher subscription fees.

To access a research database on a major online service like CompuServe, you'll usually pay an extra $20 an hour or so. For a service like Lexis or Mead Data Central you can spend up to $200 an hour. The extra money buys you extra information. Commercial services have proprietary databases you won't find on the Net, like 10K filings, the latest stock or commodities prices, and corporate credit reports. They're also easier to search through.

BBSs Government agencies like the Food and Drug Administration sponsor their own BBS systems and distribute reports and statistics through them. Some private BBSs also specialize in databases on specific topics.

Customer and supplier contacts

The online marketplace is an international one, and you can find low-cost suppliers or new markets in foreign countries if you know where to look. Business-to-business contacts are fewer and farther between than individual customer sales, but even one contact can mean more to your bottom line than dozens of single customers.

A furniture designer in Houston, Texas, uses CompuServe's International Trade Forum to find overseas manufacturers for her products. Her lower production costs mean higher profits. An electronics distributor found new customers in Europe, Asia, and Mexico by downloading inquiries from the same CompuServe forum. He only wins one bid in fifty, but each contract is large enough to make the effort worthwhile. His international contacts revived his sales during the last recession, and now they represent most of his business.

Among the major online services, CompuServe and America Online have the best selection of business-to-business forums. On the Net, business- or industry-focused discussion groups are the best places to find suppliers and customers. Sales and marketing discussion groups on the Net frequently carry messages from overseas buyers or sellers looking for North American contacts. There's even a government Gopher server that contains recent publications of the Commerce Business Daily, the newspaper that reports all U.S. Government requests for proposals.

Competitive intelligence

Every guerrilla knows that it's easier to beat your competition if you know what they're up to. Scouting the competition through anonymous store visits and customer interviews is a time-tested method of gaining valuable business intelligence. In the online world, you can get lots of competitive intelligence by shopping your competitors' storefronts and by listening to what their customers say. Discussion groups related to your business often feature comments about your competition.

When computer companies want to find out what people are saying about their latest products, they join up with a computer-related forum online. Dell, Compaq, and many other companies pay one or more employees to do nothing but prowl cyberspace for scuttlebutt about their products or their competition. Members of discussion groups are very candid in their impressions about different products and services.

Professional advice

Online services have forums devoted to professional topics like marketing, accounting, taxes, and public relations. There are also some newsgroups on the Net that cover the same fields. By joining these discussions, you can learn the latest about what's happening in these fields and get lots of free advice about running your business.

FINDING INFORMATION RESOURCES

Your ability to locate the information you want depends on whether you're using the Net, an online service, or a BBS. If you're seeking information on a BBS or online service, you use the service's menus or searching software to locate it. It's fairly easy to navigate to the database or forum you want. America Online makes it easy for small businesses with its Microsoft Small Business Center, a central repository for information and forums for small business owners (see page 289). On CompuServe, the business and professional forums are all located in one area (see page 289). There are also printed guidebooks for America Online and CompuServe that tell you what's available on them and where to locate it. CompuServe's monthly subscriber magazine also features articles about the service's information resources.

Compared with online services, the Internet is pretty chaotic. There's a lot of information available for free, as long as you can find it. There's no centralized index of files or databases that spans the whole Net, so you have to do some digging to find what you want. You use the Web, Gopher, WAIS, and FTP to access files and databases, but there are so many files and databases that it can be tough to find what you want. By mid-1994 there were some 5500 Gopher servers on the Net, and the number doubles every year. Worldwide Web sites are multiplying even more rapidly. It's much easier to locate something if you already know all or part of the file or menu option name, or if you know the server's address.

Even if you have the address you need, the Internet presents other problems. The server that hosts a particular database may be too busy doing other things when you need it, or it may be shut down for maintenance. The gateway between that server and the Net may be on the blink. And even if the equipment is working perfectly, some information resources are moved from place to place as system administrators rearrange their files. An address that's correct today may be wrong tomorrow. Online services seldom change the locations of information they offer.

Your key to finding information on the Net will be the search tools designed for that purpose. Let's take a closer look.

Finding information on the Net

The simplest way to find information on the Net is to use Gopher. Gopher servers display information in directories, and they provide access to search and retrieval tools such as WAIS, Veronica, Archie, and FTP. Your access to Gopher depends on the type of online connection you have.

- If you have a shell account with an ISP, you access Gopher by choosing a menu option or typing a command.
- If you have a subscription to an online service, Gopher is an option in the Internet services area.
- If you have a SLIP or PPP account, you run Gopher software on your own PC.

When you start Gopher, you're automatically taken to a home server. You'll see a menu of choices like this:

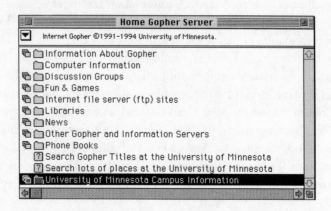

This Gopher server happens to be a computer at the University of Minnesota, where Gopher was invented. You can double-click on any of the folders to see a list of files or other folders inside them. From this one window, you can get information about using Gopher, a list of discussion groups on the Net, a list of FTP sites, a list of other Gopher servers, a list of directories, and other information. (If you're using a text-based Gopher program, each menu choice has a number, and you type the number to choose it.)

Using Veronica

Most of the information databases on the Net are accessible with Gopher, but with more than 5000 Gopher servers online, there's a lot of data in Gopherspace. In many cases you won't know which Gopher server contains the file you're looking for. That's where Veronica comes in. You use Veronica to search the menus on all Gopher servers. You type a word or phrase for the folder and tell Veronica to find all the menu items with that word or phrase in their names. To use Veronica from our Home Gopher Server, we would open the *Other Gopher and Information Servers* folder to see a window like this:

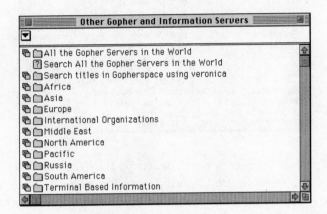

```
╔══════ Other Gopher and Information Servers ══════╗
║ ▼                                                ║
║ ┌──────────────────────────────────────────┐   ║
║ │ 🐭📁All the Gopher Servers in the World      ⬆ │ ║
║ │    ❓Search All the Gopher Servers in the World │ ║
║ │ 🐭📁Search titles in Gopherspace using veronica │ ║
║ │ 🐭📁Africa                                     │ ║
║ │ 🐭📁Asia                                       │ ║
║ │ 🐭📁Europe                                     │ ║
║ │ 🐭📁International Organizations                 │ ║
║ │ 🐭📁Middle East                                │ ║
║ │ 🐭📁North America                              │ ║
║ │ 🐭📁Pacific                                    │ ║
║ │ 🐭📁Russia                                     │ ║
║ │ 🐭📁South America                              │ ║
║ │ 🐭📁Terminal Based Information              ⬇ │ ║
║ └──────────────────────────────────────────┘   ║
╚══════════════════════════════════════════════════╝
```

We could open the folder called *All the Gopher Servers in the World*, but that option just displays a huge list of server names. We would then have to manually open each server and scan its menu to find what we were looking for.

Instead, we can click *Search all the Gopher Servers in the World* and find the server by searching for it by name. If we know the Gopher server has Microsoft in its name, we would type *Microsoft* in the search window and the program would find it.

If we don't know the server name, we'll have to look for a menu item on a Gopher server by its title. Suppose we wanted to find all the Gopher servers with a menu item called *Government Publications*. We would open *Search titles in Gopherspace using veronica*. The window opens like this:

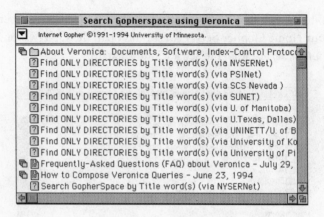

The options here let us search directories (*ONLY DIRECTORIES*) or all menu items (*Search GopherSpace by Title word(s)*). Since we're looking for a directory called *government publications* , we use the ONLY DIRECTORIES option and search for that directory by name. (If we were looking for an individual document stored on a Gopher server, we would search Gopherspace by title word.)

This window appears to list the same directory-search option several times, but each option lets you conduct your search on a different server. That's because Gopherspace is often crowded. One server you use to conduct the search may be too busy, so you'll have to try another.

Using Archie

The home Gopher server also gives us access to the Archie search utility. If you know all or part of the name of a file at an FTP site but you don't know the site's location, you use Archie to find it. To use Archie, we'll open the *Internet file server (ftp) sites* item on the Home Gopher Server. A new window opens, like this:

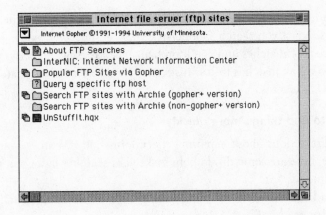

Suppose we want to find a file about the government of Zimbabwe. To search for all files relating to Zimbabwe, we would open one of the *Search FTP sites with Archie* folders and then type *Zimbabwe* in the search window that appears. Archie would search the Net and return with a list of files with Zimbabwe in their titles. We could then click on any of the titles to go to that site and retrieve the file. We would probably get quite a list of files to look at if we searched only for one country name, but by going to each FTP site and looking at the full file name, we'll know if it's the one we want or not. And we could narrow the search by including more words in the search string. Searching for *Zimbabwe government* would yield fewer matches.

The trouble with searches

Search programs like Veronica and Archie should theoretically find exactly what you want, but it's never that easy. Here are some of the problems you'll run into:

You get a bad connection. Sometimes the program can't make a connection to the server you want to search. If so, you'll see an error message. The server may also be too busy to handle your request, and you'll get a message about that.

Your search is too specific. Search programs take you quite literally: if you type *Tennis Shoes* in a search window, neither program will find a file or directory named *Tennis Shoe*, *Tennisshoe*, or *Tennis.shoes*. Fortunately, you can use wildcards in your search strings to broaden your options. For example, you could tell Archie to search for *Ten** to find any file that begins with *Ten*.

Your search is too broad. You might want to find data about the 1990 census, but if you search Gopherspace for *census,* you'll end up with hundreds of matches and you'll probably get a message that says there are too many matches to list. Instead, it would be better to search for *1990 U.S. Census.*

How to find things more quickly

If you're serious about exploring the information resources available online, here are some tips to help make your searches faster and more efficient.

Read the instructions. Before using a search utility like Archie or Veronica or even the search commands on an online service, read the manual or FAQ file. There's usually a directory on the Gopher server that contains information on how to do Veronica, Archie, and other Gopher searches. On an online service, there's a Help file you can use, and individual databases may have dictionaries of keywords you're supposed to use in searches. You'll also get advice about how to phrase search criteria, how to use wildcards, and how to use searching options to broaden or narrow your search.

Get a directory. Get a good book that describes the resources available on the Net or on an online service. One good general book is *How to Look It Up Online* by Alfred Glossbrenner. There are also books about CompuServe and America Online, and there are many books about Internet resources. Spend some time with these off-line, and your searches will go faster once you're connected.

Save addresses. Whenever you come across the address of a useful information resource on the Net, save it in a database file or write it down for future reference. It can take hours to locate a specific file on the Net, and it only takes seconds to write down an address and use it once you have it. If you're using Archie, you can also create a bookmark so you can easily find the file again.

Check spelling. Before starting a search, check the spelling of your search keywords to make sure they're correct. Remember, it's garbage in, garbage out: type the wrong thing and you'll get the wrong result.

Try different combinations. If your first search is unsuccessful, try the same words in other combinations or try adding new words to your query.

Browse. Browse Gopher servers during your travels to get a feel for how menu item names are specified. You'll get a better idea of the words

Gopher and other server administrators use to define menu choices, and your searches will be more successful.

Download. Rather than reading documents online, save them to your own disk and read them later. It's much faster and cheaper to save a group of documents to your disk and sort through them later than to read them online to find the one you really need.

WHY YOU SHOULD DO RESEARCH

Of all the weapons at our disposal, research is probably the one we overlook the most. We're usually so busy using more direct marketing weapons that research gets shoved to the bottom of the list. When we do have some extra time, research stays at the bottom of the list because it seems so academic. It reminds us too much of school or homework. We want to be out there selling, not poking through cyberspace for facts and figures.

That's a shame. The largest and most successful companies use research constantly. It helps them evaluate their market position, plan future products or services, and take advantage of new trends before anyone else. McDonald's wouldn't even think of locating a new franchise without studying the traffic past a proposed location. Home Depot doesn't open a new store until it studies the Effective Buying Income of the area's residents. Yet every day small businesses make tragic mistakes because they don't do enough research. Guerrillas know better.

Make research a regular part of your marketing arsenal. It helps you understand local market conditions, tax laws, and import customs. It helps you make better decisions and fewer mistakes. It can tell you what your customers want, and what your competition isn't giving them. It can find you new business partners or suppliers, and expand your market across the world.

The next time you have a question about your business, poke around online and look for an answer. The chances are you'll find one.

16

Leveraging Your Online Advantage

Your online attack requires its own focus, but don't forget that it's part of your overall marketing plan. Like every other part of your marketing plan, your online presence should support all your marketing efforts. Sometimes your online presence can help off-line sales, and sometimes it works the other way. The synergy is always there if you know how to take advantage of it.

- In November 1994, the Rolling Stones broadcast twenty minutes of a live Dallas concert over the Internet. Fans from Tokyo to Toronto tuned in. The band wasn't selling anything online, but the event helped polish the cutting-edge image of a group whose lead singer is past fifty.
- Well-established phone- and mail-order firms like Lands' End, Spiegel, 800-Flowers, and other vendors have joined together to offer their wares on America Online. While their printed catalogs already reach millions, going online helps them capture instant sales from well-heeled AOL subscribers.
- Federal Express and United Parcel Service let you track the progress of shipments online. You can't deliver a package in cyberspace, but an online presence gives these firms a new competitive edge in the service race.
- Ford, GM, and Chrysler can't let you drive a car online, but they offer interactive brochures and product information to whet your appetite for a dealer visit.

In this chapter, we'll see how you can increase the leverage between your off-line and online efforts. You'll learn how to use your online presence to build your off-line business, and how to promote your online presence through traditional marketing channels.

PROMOTING YOUR OFF-LINE PRESENCE ONLINE

Every good customer relationship is a human relationship. Nothing you will ever do online will achieve human contact with someone else as well as a face-to-face meeting. In a perfect world where your physical storefront could offer the same safety, convenience, price, selection, information, and twenty-four-hour access as your online presence, customers would prefer to buy from you in person. And under equal circumstances, you'd probably be just as happy to sell to them face-to-face as you would online.

Your main reason for going online is to gain customers and visibility you can't otherwise achieve, but it's much harder to form the human bonds you need for lasting relationships. Fortunately, your online presence can put you in touch with people who can visit you in person or call you on the phone. Here are some specific ways to encourage off-line contacts when you're in cyberspace:

Use your full e-mail signature. Include your phone number and your store address in your e-mail signature. Anyone who sees it online and happens to be nearby can stop in or phone. If you're offering value in your product or service, your online contact will turn into a lasting direct relationship.

Invite calls. When someone asks for help in a discussion group, respond with a private message and invite him or her to phone you.

Mention your location in messages. Find ways to give clues about your physical location in discussion group messages. When you start a message or paragraph with *As I was driving through the Lincoln Tunnel the other day*, people know you're in the New York area.

Mention off-line shows or conferences you're attending. Business trips, conferences, and trade shows can take you all over the country. When you're planning to attend an event in a different area, post a message about the event in a relevant newsgroup, or respond to another message that mentions it. Ask if anyone else in the group will be attending, and invite them to meet with you at the conference. If you've been participating in the discussion for a while and have made some useful contributions, other members will welcome the chance to meet you face-to-face.

Include printed information with orders. When you ship an order from an online customer, include a brochure, catalog, postcard, or printed information sheet about your off-line store. The printed matter becomes a mini-billboard on their desk. Invite people to stop by or phone when they're in the area.

Refer people to off-line articles, ads, and promotional events. When you're planning a promotional event at your store or a public demonstration of your products and services, mention it online so people in your area can come. Work it into your discussion group messages. Post a notice in your online store. Run a classified ad in a geographically focused newsgroup or BBS.

Participate in a local BBS. Find a BBS in your area that hosts a forum related to your business, and become active on it. Most of the BBS subscribers will be locals as well, and your online activities will alert them to your off-line presence in their community.

All of these activities will alert your online contacts to your location and give them a chance to meet you in person. In-person meetings are the best way to forge lasting human bonds. Use your online presences to facilitate them.

PROMOTING YOUR ONLINE PRESENCE OFF-LINE

Visibility is so crucial in cyberspace that you should use every means at your disposal to increase it. That includes using your physical store, mail-order catalog, print ads, brochures, stationery, invoices, TV and radio ads, and other off-line marketing weapons. Alerting your off-line customers to your online presence enhances your marketing attack in four key ways:

1. It gives your local customers another option for doing business with you.
2. It allows your local customers to refer your business to others across the state or across the world.
3. It reaches audiences you can't reach online.
4. It enhances your reputation as a modern, growing, and well-managed business.

Planning your off-line promotions

Your customers' online experiences with you should be as convenient and professional as they are off-line. Before you start inviting people to contact you online, make sure you're ready for any response your effort will generate. Make sure your mailbot, storefront, or e-mailbox is up, working, and being regularly monitored before you begin announcing it off-line.

We frequently come across e-mail addresses that aren't checked regularly, and even Web or Gopher server addresses that are no longer valid. It's easy to switch ISPs or online services and forget to change the address on your business card or stationery. If you do this, though, you'll waste your off-line promotional efforts and disappoint a lot of online customers.

Through careful planning and research, you should have established permanent e-mail or URL addresses when you prepared your online attack. But if you end up having to relocate in cyberspace, make sure you don't cut off contact with your online customers.

- If you change e-mail addresses, maintain the old address and monitor it regularly for three months after you've stopped publicizing it.
- If you change the address of your storefront, post a message at the old address that directs people to the new one. On a Web server, you can even create a link that takes people to the new address at the click of a button when they reach the old one.

Off-line marketing messages

It's fine to include your online address on signs and stationery and print ads, but if that's all you do you probably won't attract many new online customers. Most regular cybernauts will see your online promotions, so your printed messages should be targeted at people who aren't regular visitors in cyberspace. They need a reason to log on and visit your online store instead of phoning or shopping in person.

When planning how to promote your online presence in the off-line world, think about why your customers would want to shop online in the first place. Assume the people reading them are reluctant cybernauts, and give them good reasons to take the plunge. Here are some.

Convenience Your online store is open day and night. Use print ads or signs to emphasize the convenience of ordering at any time from a PC at home or at work. U.S. West ran a television ad for its yellow pages that shows a man searching for an accordion teacher at three in the morning. Tell your customers how online shopping can simplify their lives. Your in-store sign might say, *If you shopped us online, you'd be home now.* If your store has long checkout lines during peak shopping seasons, put up a sign at the register that says, *When you shop online, there's never a line.*

Information Your online presence probably offers faster access to information, or more complete information, than your customers can get over the phone or in person. An ad touting your online consumer tips or comparative product information gives people a reason to check it out.

Or how about this: *3,000 items here, 30,000 more online. Check out our online catalog and order form.*

Lower prices If you offer discounts for online shoppers, mention that in your store. You could even print price signs that say, *$3.49 here, $3.09 online. Let us show you how.*

Off-line support weapons

Once you've got some compelling reasons to shop online, you need to combine them with effective weapons. Let's look at some specific ways to promote your online presence with off-line marketing weapons.

A demo system If you have a storefront or online catalog, set up a computer in your store and display the storefront or catalog on it. Invite customers to try it out. Most of your in-person shoppers have never been in cyberspace, so educating them about your online presence is a real public service. If you set up a demo system, make sure you have an employee on hand to help customers use it and answer questions.

Your store In your physical store you have almost complete control over the size, appearance, and placement of your marketing messages. Use in-store signs, placards, window signs, banners, and even cash register tape to display your online address and invite customers to visit. The information highway is a hot topic. You'll draw new customers out of curiosity with a window sign that says, *See us on the information highway!*

Stationery Put your online address on your letterhead, business card, invoice, and packing list. If you have an online storefront, make sure your stationery tells people they can reach you twenty-four hours a day online. Invite customers to send in billing questions via e-mail.

Print ads Include your e-mail or storefront address in all your display ads in newspapers, magazines, and on buses, taxis, benches, and billboards. When you first begin using the online address, call attention to it by playing up the themes of convenience, information access, or lower prices. If you're on an online service like Prodigy or CompuServe, put *See us on Prodigy* in a highlighted box in your ads. The major online services are spending millions to promote themselves, and mentioning your online presence leverages all that promotion.

Radio and TV ads Include your e-mail or URL address in all your radio and TV ads. Here, too, you can start with special ads promoting your online launch and the benefits of shopping online. Your radio ad might depict someone buying your product from the PC at home instead of going out in the rain. Your TV ad might show a session at your storefront, highlighting the wealth of information available there.

Postcards and direct-mail letters Send out direct-mail postcards. Announce your online presence and offer a special discount or gift for those who visit you there. If you send a direct-mail letter, include a color screen photo of your electronic storefront to entice customers into it. If you're marketing mostly to computer users, try mailing a postcard teaser with just your online address on it; people will visit your store out of curiosity.

Free software If you have a BBS, make up floppy disks containing a freeware communications program or your custom BBS interface program. Mail the disks out with an invitation to shop online. This strategy has worked fabulously for America Online. AOL used free disks to build its subscriber base from zero to more than a million within three years, passing up long-established competitors like Delphi and GEnie in the process.

Advertising specialties Print your company name and online address on pens, pencils, coasters, floppy disk holders, mouse pads, screen dustcloths, or other computer-related giveaway items. People will put them by their computers, and your ad message will remind them about your online presence at the right time and in the right place.

CAPTURING OFF-LINE PUBLICITY

There may be 30 million or more people in the online marketplace, but most of them won't hear about your business there. Of the millions of people who explore the online world, most barely have their toes in the water. Most of the people online, like most of the people who use computers, are technically timid. They learn to do one or two useful things online and then stick with those, hesitant to venture farther into cyberspace. Publicity brings news about your company or activities in front of the reading public, whether or not they're online, whether or not they even have computers.

If news about your company appears in a magazine devoted to online trends, it gives readers an incentive to seek you out. Most of them need one. CompuServe and Prodigy have recognized the need to promote themselves off-line since they were founded. CompuServe publishes *CompuServe* magazine, a monthly publication that covers news about CompuServe and features articles about different services or businesses you can explore when you connect. Prodigy mails out a newsletter emphasizing new services or online events. Prodigy also uses telemarketers to phone new subscribers to see if they need help using the service.

When news about your company appears in a general-interest publication, it alerts people to your online presence and may win you some online converts who had remained on the sidelines until then. Every time a story about the online world appears in *Time*, *Newsweek*, or the *New York Times*, online activity jumps.

Magazines and other print media also offer two benefits you can't get online: portability and distribution. In a magazine or newspaper, people can read news about your online company on a subway train, at a lunch counter, or on an airplane. Print articles in major publications have millions of readers. Print articles can be photocopied and easily distributed to millions of others who can read them immediately without having to fire up a computer and connect. Finally, articles in targeted media let you tell your customers about your online activities with the credibility of a publication rather than the self-promotion of an ad.

If you're a true guerrilla, you're already pursuing publicity outlets for your business. Your new online presence can give you new exposure, or new reasons for repeated exposure in media that have covered your company in the past. The keys to success are coming up with the right weapons, and then aiming them at the right media targets.

Publicity weapons

The basic weapons you'll use in media campaigns are:

- press releases
- story ideas or pitches
- contributed articles and columns
- press demonstrations

Let's take a closer look at these.

Press releases A press release is a brief document announcing news about your company. This is the first salvo in your campaign for publicity. Properly written, the release reads like a news story to help the reporter or editor who gets it visualize your news as an article or story. The news in this case is that you've gone online, but there are many different spins you can put on this news, depending on your media target. Here are four natural angles you can apply to your news release:

- Your new online presence offers new convenience or lower prices for your customers.
- Your business delivers special information that can't be gotten off-line.
- Yours is the first online business to offer a particular product or service.
- Yours is the first business in your geographic area to expand into cyberspace.

Begin the news release with one of the major news hooks above, and then expand with a few paragraphs of details. Include specifics of what you're offering online, why it's important for online customers, and how it expands your off-line business. Quote yourself or another key employee about the importance of going online. Include your online address. At the end of the release, include a paragraph that describes your business mission, your market, and how long you've been in business. Here's a brief example:

FOR IMMEDIATE RELEASE

Contact:

Jackie Raley, Marketing Director
Wayland Fruit Company
502-555-5521
jackier@pomegranates.com

EXOTIC FRUIT GOES ONLINE
SEEKS INTERNATIONAL MARKET

Wayland, Florida—July 17, 1995—In a bid to gain an international market for its pomegranates, kumquats, and other exotic fruits, Wayland Fruit today announced the opening of Pomegranates Online, the information highway's first exotic fruit stand. Located on the Worldwide Web at URL http://www.pomegranates.com, the Pomegranates Online storefront displays color graphics of exotic fruit baskets and assortments and allows customers across the world to order at discount prices via the Internet. In addition, the storefront offers a database of exotic fruit recipes, daily bulk pricing

updates, a holiday and birthday gift register, and an international
fruit newswire.

"Our institutional marketing efforts have brought pomegranates
and other exotic fruits to the tables of restaurants across America,"
said Laurie Mendoza, president of Wayland Fruit. "By moving onto
the Internet, we can bring these exotic fruits within reach for
millions of international customers who have never seen them
before."

Wayland Fruit is Florida's leading purveyor of exotic fruit for
restaurants, institutions, and individual customers around the world.
Founded in 1981, the company specializes in premium-quality
pomegranates and kumquats for discerning palates.

*   *   *

This is the standard format for a press release, with a title, a contact
name and phone number, and FOR IMMEDIATE RELEASE at the top.
Notice the first paragraph. It contains two news hooks: Pomegranates
Online is the first exotic fruit stand in cyberspace, and the online move is
a bid by Wayland Fruit to go international. The next paragraph is a
quote about why the move is important, and the last paragraph is a boil-
erplate that describes the company, its markets, and its market position.

Your press release can be two or three pages long, but don't make it
any longer than necessary. The point is to tempt the press with some
interesting news and get them to follow up with a phone call and
interview. If you have a Web storefront with an appealing graphical look,
include a color photo or slide of it.

Story ideas and pitches A press release may result in a full-blown feature
story or article about your business, but often it's just published as a news
item. If you're after a longer, more detailed article about your online
business, come up with an idea for such a story and pitch it in a letter or
phone call to the appropriate editor at your media target.

The key to a pitch is broadening the focus of your message so it
encompasses a trend rather than just your own news. Wayland Fruit's
marketing or PR manager might target a magazine that goes out to
restaurant or hotel managers, like this:

James Banuelos
Features Editor
Restaurant Manager Magazine
111 Front Street
Boston, MA 02190

July 24, 1995

Dear Mr. Banuelos:

A year of frosty weather in the southern United States has pushed up prices of exotic fruit, yet restaurant owners are reluctant to raise prices during today's climate of low inflation. What's a buyer to do?

Wayland Fruit is one of a handful of fruit purveyors who are helping restaurants stabilize costs. Wayland recently launched Pomegranates Online, a new interactive buying service in the Internet that allows institutions to use personal computers to place orders, and track shipments, and get the latest international grower news twenty-four hours a day. Other purveyors are offering fruit shipment futures contracts for regular customers as a way to hold down costs.

Please phone me at the number below for more information about this trend, references to some of our electronic customers, and contacts at other firms who are helping cut exotic fruit costs.

Sincerely Yours,

Jackie Raley
Marketing Director
Wayland Fruit Company
502-555-5521
jackier@pomegranates.com

This pitch focuses on an industry trend toward higher exotic fruit costs, and explains how Wayland Fruit is helping restaurants hold them down. Notice that it's addressed to a specific editor at a specific magazine. Each pitch must be tailored for a particular magazine and even for a section in that magazine. If the media target was a mass-market consumer magazine like *Good Housekeeping* or *Gourmet*, the focus might be on how consumers are going online to obtain exotic fruits and recipes.

If you're pitching a story by mail, find out which specific editor is in charge of the magazine section or TV or radio show segment you want to reach, and write it up in a letter. Along with the basic story idea, offer to provide references to customers of yours who might be interviewed for the story, and enclose the press release announcing your online business. If you're pitching the story by phone, have the pitch organized and ready to deliver, and have your customer references ready.

Contributed articles and columns If you're going after an industry-specific magazine or a local newspaper, you can usually write a column or article sharing your expertise. Publications like this are usually hungry for material. They often print reader contributions. As with a pitch, write an article or column that highlights a trend rather than one that blatantly praises or focuses on your own business.

When you're targeting a local newspaper, write an article sharing your experience as the first online business in your area. If the article is well-received, pitch the paper about doing a regular column about cyberspace. Your credibility as an expert and the weekly appearance of your online address will draw customers.

When your target is a special-interest magazine, write about online information sources for people with those interests, and include your company as one of them. Your exercise equipment business would benefit if you wrote an article about online fitness forums and sources of equipment.

Think about the benefits of your product or service, and turn each benefit into an article for a specific audience.

Press demonstrations If you're an online pioneer in your business or geographical area and you have an interesting online storefront, set up a demonstration for the press. You may get some air time on the local TV station as you demonstrate online shopping. The manager of an equipment rental company recently got a feature story on a Phoenix TV news station by demonstrating techniques for winter lawn care.

Follow-up calls Unless you're lucky enough to hit a slow news period or find just the right angle, you'll need to follow up your mailed release or pitch with a phone call. Most of the stories that get done are prodded to life with a follow-up call. Call the editor to whom you sent your release or pitch and find out if they got it. If they did, ask if they read it and offer to help supply more information. Editors at busy newspapers see dozens of press releases every day; the ones that are boosted by a follow-up call are more likely to get published.

Choosing media targets

To find the right targets for your publicity campaign, study the media outlets you use now and think about the kinds of stories they run. Every outlet has different types of stories, or different departments. Your city paper has national news, local news, lifestyle coverage, sports, business, society, religion, and other departments. Think about how and where your story will fit into the paper. Do the same thing for TV and radio stations. Every TV news or magazine show is broken into segments that are like sections in a printed newspaper or magazine. Each segment has its own focus.

While noting the different types of stories in each media outlet, look at the stories themselves and think about how they're written. What angles do they cover? How many different companies or information sources are mentioned or quoted? How might an article about your business be packaged to fit the format of the media outlet you're trying to reach?

To get an idea of how this works, let's look at some target categories and see how you could attack each one with the weapons covered earlier.

Local newspapers, radio, or TV stations Set up demonstrations, pitch stories, and offer interviews for radio and TV stations. Send press releases to all your local media. Come up with article pitches for your local paper, or write your own company profile and submit it. Many local papers make local business profiles a regular feature, and some of them are written by the business owners themselves. Pitch yourself as a guest on local radio or TV interview shows.

Online magazines Send out a press release announcing your business, with a special focus on why it's unique in cyberspace. Online magazines cover the whole online market but they only have a limited amount of space. If you want to see your news in print, find an angle to use in your press release or story pitch that will make it especially newsworthy.

Special-interest publications Magazines that focus on your customer base will be interested in stories about your online presence. If you're one of the first to do computer training on the Net, your training industry magazine will be interested in that. Send a press release announcing the opening of your business. Focus your pitches on the benefits of going online for this industry segment's particular group of consumers.

*   *   *

Your online marketing attack will bring a powerful new dimension to your business. You now know all you need to make it work. But guerrillas understand that knowledge is nothing without the willingness to use it. So choose your weapons, target your battlegrounds, and write your own success story in the online marketplace.

GLOSSARY

APPENDIX

INDEX

Glossary

When a definition contains a word in italics, that word is also defined.

Acceptable Use Policy (AUP) — A code of rules for using an *ISP* account or a portion of the *Internet*.

address book — A personal directory of *e-mail* addresses stored and maintained with one's e-mail program.

alias — A collection of *e-mail* addresses stored under one name to facilitate addressing mail to a particular group of users.

Archie — A search utility that surveys all *FTP* sites once a month and builds an index of all software at those sites. The index is stored on an Archie *server* on the *Net*. Short for "archiver," it was written by Peter Deutsch and Alan Emtage at McGill University in Montreal in 1990. There are dozens of Archie servers worldwide.

backbone — A communications pathway that carries *Internet* traffic between individual networks.

bit — One binary digit, either 0 or 1.

browser — A program used to access and view information on *Worldwide Web, Gopher,* or *WAIS servers.*

Bulletin Board Service or **Bulletin Board System** (BBS) — Any computer system and software with one or more telephone lines that will accept a phone call from another computer at any time with little or no prior arrangement for access.

byte — The basic unit of information storage in a computer, usually 8 *bits.*

Cello — The name of a *Worldwide Web browser.*

channel — A specific discussion carried via *Internet Relay Chat.*

chat room — An area in an *online service* or *BBS* where several users can meet simultaneously and exchange typed messages.

CIX — Commercial Internet Exchange, an organization of *Internet Service Providers* through which they agree to cooperate with one another to provide interconnections among regional portions of the *Internet backbone.*

conference — A large *chat* session that features a main speaker and an audience that asks questions.

continuous connection — A high-speed telephone connection to the *Internet* that doesn't require dialing a phone number and which is never broken.

cross-posting — Sending the same message to several different *discussion groups.*

dial-up connection — A connection to the *Internet* that requires dialing a telephone number.

direct connection — A *continuous connection.*

directory — A named subsection of the storage space on a *server* or computer storage disk.

discussion group — An electronic message board on an *online service, BBS,* or the *Net* that contains messages focusing on a specific topic.

domain — A category of *network* on the *Internet,* or a specific network name, called a *domain name.* Every Internet address has a suffix that indicates its domain. Some common domain suffixes are *.com* (commercial organizations), *.edu* (education), *.gov* (government), and *.net* (network).

domain name service — A service offered by an *ISP* or *IPP* that registers customers' servers as distinct *Internet domains.*

download — To retrieve a file from an *online service, BBS,* or *Internet server,* transferring it to a disk on your own computer for local use.

e-mail (electronic mail) — A means of exchanging typed messages between computer users in which messages are sent to specific addresses and stored in mailboxes.

emoticon — A combination of keyboard symbols that, when looked at sideways, resembles a facial expression, such as ;=).

FAQ (Frequently Asked Questions) — A collection of frequent questions about a particular discussion group, bulletin board, *SIG, Internet* service, or other subject.

firewall — An *Internet* server that is isolated from the rest of an organization's *network* and so prohibits outside callers from accessing information the organization wants to keep private.

flame (*v.*) — To send a poison-pen *e-mail* letter to another *Internet* user, usually someone who has violated *netiquette; (n.)* A poison-pen e-mail letter.

forum — The name used for a *discussion group* on an *online service* or *BBS*.

FTP (File Transfer Protocol) — A service that allows you to transfer files to and from other computers on the *Internet*.

gateway — A communications link between a *network* and the *Internet*.

geographic names — Suffixes at the end of an *Internet* address that denote the country in which a *server* is located. For example, *.us* (United States), *.uk* (United Kingdom), and *.ca* (Canada).

gigabyte — Roughly one billion *bytes* of computer data.

Gopher — A method of locating information on the *Internet*. Also, a type of server that uses that location method, and a software program used to locate such servers. Created in 1991 at the University of Minnesota, Gopher was the first easy-to-use Internet searching and browsing system.

handle — A pseudonym used by an individual participant in a *chat room* or *conference*.

header — The portion of an *e-mail* document that contains the mailing address and subject information.

hierarchy — A category of *Usenet newsgroup*. Usenet is divided into more than a dozen hierarchies, including *alt* (alternative topics), *biz* (business topics), and *rec* (recreational topics).

hit — A specific occurrence of a user accessing a *server*. Server traffic is sometimes measured in hits per hour or hits per day. An active *Net* server has thousands of hits per day. That is, it is accessed thousands of times per day by various users.

home page — The introductory or menu page of a *Web* site. A home page usually contains the site's name and a directory of its contents.

HTML (Hypertext Markup Language) — The programming language used to store and present information on *Worldwide Web servers*.

HTTP (Hypertext Transfer Protocol) — The communications protocol, or set of technical rules, through which *Worldwide Web* information is linked on the *Internet*.

hypertext — A method of cross-referencing computer data through automatic links between words, pictures, or phrases. For example, a paragraph about the history of opera might mention Verdi as one of the great opera composers. Hypertext could be used to link Verdi's name with a page that lists his major compositions, so that someone reading the general paragraph could select Verdi's name to activate the link and get more details about him rather than having to look them up elsewhere.

hypertext link — An automatic link on the *Worldwide Web* that connects a word, phrase, or picture with other information elsewhere. When a user selects a linked phrase or picture, that user is automatically connected to the other data to which it is linked.

Internaut — One who uses the *Internet*.

Internet — An international data communications pathway that links thousands of computer *networks* together. Also called the *Net*.

Internet Access Provider (IAP) — See Internet Service Provider.

Internet mail gateway — A communications path that connects a *network* to the *Internet*, and which allows *e-mail* to pass between the network and other networks via the *Net*.

Internet Presence Provider (IPP) — A company that specializes in establishing storefronts and other *servers* for businesses that want to locate on the *Internet*.

Internet Service Provider (ISP) — A company or organization that offers *Internet* access to customers for a fee. Also called an *IAP*, or *Internet Access Provider*.

IRC (Internet Relay Chat) — A *chat* function on the *Internet* that has many different *channels*, each of which is topic-specific.

kilobyte — 1024 *bytes*.

Listserv — One of the best-known *mailing list manager* programs; sometimes used as a generic name for a mailing list manager.

lurker — Someone who monitors a *mailing list, forum*, or *newsgroup* without *posting* to it.

Lynx — A graphical *Worldwide Web* browser that runs under the MS-DOS operating system.

mailbot — A program that responds automatically to incoming *e-mail*. A mailbot receives e-mail messages and then replies to them automatically by sending messages or files to their authors.

mailer — A program that sends and receives *e-mail*.

mailing list — An electronic discussion carried out with *e-mail* messages rather than with an electronic message board. Rather than *posting* a message to a discussion board, you send it to a mailing list's e-mail address. All subscribers to a mailing list receive copies of all messages sent to that list's address.

mailing list manager — A program that collects and distributes *e-mail* messages to a mailing list.

megabit — Roughly one million *bits* of computer data.

megabyte — Roughly one million *bytes* of computer data.

modem — A device that allows a computer to connect with other computers over standard telephone lines by dialing phone numbers.

Mosaic — A program that provides a graphical interface to the *Internet* that allows users to view text, sounds, video, and photos on *Worldwide Web* sites. It also provides access to *FTP* sites and to *Gopher* servers.

navigator — A *browser* used to search for and display information on the *Internet*.

Net — Nickname for *Internet*.

netiquette — Rules of conduct for *Internet* users.

netizen — Someone who uses the *Internet*. A member of the Internet community of users.

newbie — A newcomer to the *Internet* or to an *online service*.

newsgroup — A message board on the Internet that focuses on a particular subject. Also known as a *Usenet* newsgroup.

newsreader — A program that allows you to read *newsgroups* on the *Internet*.

online service — A large commercial *bulletin board system* that accommodates hundreds or thousands of users at once, offers a wide variety of services and information, and charges a monthly subscription fee.

POP (Point of Presence) — A telephone number through which an *Internet Service Provider* can be reached by a customer. Larger ISPs have dozens of POPs across the country. Also used to describe a *server* or other business location on the *Internet*.

post — (v.) To send a message to a *discussion group* or *mailing list*; (n) a message posted to a *discussion group* or sent to a *mailing list*.

PPP (Point-to-Point Protocol) — A communications *protocol* that allows a computer to become an *Internet* site via a *dial-up connection*. Also a type of Internet connection. When using a PPP connection, you run software on your own computer to navigate the Internet.

protocol — A set of technical rules that defines a specific method of doing something. A communications protocol governs a particular method of communicating.

Roundtable — The name used for *forums* on the GEnie *online service*.

RTFM — An acronym standing for "Read The F—— Manual," a suggestion to a new user to read the online manual about a program or *Internet* service before asking questions about a particular command or procedure.

server — A computer that stores files and makes them available to other users on a network or on the *Internet*.

server log — A record of users accessing a particular *server*.

shell account — A type of *Internet* connection through which your computer establishes a *dial-up connection* with an *ISP*'s computer, and you then use software on the ISP's computer to navigate the Internet.

signal-to-noise ratio — Technically speaking, the relative strength of an electronic signal to the amount of electronic static or interference on a circuit. On the *Internet*, this is the ratio of useful information to meaningless blather.

signature (.sig) — A block of information used to sign the end of an *e-mail* or *discussion group* message. It usually includes an author name, company name, e-mail address, and other information.

site — A distinct *server* or *virtual server* on the *Internet*.

SLIP (Serial Line Internet Protocol) — A communications *protocol* or method that allows a computer to connect directly to the *Internet* via a *dial-up connection*. Once you get on the *Net* with a SLIP connection, you run programs on your own computer to navigate the Internet.

smiley — An *emoticon*.

snail mail — An *internaut*'s term for paper or postal mail.

spam — (*v.*) To *cross-post* or mass-mail unsolicited electronic messages to a large number of *discussion groups* or individuals on the *Net*.

special interest group (SIG) — Another name for a *forum* or discussion group; often used on *CompuServe*.

sysop — The person responsible for maintaining the hardware, software, or content of a *forum* or *BBS*.

T1, T2, T3, and T4 lines — High-speed telephone lines leased from a telephone company that provide an ongoing connection for data transfers.

Telnet — A program that allows you to log onto other computers on the *Internet* and run programs on them remotely.

thread — A group of *newsgroup* messages on the same topic, often a sequence of replies and comments about an initial message.

top menu — The menu on a *server* that functions as its table of contents.

Unix — A powerful computer operating system that is used on many *Internet servers*.

upload — To transfer a file from your PC to a *BBS, online service,* or a *server* on the *Net.*

URL (Universal Resource Locator) — A standardized address format used for *Internet* addresses.

Usenet — The largest collection of *newsgroups* on the *Internet.*

UUCP connection — A type of *Internet* connection between two *Unix*-based computers that allows the transfer of data in large batches at specific intervals.

Veronica — A program that locates information stored on *Gopher servers.* The name is an acronym for Very Easy Rodent-Oriented Net-wide Index to Computerized Archives.

virtual server — A *directory* on a *server* that has its own *Net* address and appears as a standalone server to outside users.

WAIS (Wide Area Information Servers) — A system for searching for files or programs via groups of keywords. Also, *servers* that are set up to be accessed by that system.

workstation — A powerful desktop computer, usually one designed for engineering or scientific uses that runs the *Unix* operating system.

Worldwide Web (also WWW, or the Web) — A collection of information located on many *Internet servers* that can be accessed with a *browser* or by navigating via *hypertext links.*

zine — An electronic publication on one very specific topic, published by one person or a handful of people, and distributed at intervals for free over the *Internet.*

Appendix:
The Information Arsenal

Books

Bryant, Alan D. *Creating Successful Bulletin Board Systems*. Reading, MA: Addison-Wesley, 1994.

Cronin, Mary J. *Doing Business on the Internet*. New York: Van Nostrand Reinhold, 1994.

Ellsworth, Jill H. and Matthew V. *The Internet Business Book*. New York: John Wiley & Sons, 1994.

Engst, Adam. *Internet Starter Kit for Macintosh*, Second Edition. Indianapolis, IN: Hayden Books, 1994.

Engst, Adam and Dickson, Bill. *Internet Explorer Kit for Macintosh*. Indianapolis, IN: Hayden Books, 1994.

Engst, Adam; Low, Cory; and Simon, Mike. *Internet Starter Kit for Windows*. Indianapolis, IN: Hayden Books, 1994.

Gilder, George. *Life After Television*. New York: W.W. Norton, 1992.

Gilster, Paul. *The Internet Navigator*. New York: John Wiley & Sons, 1994.

Hahn, Harley and Stout, Rick. *The Complete Internet Reference*. Berkeley, CA: Osborne/McGraw-Hill, 1994.

———. *The Internet Yellow Pages*. Berkeley, CA: Osborne/McGraw-Hill, 1994.

Internet World Magazine, *On Internet*. Westport, CT: Mecklermedia Corp., 1994.

Kehoe, Brendan. *Zen and the Art of the Internet*, Third Edition. Englewood Cliffs, NJ: Prentice-Hall, 1994.

Krol, Ed. *The Whole Internet: User's Guide and Catalog*, Second Edition. Sebastopol, CA: O'Reilly & Associates, 1994.

Levinson, Jay Conrad. *Guerrilla Marketing*. Boston: Houghton Mifflin, 1993.

———. *Guerrilla Marketing Attack*. Boston: Houghton Mifflin, 1989.

———. *Guerrilla Marketing Excellence*. Boston: Houghton Mifflin, 1993.

———. *Guerrilla Marketing Weapons*. New York: Plume, 1990.

Naisbitt, John and Aburdene, Patricia. *Megatrends 2000*. New York: Avon Books, 1990.

Notess, Greg R. *Internet Access Providers*. Westport, CT: Mecklermedia Corporation, 1994.

Popcorn, Faith. *The Popcorn Report*. New York: Harper and Row, 1992.

Resnick, Rosalind and Taylor, Dave. *The Internet Business Guide*. Indianapolis, IN: Sams Publishing, 1994.

Ries, Al and Trout, Jack. *The 22 Immutable Laws of Marketing*. New York: Harper Business, 1993.

Magazines and newsletters

Advertising Age, 740 N. Rush St., Chicago, IL 60611 (800-678-9595)

Adweek, 5757 Wilshire Blvd., Los Angeles, CA 90036 (800-722-6658)

BBS, Callers Digest, Inc., 701 Stokes Rd., Medford, NJ 08055 (800-822-0437)

Boardwatch, 8500 W. Bowles Ave., Suite 210, Littleton, CO 80123 (800-933-6038), or via e-mail at: subscriptions@boardwatch.com

Guerrilla Marketing Newsletter, Guerrilla Marketing International, 260 Cascade Dr., P. O. Box 1336, Mill Valley, CA 94942 (800-748-6444) or (415-381-8361)

Internet Business Advantage, Wentworth Worldwide Media, Inc., 1866 Colonial Village Lane, P. O. Box 10488, Lancaster, PA 17605-0488 (800-638-1639), or via e-mail at: success@wentworth.com

Internet Business Journal, Strangelove Internet Enterprises, Inc., 208 Somerset St. East, Suite A, Ottawa, Ontario, Canada K1N 6V2 (613-565-0982), or via e-mail at: curtin@hookup.net

Internet World, Mecklermedia Corp., 11 Ferry Lane West, Westport, CT 06880 (203-226-6967), or via e-mail at: info@mecklermedia.com

NetPages, Aldea Communications, Inc., 7720 B El Camino Real, Box 117, Carlsbad, CA 92009 (619-943-0101)

Online Access, Chicago Fine Print, Inc., 900 N. Franklin, Suite 310, Chicago, IL 60610 (312-573-1700)

Wired, Wired Magazine, 520 Third St., Fourth Floor, San Francisco, CA 94107 (415-222-6200)

Newsgroup, mailing list, and FAQ information

FAQ locations The following newsgroups are storage locations for FAQs: *alt.answers, comp.answers, misc.answers, news.answers, rec.answers, sci.*

answers, *soc.answers*, and *talk.answers*. For more beginner information about the Net, see *news.announce.newusers*. Also, you can download a copy of any FAQ via anonymous FTP from *rtfm.mit.edu*.

List of Internet mailing lists This directory lists thousands of mailing lists on dozens and dozens of topics. You can get it via anonymous FTP from: *ftp.nisc.sri.com* (look in *netinfo/interest groups*); or by sending the message *send netinfo/interest groups* to the address: *mail-server@nisc. sri.com*. You can also search for mailing lists by category via Gopher at: *nstn.ns.ca* (look in *Internet Resources/Mail Lists*).

New Gopher, Telnet, and WAIS sites This server has a regularly updated list of new Gopher, Telnet, and WAIS sites. Gopher to: *liberty.uc.wlu.edu* and look in *Explore Internet Resources/New Internet Sites*.

Online services

America Online, 8619 Westwood Center Dr., Vienna, VA 22182 (800-827-6364)

CompuServe, 5000 Arlington Centre Blvd., Columbus, OH 43220 (800-848-8990)

Delphi Information Service, (800-695-4005) or e-mail: info@delphi.com

eWorld, Apple Computer, Inc., P. O. Box 4493, Bridgeton, MO 63044-9718 (800-775-4556)

GEnie, P. O. Box 6403, Rockville, MD 20849-6403 (800-638-9636)

Prodigy Services Co., 445 Hamilton Ave., White Plains, NY 10601 (800-PRODIGY)

Internet services providers

InterNIC Information Services maintains a list of U.S. service providers and their rates. Call them at 619-455-4600 and ask for the Public Dialup Access List, or ask for it via e-mail at *info@is.internic.net*.

Mary Morris of Finesse Liveware maintains a list of Worldwide Web service providers. The list is available via e-mail by sending the message GET INET-MARKETING WWW-SVC-PROVIDERS to *listproc @einet.net*.

Internet consultants

Automatrix, e-mail Skip Montanaro at skip@automatrix.com

Branch Information Services, 2607 Patricia, Ann Arbor, MI 48103-
2647 (313-741-4442) or e-mail branch-info@branch.com
CommerceNet's consultants directory, available at http://www. com-
merce.net/directories/consultants/
CyberMall VirtualNet, consulting from NSTN, Canada's Internet
provider. E-mail to services@cybermall.com
Cyberspace Development, Inc. (303-759-1289) or http:/ /mar-
ketplace.com
International Association of Independent WEB Consultants, contact
Barclay Hambrook, World Tel Internet Canada, 810–675 West Hast-
ings St., Vancouver, BC, Canada, V6B 1N2 (604-685-3877) or e-
mail: hambrook@worldtel.com
The Internet Company, 96 Sherman St., Cambridge, MA 02140 (617-
547-4731) or e-mail to info@internet.com
The Internet Group, 245 Lehigh Ave., Pittsburgh, PA 15232 (412-661-
4247) or e-mail bauer@tig.com. On the Web at http://tig.com
Internet Presence and Publishing, 1700 World Trade Center, Norfolk,
VA 23510 (804-446-9060), www: http://www.ip.net or e-mail
keith@tcp.ip.net
Mary Morris, Finesse Liveware, e-mail at marym@finesse.com
Point of Presence Co., Seattle, WA (206-860-0789) or e-mail Todd
Haedrich at todd@popco.com

Online business directories, shopping malls, and news

Apollo, an Internet shopping mall. http://apollo.co.uk
BizNet http://128.173.241.138/
BizWeb, http://www.bizweb.com/
Branch Mall, an Internet shopping mall. http://branch.com:1080/ or
send e-mail to info@branch.com
CommerceNet, a Web site with a business directory. http://www.com-
merce.net, or send e-mail to info@commerce.net
EINet Galaxy, a directory of shopping and information. http://galaxy.
einet.net/
IndustryNet, a directory of business-to-business services. Automated
News Network, Pittsburgh, PA (412-967-3500), http://www. indus-
try.net
The Internet Business Directory, Internet Business Services, 1250
Oakmead Pkwy., Suite 210, Sunnyvale, CA 94088 (408-524-2979)
or e-mail to: info@ar.com

The Internet Mall, a list of stores accessible via the Internet. On the Web at http://www.mecklerweb.com/imall

Internet Shopping Network, an Internet shopping mall. http://www.internet.net/

MarketPlace, an Internet shopping mall. http://marketplace.com

NetMarket, an Internet shopping mall. http://www.netmarket.com

Netsurfer Digest, a weekly zine about Net news. http://www. net-surf.com

Open Market, an Internet shopping mall. http://www.directory.net

Note: The names and addresses of the databases listed here are accurate at this writing, but things change on the Net. If you don't find the resource at the location we've listed, use a search utility or ask around in your favorite discussion group; someone will probably know the new address.

Online information directories

One way to zero in quickly on the information you want is to get a directory. Your home Gopher server or Web site will probably have one or more directories. Here are some others that specifically list business and government information. To find these resources, use the search tool we specify (usually Gopher) and then follow the specified path through menu items. Each menu is separated from others by a slash (/). When we tell you the resource *Business* is inside the directory *Other Info*, we'll say, "look in *Other Info/Business*."

Business and Academic Related E-mail Addresses lists names, e-mail addresses, and descriptions for hundreds of businesses. Gopher to: *nysernet.org* and look in *Special Collections: Business and Economic Development*.

Government BBS list is a database that lists dozens of BBSs operated by government agencies for the purpose of providing online information. You can get this list via gopher at: *gopher.panix.com* (look in *Society for Electronic Access/List of U.S. Gov.*).

Government Gophers list provides gopher servers operated or funded by the U.S. government, listed by agency. Gopher to: *stis.nsf.gov* and look in *Other U.S. Government Gopher Servers*.

Business Resources on the Net is a directory containing a series of files, each of which lists resources in categories like finance, economics, and statistics. This directory is available via anonymous FTP from *ksuvxa.kent.edu* (look in the *library* directory) or via Gopher at *refmac. kent.edu*.

Government Sources of Business and Economic Information on the Internet is another good starting place. Use Gopher to go to *Niord. SHSU.edu*. This directory lists government as well as business databases.

Internet Sources of Government Information lists hundreds of government databases and their locations. You can get it from four different Gopher servers:

nysernet.org (look in *Special Collections: New York State and Federal Info*)

gopher.oar.net (look in *beginning unix and the internet*)

gopher.lib.umich.edu (look in *clearinghouse*)

gopher.virginia.edu (look in *library services*)

Reports and statistics

The U.S. government maintains hundreds of online databases, reports, and books. Here's a small business-oriented sampling:

Census information For detailed results from the 1990 U.S. Census, there are three possibilities. Gopher to:

gopher.micro.umn.edu (look in *Libraries/Electronic Books/By Title*)

bigcat.missouri.edu (look in *Reference and Information Center*)

riceinfo.rice.edu (look in *Information By Subject Area, Census*)

CIA World Fact Book This book contains detailed information about every foreign country. Gopher to: *wiretap.spies.com* (look in *Electronics Books*) or to *gopher.micro.umn.edu* (look in *Libraries/Reference Works, CIA World Fact Book*).

Department of Agriculture Economics and Statistics This contains data on food consumption and consumer spending, among other topics. Gopher to: *usda.mannlib.cornell.edu*.

Department of Commerce economic data The Department of Commerce maintains the Economic Bulletin Board that offers files about current economic conditions (some updated every day). Gopher to: *gopher.lib.umich.edu* (look in *social sciences resources, economics*).

Department of Justice Statistics Get data on crimes, inmate populations, and other such topics via Gopher at: *uacsc2.albany.edu* (look in *United Nations Justice Network/Bureau of Justice Statistics Documents*).

Economic Bulletin Board This BBS from the Department of Commerce offers information on economic and trade conditions such as Treasury auction results and current economic indicators. When you're on the Net, you can reach it via Gopher at: *gopher.lib.umich.edu* and look in *Social Sciences Research/Economics*.

Economic Conditions Summary This server offers statistical summaries on the balance of payments, the consumer price index, retail sales, durable goods sales, construction, plant and equipment spending, and other indicators. Gopher to: *infopath.sdsu.edu* and look in *News & Services/Economic . . . /Summaries of current . . .*

International Business Practices This Department of Commerce report spells out import regulations, tax laws, and other information for over 100 countries. Gopher to: *umslvma.umsl.edu* (look in *library, government information*).

Library of Congress The online Library of Congress catalog is available by Telnet at: *locis.loc.gov.* There's also a catch-all information service from the Library of Congress called Marvel. You can find it via Gopher at: *marvel.loc.gov.*

National Trade Data Bank This contains over 300,000 documents from the Commerce, State, Treasury, Defense, Agriculture, Labor, and Energy Departments, as well as the CIA, Federal Reserve Board, and International Trade Commission. Gopher to: *gopher.stat-usa.gov*, or use a Web browser to go to: *www.stat-usa.gov.*

National Weather Service Forecasts This site offers regional weather reports, updated constantly. Gopher to: *wx.atmos.uiuc.edu* or to: *ashpool.micro.umn.edu* (look in *Weather*).

Opinion poll results The University of North Carolina maintains an archive of results from polls conducted by *USA Today*, Louis Harris, and other organizations. Telnet to *uncvml.oit.unc.edu*, log in as *irss1* with the password *irss*, and then look for the *Public Opinion Item Index* in the *IRSS* directory.

SBA Home Page This Small Business Administration's server offers information about the agency's programs and services. Soon the SBA hopes to allow electronic filing of SBA loan applications here. Reach it via Gopher at: *sbaonline.sba.gov*, or with a Web browser at *http://www.sbaonline.sba.gov.*

State Department Travel Advisories Get travel advisories for foreign countries issued by the State Department. Gopher to: *gopher.stolaf.edu* (look in *internet resources, us-state-department-travel-advisories*).

Stock prices You still have to pay for up-to-date stock information, but you can get a daily market summary report via Telnet at *a2i.ra-hul.net* (log in as *guest*). For a selection of recent closing quotes on specific dates, Gopher to: *lobo.rmhs.colorado.edu* and look in *Other Information Services/Stock Market Closing Quotes*.

Contacts

If you're hunting for customers or suppliers, the Net offers several newsgroups and a couple of databases that can help.

Commerce Business Daily This is the government's publication that requests bids on government projects. There's a database on the Net that stores the most recent issues. Gopher to: *cns.cscns.com* (look in *The Library, Government Information*).

CommerceNet This is a Worldwide Web site that includes a business-to-business directory. Use a Web browser like NetScape, Mosaic, or Lynx to find it at: http://www.commerce.net.

IndustryNet This online service is a directory of business suppliers for various manufacturing industries. Use a Web browser to find it at: *http://www.industry.net*.

Newsgroups You should be participating in newsgroups related to your business as part of your guerrilla marketing strategy, but you'll also want to browse some other groups. The *alt.business.misc, biz.misc,* and *misc.entrepreneurs* groups have a lot of useless messages on them, but occasionally there's a good lead among them. We've seen overseas manufacturers looking for U.S. distributors and overseas buyers looking for everything from Internet consulting to copper wire. Also, check the geographically specific newsgroups for foreign countries for ones related to your business.

Small Business Administration Industry Profiles The SBA offers reports on small business opportunities in various industries. Gopher to: *umslvma.umsl.edu* (look in *library, government information/small business administration industry profiles*).

Competitive intelligence

The industry-specific discussion groups and mailing lists where you participate will help you gather opinions about your products or services and those of your competitors. But you may also want to know financial details about your competition. Here are two sources:

Industry statistics This database offers performance statistics for various industry segments, including quarterly financial reports. Gopher to: *infopath.ucsd.edu* and look in *News & Services/Economic . . . /Industry Statistics.*

Securities and Exchange Reports The SEC's EDGAR system offers stock sales and corporate reports that were filed electronically from 1994 on. Gopher to: *vaxvmsx.babson.edu* (look in *business resources*).

Professional advice

To find out what the pros have to say, participate in a professionally oriented discussion group or mailing list. Here are three options:

Law The *misc.legal* newsgroup is a good place to learn what lawyers are saying about the law.

Marketing The Free-Market, Inet-Marketing, and HTMARCOM mailing lists are all good sources of information for marketing, with a special emphasis on Internet marketing. To subscribe to Free-Market, send the message *sub free-market <your name>* to the address *listserv @ar.com*. Subscribe to Inet-Marketing by sending the message *subscribe inet-marketing <your name>* to the address *LISTPROC@einet.net*. Subscribe to HTMARCOM by sending the message *SUBSCRIBE HTMARCOM <your name>* to the address *listserv@cscns.com*.

Taxes The *misc.taxes* newsgroup offers some advice and professional contacts from accounting professionals, although there's also a good bit of whining about the IRS.

Business information on online services

If you don't find the information you need on the Net, you can probably get it from an online service. You won't find the same wealth of databases, but there are more specific services for small businesses. Here's a sampling from the five largest online services:

America Online (AOL) The Personal Finance area on AOL features business information databases, business news, company profiles, stock information, and more. Access it from the main AOL menu.

Inside the Personal Finance area, the Microsoft Small Business Center has a library of articles in many categories, including finance, legal issues, management, marketing and advertising, sales, and starting a business. The center also features a message board, frequent conferences with business gurus, and a directory of business resources.

AOL's **Reference Desk** (also on the main menu) is mostly a collection of periodicals and investor-related services, but **Hoover's Company Profiles** lists detailed information on more than 1000 of the largest U.S. companies. The **Media Information** network has news and information about business activities in radio, TV, and publishing.

CompuServe CompuServe is the place for professional discussion groups, where you can get professional advice straight from the horses' mouths. In the Professional Forums area, you'll find such forums as Legal, PR and Marketing, International Trade, Office Automation, and Engineering Automation. Also, Entrepreneur's Small Business Forum features a world of business advice by itself.

CompuServe has a good selection of information databases, too. The **IQuest** database service alone offers more than 850 databases. Many of the databases offer detailed business information such as company profiles and credit reports. **Knowledge Index** offers full-text and bibliographic indexes to articles in more than 50,000 journals.

Prodigy Prodigy's business services are geared more for individual investors.

The Business/Finance area features articles on various topics in the For Business section. You can click the Research button there to browse an online version of *Advertising Age*. Most of the other topics are about stocks, municipal bonds, and electronic banking, bill-paying, and brokerage services.

GEnie GEnie has a relatively small subscriber base, but when it comes to business information, it's bigger than the Big Three. There are dozens of business-related databases and forums (GEnie calls them *roundtables*). Here's a sampling:

Commerce Business Daily, which features announcements for product and service procurements by the U.S. government.

Dialog Databases, which offer access to over 400 databases from the Dialog Information Service.(Dialog itself is a separate online service that offers thousands of databases to corporate customers at hefty hourly rates.) Topics in the selection of Dialog databases available on GEnie include government regulations, business, finance, and copyrights.

Dun & Bradstreet Company Profiles include sections for the U.S.,

Canada, Asia/Pacific region, Europe, and International, covering millions of public companies everywhere. Information includes SIC codes, sales, employees, products, and more.

Public Opinion Online Database is a vast collection of surveys conducted by such organizations as Gallup Polls, Harris Polls, ABC, NBC, CBS, CNN, the *Washington Post*, the *New York Times*, the *Wall Street Journal*, and *USA Today*.

The Law Roundtable is a message board for legal professionals and others interested in the law, plus a Law Center database containing the texts of laws, government regulations, and news about court decisions, tax changes, and more.

The Home Office/Small Business Roundtable has libraries and bulletin boards on finance, marketing, management, and other topics.

The Tax Roundtable features tax information, IRS forms, and a bulletin board where you can talk with tax professionals.

Thomas Register of North American Manufacturers lists names, addresses, and phone numbers by product type, product trade name, or company name.

Trade Names Database lists nearly 300,000 consumer brand names and their makers or distributors.

Trademark Center tells you whether or not a trademark has been registered at the state or federal level. There's also a patent register where you can get information about patents in the United States and thirty foreign countries.

TRW Business Credit Profiles features credit information on millions of U.S. businesses.

Delphi Delphi is the smallest of the five major online services (with about 150,000 subscribers), but it has gained a lot of visibility in the past year or so by advertising a free five-hour trial of its service in magazines far and wide. For a long time, Delphi offered its subscribers far more complete access to the Internet than its competitors, but that's not the case today. When it comes to business information, Delphi is about average. Here's a sampling:

The **Business Forum** offers libraries of files, a collection of business newsletters, the Reuters Business News, a conference room, a shopping service, and a message area. The forum also gives you access to business-related Usenet newsgroups.

Business Wire and **PR Newswire** are wire services that carry press releases from companies.

The **Register of Public Corporations** features names, addresses, and basic information about public companies in the United States.

Delphi also has databases of stock prices, investment ratings, money fund reports, and other investment information.

Index

A *Brief History of Time* (Hawking), 165
acceptable use policies, 27, 199
Ace Hardware, 212
acronyms, 73
added value, 210–211
Adobe Systems, 19, 48
advertising
  classified, 6–37, 113, 114–119, 184
  online, 113–114, 121–127, 184
  print, 184
Adweek magazine, 243
Alain Pinel Realtors, 7–8
alt.architecture 22
alt.bbs.lists, 22
alt.beer, 22
alt.business, 44–45
alt.business.misc, 22, 117
alt.dads.rights, 22
alt.music.progressive, 22
alt.sci.physics.new-theories, 22
America Online, 4, 5, 6
  Aviation Forum, 37
  BBS Corner, 150
  classified ads, 36, 114
  conferences, 41, 169
  demographics, 199
  goodbye screen, 125
  Guerrilla Marketing mailbox, 59
  Internet Center, 44, 47
  mail program, 58–60
  Send Later icon, 60–61
  Send Now icon, 60
  store, 39
  welcome screen, 124
Anarchie, 46, 90
apathy, 240–244
Apple Computer, 9, 19, 35, 237
AppleLink, 71, 103
APS Technologies, 176
Archie, 46, 90, 253, 256–257
ARPAnet, 17
article pitches, 268–270
articles, publishing, 184
ASAP magazine, 243
Ascii graphics, 78
Asprey, Dave, 246
attack calendar, 223–229
attack
  choosing a launch date, 226, 227
  organizing, 232–234
  scheduling activities, 227–229
audiovisual aids, 185
AutoVantage Online, 231–232
Avis Rent A Car, 180

backbone, 15, 17, 18
backups, 239–240
bandwidth, 183, 194–195
BARRnet, 18
Barron's magazine, 243
battle, organizing, 232–234
battlegrounds, active and passive, 221–222
Bauer, Mike, 211

BBS magazine, 155, 158, 161, 199

billboards, 40–41, 88, 113–114, 121–127, 128
  estimating costs, 220

biz.misc, 117

Boardwatch magazine, 5, 51, 150, 155, 158, 161, 199, 225, 243, 247

Book Stacks Unlimited, 211

bookmarks, 233–234

Branch Mall, 50, 92, 104, 105, 127, 180

brochures, 184

BTW, 73

bulletin board systems, 4, 16, 19, 51, 148, 149, 151–155, 159, 161
  choosing hardware/software for, 159–160
  classified ads, 114, 149
  conferences, 164–170
  connecting to, 151, 159, 162
  e-mail features, 149
  estimating costs, 221
  evaluating as a battleground, 150–155
  evaluating results, 238
  finding, 150
  forums, 130, 149, 153–154
  gateways to online services, 161–162
  government-sponsored, 251
  hardware requirements, 158
  interfaces to, 154, 159–160
  libraries, 149, 152–153
  marketing advantages, 51–53; opportunities, 148–149; techniques, 155–157, 162
  newsgroup that lists, 22
  promoting, 161–162
  promotional services in, 23
  rules of behavior, 154–155
  setup costs, 158
  starting, 51–52, 157–162

Burger King, 211

business identity, 180, 189

business name, 179

Business Week magazine, 243

buying comfort, 230–231

Canter & Siegel, 10, 192

capitalization, 72

catalogs, 184

Cello, 21

census figures, 250

Ceram Corp., 7

CERFnet, 18

CERN, 23

Charles Schwab and Co., 211

chat rooms, 22, 41, 149

Cheerios, 244

Chevrolet, 21

Chrysler Corp., 260

clarity, 197

classified ads, 36–37, 113, 114–121, 120, 185
  on bulletin board systems, 114
  checking replies, 121
  content, 116, 120
  costs, 117
  duration, 117, 118
  estimating costs, 220
  evaluating results, 238
  on Internet, 117–119
  in newsgroups, 117–119
  on online services, 114–117
  placement order, 115–116, 118–119, 120–121
  Reply button, 116
  response options, 116, 120
  testing 119–120, 128
  titles, 115, 119–120

club memberships, 186

.com, 29
columns in publications, 185, 270
co-marketing, 186
Commerce Business Daily, 252
CommerceNet, 50
commercial networks, 17–18, 29–
30
community involvement, 186,
189
Compaq Computer Corp., 214,
252
competitive advantages, 210–212
competitiveness, 189
CompuServe, 4, 5, 6
classified ads, 114–117
Electronic Mall, 123–124
forum Browse Libraries button,
132
forum Enter Room button, 131
forum Newsflash button, 131
forum Who's Here button, 131
Health and Fitness forum, 130–
135
International Trade forum,
251–252
marquees, 88, 123–124, 220
PR/Marketing Forum, 38
Special Events/Contests area,
35, 109
storefront costs, 124
What's New window, 35, 104,
109, 124
CompuServe magazine, 185, 265
computer literacy, 10
Computer Shopper magazine, 243
conferences, 41–42, 131, 164–
170, 184
archives and transcripts, 170,
185
pitching, 168–169
promoting publications in, 177
confidence, 189, 190

contests, 109, 187, 236
contributed articles, 270
convenience, 182–183, 190, 210,
231
costs, estimating, 216–217
Country Fare Restaurant, 210
credibility, 180, 189, 211
credit card purchases, 96, 106
crime statistics, 250
cross-posting, 118
curiosity, 188, 204
customer
comfort, 230–231
contact information, 251–252
involvement, 235–238
needs, 230–232
recourse, 183
CyberMall, 50, 92

decor, 181
dedicated server, 90, 100
Dell Computer Corp., 9, 252
Delphi, 5
demographic information online,
250
demonstrations, 185
dial-up connection, 15, 25–26
Digital Equipment Corp., 19,
140, 193
direct-mail postcards, 186
directories, 184, 186
discussion groups, 9, 45, 129–
130, 133–134
archives, 188
estimating costs, 221
evaluating results, 238
organizing messages in, 233
domains, 27, 29–30, 78–79
Domino's Pizza, 4, 210

e-mail, 20, 57–64, 65
acronyms in, 73

Ascii graphics in, 78
bozo filtering, 65
on bulletin board systems, 149, 153–154
customer mailing lists, 82–83, 188
customizing messages, 81
effective messages, 72–73, 75–76, 196–198
estimating costs, 219
follow-up messages, 206
junk, 79, 196, 199–200
marketing with, 70–84
multiple mailboxes, 233
per-message charges, 71
prewritten messages, 80–81
promoting publications with, 177
promotion-oriented addresses, 78–79
prospecting with, 82–83
recycling messages, 80–81
saving customer addresses, 82–83
saving messages, 60, 64, 80–81
signature tips, 76–78
subject line, 59, 73–75
testing messages, 81
economy, 198
.edu, 29
educational networks, 17–18, 29–30
Educom, 173
Edupage, 173, 174
800-Flowers, 260
800-THE-ROSE, 7
electronic publications
evaluating results, 238
organizing and tracking, 233
electronic publishing, 45–47, 170–178
electronic shopping malls, 15–16, 123–124

electronic storefront
buyer demographics, 87
buying comfort, 104–105, 106
changing, 87, 88–89, 108
checking out competitors, 108
choosing, 96–102, 110–111
consultants, 89, 90, 91, 97
contents, 102–107
costs, 100–101, 220
credit card purchases, 96, 106
customer involvement, 104–105
customer referrals, 109
departments, 94–95
designing, 28, 102–107
disk space, 91, 101
ease of use, 102–103
evaluating results, 238
faxing orders from, 204
feedback area, 106
front door, 92–93
FTP site, 90–91, 97
fusion marketing, 109
via gateways, 86–87
Gopher server, 91–92, 97
grand opening notices, 124
graphics in, 89, 95–96, 103, 104
guarantees, 105, 182
home page, 93
on Internet, 89–92
locations, 85–92, 181, 210, 247
maintenance, 101
monitoring, 203–204
navigating, 93–95
offering free information, 105, 111, 177
off-line promotions, 110
online services, 86–89, 97
options for, 85–92
ordering, 96, 106, 182
organization, 102–103
payment options, 182
presentation, 92–96

electronic storefront *(cont.)*
  press announcements, 109
  production services, 88, 89, 90, 91
  promoting, 88, 99, 108–110, 112
  promoting publications in, 177
  provider track record, 101–102
  reviving interest in, 109–110
  seasonal promotions, 110
  speed, 99–100, 102, 183
  testing, 107, 108, 111–112
  tip of the day, 108
  top menu, 93
  traffic, 99–100
  visibility, 102
  Worldwide Web server, 92, 97
emoticons, 72
encrypted transfers, 96
Engst, Adam, 176
Engst, Tonya, 176
enthusiasm, 189, 242–244
eWorld, 5, 35
EXEC-PC bulletin board, 53
expectations
  customer, 194–195
  realistic, 188

fame, 163
FAQ, 73, 117
fax-on-demand, 3
Federal Express, 260
federal laws, 250
Fetch, 90
file transfers, 30–31
flames, 10, 143, 192
follow-up, 183, 206
  calls, 270
  techniques, 234–235
Food and Drug Administration, 251
Ford Motor Co., 260
Fortune magazine, 243
Fortune 1000, 214

forums, 22–23, 37–38, 130–135
  administrators, 131
  advertising in, 23, 38
  on bulletin board systems, 149, 153–154
  conferences in, 131
  effective messages in, 143–145, 146–147
  estimating costs, 221
  evaluating, 130
  lurking in, 142–143, 144, 146
  marketing in, 142–147
  marking messages, 133–135
  participating in, 146, 147
  pitching conferences in, 146
  promoting publications in, 177
  proposing, 135
  signatures in, 145, 147
  starting your own, 135
  subgroups within, 37
  targeting, 145
  topic names, 143
  What's New area, 146
free information, 184, 190
FTP servers, 21, 30–31, 32, 45–47, 90–91, 97
fusion marketing, 109
Future Fantasy Bookstore, 200
FWIW, 73

gateway, 86, 87
General Motors Corp., 260
GEnie, 5, 199
gift certificates, 185
Glossbrenner, Alfred, 258
Good Housekeeping magazine, 269
goodbye messages, 124–125
gopher server, 18, 21, 30, 32, 45–47, 91–92, 256
Gore, Al, 4
Gourmet magazine, 269

gov, 29
government networks, 18, 29–30
Grant, Larry, 104
Grant's Flowers, 93, 96, 104, 180, 226
graphics, presenting, 48, 89, 95–96, 103, 104
guarantee, 182
guerrilla marketers, why going on-line, 5, 6–9
Guerrilla Marketing Interna-tional, 28–29, 52
  e-mail address, 29
Guerrilla Marketing Online bul-letin board system, 52, 154
guerrilla vocabulary, 74

hackers, 12, 96
Hahn, Harley, 247
handles, 41
Hawking, Stephen, 165
hits, 34, 100
Home Depot, 212
Home Office Computing maga-zine, 203
home page, 93
Hot Hot Hot, 248
hot lists, 234
hours of operation, 181
How to Look it Up Online, 258
HTMARCOM mailing list, 242
http-compatible software, 21, 30
humor, 189
hypertext link, 48, 92
Hypertext Transfer Protocol (http), 21

IBM, 122, 214
identity, promoting, 244
imagination, 189
IMALL-CHAT mailing list, 242
IMHO, 73

Inc. magazine, 243
income projection, 215
IndustryNet, 98
Inet-Marketing mailing list, 67, 68, 242
information
  finding, 252–259
  classifying, 249–252
  organizing, 232–234
information publishing, 45–47, 170–178, 184, 190
Information Week magazine, 230, 231
Intercon, 25
international laws, 250
Internet, 5, 6, 16–17, 23–26, 31–32, 42–51, 89–92
  addresses, 28–31
  backbone, 15, 17, 18
  billboard costs, 127
  classified ads, 117–119
  connections, 24–25
  directories, 126
  graphics and sound on, 48, 89, 95–96, 103, 104
  literacy, 10
  mail communications proto-col, 60
  mail gateway, 57–58
  networks connected via, 17–19
  newsgroups, 135–142
  presence provider, 27–28, 89, 90, 91, 96, 97
  server hits, 34, 100
  service provider, 19, 25, 26–28
  shopping malls, 49–51, 92, 104, 105
Internet Business Journal, 47
Internet Business Report, 6
Internet Group, The, 211
Internet Mall, The, 42, 50, 51, 109, 248

Internet Relay Chat (IRC), 22, 25
Internet World magazine, 5, 109, 161, 203, 205, 225, 226, 243, 247
Internet Yellow Pages, The, 140, 247

J.C. Penney, 87
Jiffy Lube, 211
junk e-mail, 79, 196, 199–200

Kentucky Fried Chicken, 180
key messages, 244–246

Lands' End, 260
leased telephone lines, 19, 24, 28
Lexis, 251
limited offers, 236
links
    gopher, 125–126
    Worldwide Web, 125–126
Listproc program, 67
Listserv program, 67
Local Area Network (LAN), 24–25
logo, 180–181
lurking, 32, 142–143, 146
Lynx, 21

McDonald's, 211
Macintosh, 237
MacWeb, 21
MacWorld conference, 237
MacWorld magazine, 243
magazine inserts, 185–186
mail reflector programs, 20, 27, 65, 183–184
mailbots, 20, 27, 65, 183–184
mailing lists, 20–21, 32, 43–44, 66–70, 237–238
    estimating costs, 219–220
market research, 45, 187
marketing goals, 213–215

marketing plan, 180, 209
marketing results, evaluating, 238
MarketPlace, 49–50, 92, 95–96
marquees, 88, 123–124, 220
MCI Mail, 19
Mead Data Central, 251
MecklerWeb, 205
media targets, 271–272
Merrill Lynch, 212
message thread, 45, 133–134
messages, repackaging, 244–246
Meyer Boswell Books, 51
Microsoft, 9, 35
Microsoft Network, 35
.mil, 29
Milne, Sherry, 94
Milne Jewlery Co., 94, 103, 105
misc.entrepreneurs, 117
misc.forsale.computers.pc-clone, 118
mission statement, 209–213
modem, 15
Monday Night Football, 79
Mosaic, 19, 22, 30, 34, 126

Nando Land, 158
NandO.net, 157–158, 160
National Association of Cave Divers, 152
National Center for Supercomputing Applications (NCSA), 19, 109, 126
National Information Infrastructure, 4
National Science Foundation, 17
NBC Nightly News, 29
NCSA Mosaic What's New page, 109, 126
neatness, 182
.net, 29
Net-happenings mailing list, 242
Netcom, 19, 25, 30, 140

Netscape, 21, 136
network addresses, 27, 28–31
New York Times, 266
newbie, 31
News & Observer, 157–158
news.announce.newgroups, 140, 141
news.announce.newusers, 144
newsgroups, 22–23, 32, 44–45, 135–143
  effective messages in, 143–145, 146–147
  estimating costs, 221
  lurking in, 142–143, 146
  marketing in, 142–147
  moderated, 137, 142
  participating in, 146, 147
  personal group list, 138–139
  promoting publications in, 177
  signatures in, 145, 147
  software to access, 44–45, 136
  starting, 140–142
  targeting, 145
  unmoderated, 137, 142
newsletters, electronic, 173, 184
newsreader software, 44–45, 136, 137–138
Newswatcher, 46, 136, 137–138
Newsweek magazine, 186, 226, 266
Norstad, John, 138
Northwestern University, 138
NSFnet, 17

off-line marketing weapons, 264–265
off-line presence, promoting on-line, 260–262
Oil Changers, 211
ONE BBS Con, 159
online

advertising, 113–114, 121–127, 183, 184
business directories, 50
computer service networks, 19
conferences, 22–23, 41–42, 131, 164–170, 184
marketing attack, 200–205
marketing plan, 180
marketplace, 3–12, 16–17, 19–23, 192–197; advertising, 8, 113–114, 121–127, 184; competitive intelligence, 9, 252; credit card transactions, 12; exploring, 198–200
news, 242
presence, promoting off-line, 262–265
services, 4, 6, 15–16, 24–25, 33–42, 86–89, 97, 199; billboards, 40–41, 122–125; chat rooms, 22, 131; conferences, 41, 131, 164–170; forums, 130–135; user name, 28
shopping malls, faxing orders from, 204
Online Access magazine, 109, 161, 203, 243
Online Bookstore, The, 49
Oracle, 140
order form, 105–106, 182
.org, 29

package, 181
Panix, 19
patent information, 250
patience, 205
payment options, 106, 182
PC Computing magazine, 243
Penny Wise Office Products, 88, 157, 160, 182, 202, 211
Performance Systems International, 30, 140, 202

personal contacts, 204–205
personal voice, 198
Pipeline, 25
Pizza Hut, 210
poison pen letters, 10, 143, 192
Portal, 19
power words, 74, 119, 128
PPP connection, 25–26
precision, 197–198
preparation calendar, 224–227
press demonstrations, 270
press releases, 266–268
pricing, 181, 211–212, 231
print advertising, 184
Procter & Gamble, 244, 245
Prodigy, 4, 5, 6, 199
    billboards, 23, 40–41, 88, 122–
      123, 220
    classified ad rates, 117
    conferences, 169
    goodbye screen, 125
    welcome screen, 124
product/service niche, 179
products, repackaging, 246–247
PSIlink, 25
public relations, 186
publicity, 265–272
publicity contacts, 186–187
publishing, electronic, 170–178

Q&A documents, 170, 172, 185
quality, 212

Racquet Workshop, The, 105, 211
reality check, 213
reconnaissance, 198–200
regional backbone providers, 18
reprints, 184
reputation, 163, 180
research studies, 184
resources, allocating, 215–219
return on investment, 215

rn, 136
Rolling Stones, The, 260
ROTFL, 73
roundtables, 37
RTFM, 73

safety, 230–231
Sales & Marketing Management
    magazine, 243
samples, 185
satisfied customers, 187, 190
Sears, 122
Seaside Book & Stamp, 51
secure payment methods, 12,
    96
Securities and Exchange Com-
    mission, 250
security, 96
selection, 212
self-confidence, 165–166
server(s), 19, 46–50, 89–92
    addresses, 28–31
    logs, 188
service, 182, 190, 211, 231
7-Up Co., 104
shell account, 25
Shoppers' Advantage, 232
.sig, 43
signal-to-noise ratio, 79
signatures, 43, 76–78, 145, 177,
    180, 189
Silicon Graphics, 19, 193
SLIP connection, 25–26
Small Business Administration,
    250
smileys, 72
snail mail, 76
software agents, 4
Software Creations bulletin
    board, 51
Software Publishers Association, 6
sounds, 48

spam, 10, 142
spam attack, 10, 79, 142, 192
special events, 187
special interest groups, 37–38
Specialty Bookseller, 51
speed, 183
Spiegel, 260
sponsorships, 187
SprintNet, 28
standard advertising units, 122
stationery, 183
story ideas, 268–270
Stout, Rick, 247
Strangelove, Michael, 211
Strangelove Enterprises, 211
supplier contact information,
    251–252
surveys, 235–236
Sutton, Willie, 5
sysop, 155

targets, choosing, 219–222
Taylor, Dave, 42, 50, 51, 248
teasers, 236–237
telephone number information,
    251
Telnet, 23, 25, 30
testimonials, 187
theme, 180
thread, 45, 133–134
Tidbits, 175–176
Tide, 244, 245
tie-ins, 186
Tiffany's, 181
Time magazine, 186, 266
time, estimating, 217–219
tin, 136
T1 line, 99
top menu, 93
trademark information, 250
True Value Hardware, 212
Tymnet, 28

U.S. Department of Agriculture,
    250
U.S. Department of Commerce,
    250
uniqueness, 211
United Parcel Service, 260
Universal Resource Locators
    (URLs), 30–31
University of Illinois, 19
University of Minnesota, 18, 254
Unix, 25, 141
Usenet, 136–137
Usenet Volunteer Votetakers, 141
UUCP connection, 26
UUNet Technologies, 18

Veronica, 18, 91, 253, 256
virtual server, 47, 90, 97, 100, 101
visibility, 211

WAIS, 253, 254
Wall Street Journal, 243
weapons
    checking, 239
    choosing, 190–191, 222–223
    estimating preparation time, 223
    ten most important, 189–190
welcome messages, 124–125
Wendy's, 211
West American T-Shirt Com-
    pany, 246
What's New messages, 23, 124–
    125
WinWeb, 21
word-of-mouth marketing, 80, 187
Worldwide Web, 48, 50, 92, 93–95
    server, 21–22, 30–31, 47–50
written expression, 196–198

Ziffnet, 5
zines, 173, 184
Zip codes, 250

You can continue to be a guerrilla with
The Guerrilla Marketing Newsletter!

The Guerrilla Marketing Newsletter provides you with state-of-the-moment insights to maximize the profits you will obtain through marketing. The newsletter has been created to furnish you with the cream of the new guerrilla marketing information from around the world. It is filled with practical advice, the latest research, upcoming trends, and brand-new marketing techniques—all designed to pay off on your bottom line.

A yearly subscription costs $49 for six issues.

All subscribers to *The Guerrilla Marketing Newsletter* are given this unique and powerful guarantee: If you aren't convinced after examining your first issue for 30 days that the newsletter will raise your profits, your subscription fee will be refunded—along with $2 just for trying.

To subscribe, merely call or write:

> Guerrilla Marketing International
> 260 Cascade Drive, P.O. Box 1336
> Mill Valley, CA 94942, U.S.A.
> 1-800-748-6444
> In California, 415-381-8361

Charles Rubin offers seminars, custom online marketing plans, and hourly consulting to help you apply the strategies and tactics discussed in this book. For more information, contact:

> Guerrilla Marketing Online Strategies
> 2675 W. Hwy 89A, Suite 1140
> Sedona, AZ 86336
> phone: 520-204-1057   fax: 520-204-1190
> e-mail: crubin@sedona.net
> worldwide web: http://www.sedona.net/crubin

Get the Complete Guerrilla Arsenal!

Guerrilla Marketing: Secrets for Making Big Profits from Your Small Business   ISBN 0-395-64496-8 $11.95

The book that started the Guerrilla Marketing revolution, now completely revised and updated for the nineties. Full of the latest strategies, information on the latest technologies, new programs for targeted prospects, and management lessons for the twenty-first century.

Guerrilla Financing: Alternative Techniques to Finance Any Small Business   ISBN 0-395-52264-1 $10.95

The ultimate sourcebook for finance in the 1990s, and the first book to describe in detail all the traditional and alternative sources of funding for small and medium-size businesses.

Guerrilla Marketing Attack: New Strategies, Tactics, and Weapons for Winning Big Profits   ISBN 0-395-50220-9 $9.95

A companion to *Guerrilla Marketing*, this book arms small and medium-size businesses with vital information about direct marketing, customer relations, cable TV, desktop publishing, ZIP code inserts, TV shopping networks, and much more.

Guerrilla Marketing Excellence: The Fifty Golden Rules for Small-Business Success   ISBN 0-395-60844-9 $9.95

Jay Levinson delivers the 50 basic truths of guerrilla marketing which can make or break your company, including the crucial difference between profits and sales, marketing in a recession, and the latest uses of video and television to assure distribution.

Guerrilla Selling: Unconventional Weapons and Tactics for Increasing Your Sales   ISBN 0-395-57820-5 $9.95

Today's increasingly competitive business environment requires new skills and commitment from salespeople. *Guerrilla Selling* presents unconventional selling tactics that are essential for success.

The Guerrilla Marketing Handbook   ISBN 0-395-70013-2 $14.95

The Guerrilla Marketing Handbook presents Jay Levinson's entire arsenal of marketing weaponry, including a step-by-step guide to developing a marketing campaign and detailed descriptions of over 100 marketing tools.

Guerrilla Advertising: Cost-Effective Tactics for Small-Business Success   ISBN 0-395-68718-9 $11.95

Jay Levinson applies his proven guerrilla philosophy to advertising. Teeming with anecdotes about past and current advertising successes and failures, the book entertains as it teaches the nuts and bolts of advertising for small businesses.

These titles are available through bookstores, or you can order directly from Houghton Mifflin at 1-800-225-3362.